A

BOXING
LEGACY

A
BOXING
LEGACY

THE LIFE AND WORKS OF WRITER AND CARTOONIST
TED CARROLL

EDITED BY

IAN PHIMISTER
DAVID PATRICK

ROWMAN & LITTLEFIELD
Lanham • Boulder • New York • London

Published by Rowman & Littlefield
An imprint of The Rowman & Littlefield Publishing Group, Inc.
4501 Forbes Boulevard, Suite 200, Lanham, Maryland 20706
www.rowman.com

86-90 Paul Street, London EC2A 4NE, United Kingdom

British Library Cataloguing in Publication Information Available

Library of Congress Cataloging-in-Publication Data
Names: Phimister, I. R. (Ian R.) editor.
Title: A boxing legacy : the life and works of writer and cartoonist Ted Carroll /
    Edited by Ian Phimister, David Patrick.
Description: Lanham : Rowman & Littlefield, [2023] | Includes bibliographical
    references and index. | Summary: "This book is a celebration of legendary African
    American sports writer and boxing cartoonist Ted Carroll, whose career spanned
    one of the most exciting periods of boxing's past, from Joe Louis to Muhammad Ali.
    His experiences and commentary are of great historical significance, encompassing
    issues of race, sport, culture, and society"—Provided by publisher.
Identifiers: LCCN 2022020755 (print) | LCCN 2022020756 (ebook) |
    ISBN 9781538164792 (cloth) | ISBN 9781538164808 (epub)
Subjects: LCSH: Carroll, Theodore, 1904–1973. | African American sportswriters—
    Biography. | African American cartoonists—Biography. | Boxing—United States—
    History.
Classification: LCC GV742.42.C382 B68 2023 (print) | LCC GV742.42.C382 (ebook) |
    DDC 796.83092 [B]—dc23/eng/20220624
LC record available at https://lccn.loc.gov/2022020755
LC ebook record available at https://lccn.loc.gov/2022020756

CONTENTS

ACKNOWLEDGMENTS

Ian and David are most grateful for the interest and support this project received all along the way from Doug Fischer, editor-in-chief of *The Ring*. We are also much in debt to Christen Karniski, Rowman & Littlefield's senior acquisitions editor, for obliging us to be clear about what we were trying to do.

INTRODUCTION

Ted Carroll (1904–1973)

Ted Carroll with a cartoon portrait of himself, gifted to him by friend and fellow artist Burris Jenkins Jr. *Ebony* magazine profile (December 1959), courtesy of the Ford Foundation, J. Paul Getty Trust, John D. and Catherine T. MacArthur Foundation, Andrew W. Mellon Foundation, and Smithsonian Institution

For more than thirty-five years, Ted Carroll contributed to *The Ring* magazine, widely regarded in its day as the most prominent and influential of all boxing publications. As well as writing a regular column discussing virtually every aspect of the sweet science, Carroll was a hugely talented illustrator. His detailed drawings and matchless cartoons captured a kaleidoscope of boxing personalities and events. Respected and admired by the best sports journalists and illustrators of his era, Carroll enjoyed close contact with some of the greatest pugilists of the time. He counted among his friends and acquaintances Jack Dempsey, Sugar Ray Robinson, and Joe Louis. Despite these credentials, however, Ted Carroll has been forgotten by all but a handful of boxing historians.

Though fleeting references to Carroll and his work appear in a tiny number of boxing books, his major contribution to sports journalism has generally been overlooked where it has not been entirely ignored. Even the autobiography of the legendary Nat Fleischer—founder and editor of *The Ring* for fifty years from its first appearance in 1922—makes no mention at all of Carroll, for all that the two men were close colleagues for almost four decades.[1] Indeed, there are only three publications devoted solely to Carroll: an illustrated article carried by *Ebony* magazine in December 1959, followed in March 1960 by three short letters to the editor; his obituary published in the August 1973 issue of *The Ring*; and in 2013 an online entry in the Observer Category of the International Boxing Hall of Fame's website. None of them run to more than a page of text; and the Hall of Fame entry itself essentially repeats the obituary, even as it acknowledges the *Ebony* portrait. A book on *Pioneering Cartoonists of Colour* devotes a grand total of four sentences to Carroll.[2]

EARLY LIFE

Theodore (Ted, Teddy) Carroll was born on July 6, 1904, to parents Jesse and Elizabeth. Along with his brother, John, he grew up in the Greenwich Settlement area of New York. The locale, close to Greenwich Village, was known as the old American quarter. As described by John Hansan, citing the *Handbook of Settlements, 1911*, its outward signs were "the small three-story house, the small shop, the picturesque and winding streets; and, permeating all, the note of torpor and decay."[3] But crowding into the old district, continued the *Handbook*, "come great factories, with swarms of working people, and taking the place of the old private dwelling the new five-story tenement with stores on the ground floor, often as an improvement on the mouldy building it replaces, though frequently also introducing an overcrowding, hitherto foreign to this quarter. . . . The population is American in the sense of being second and third generation Irish, with some Germans, a growing army of Italian incomers and a group of colored people." Gerald McFarland's finely observed *Inside Greenwich Village: A New York City Neighborhood, 1898–1918* puts the number of African Americans living in the area at the turn of the twentieth century at about 1,200.[4]

In 1917, when Carroll was thirteen, Greenwich Settlement House, with which he retained ties well into the 1930s, opened an arts school. The original Art Committee, as recorded in the Tamiment Library Archives, included renowned artists like Daniel Chester French, John Sloan, James Fraser, and Guy Pene du Bois, soon bestowing on Greenwich House a reputation as a leading center of fine arts education and production.[5] Carroll, though, graduated from the High School of Commerce, not the arts school. He nonetheless showed an early interest in sketching and painting and subsequently applied to the Arts Student League but failed to gain entry.

A voracious reader and an autodidact, Carroll steeped himself in classical literature—"the old writers," as one friend had it—spending many pleasant hours discussing authors such as Samuel Johnson and Samuel Boswell, Oliver Goldsmith, Charles Dickens, and William Faulkner. His work was peppered with references to Shakespeare, Melville, and other writers too numerous to mention. "There are two requisites for success in the specialised profession of sports cartooning," the *Ebony* article insisted, "a passion for drawing and an ardent love of sports. Ted Carroll possesses both these qualities in abundance."[6] The fact that Carroll was very largely self-taught—the influence of fellow illustrators and friends like Tad Dorgan and Bob Edgren notwithstanding—makes his artistic ability in terms of technique, simplicity of composition, sense of perspective, and range across different mediums quite extraordinary. As an artist, observed historian Tim Jackson, Carroll "never employed the negative blackface images often used for comic relief in other sports cartoons of the era, including sports comics drawn by Black illustrators."[7] In 1972, one year before Carroll's death, his close friend and colleague at *The Ring* Dan Daniel recommended that Howard University bestow an honorary degree on Carroll, but this was never acted upon. In September of that same year, Carroll and two other members of *The Ring*'s staff were awarded silver medals by the New York Boxing Writers Association.

Carroll's career as a professional artist and journalist—his talent showcased in depictions of horse racing, baseball, golf, cycling, motorsports, and especially boxing—began in his early twenties. From 1926 to 1933, he was a regular illustrator for the *Brooklyn Daily Times*, a popular weekday newspaper of the day. From 1933 to 1937, he also contributed to the *Brooklyn Daily Eagle*, and it is likely that his output during this time was what brought him to the attention of Fleischer and *The Ring*. His first illustrated article in the "Bible of Boxing" appeared in June 1936. Jackson's claim that *The Ring* carried a cartoon by Carroll in 1924 "to honour African American athletes who competed in the Summer Olympic Games" is without foundation.

CAREER AT *THE RING*

Although it is occasionally asserted that Ted Carroll worked for *The Ring* almost from its very first issue in February 1922, this is not true. His written columns for the magazine only started appearing in the mid-1930s. Published in June 1936, his debut article, "Fighters Who Fight," celebrated lightweight champion Tony Canzoneri's willingness to take on the toughest opponents around. Over nearly four decades to follow, Carroll would contribute more than a million words to *The Ring*, spread over some four hundred articles, columns, and commentaries. During the same period, he produced several thousand illustrations and graphic accompaniments. One of the first major works that he illustrated was *Black Dynamite* (1938–1947), Nat Fleischer's five-volume study of the history of black American boxers.

Starting with his first column in *The Ring* in 1936 to his final article published toward the end of 1972, Carroll's authoritative voice, invariably infused with a gentle wit, addressed just about every aspect of the sport he loved. Whether focusing on individual fighters or examining thematic issues that shaped the wider landscape of the sweet science, his contributions over the years built up a rich, complex, and comprehensive history of the art and business of boxing. No leading boxer escaped his attention. From his typewriter flowed portraits of Jack Johnson, Joe Gans, Jack Dempsey, Joe Louis, Billy Conn, Henry Armstrong, Sugar Ray Robinson, Jimmy Wilde, Ted Driscoll, Ruby Goldstein, Tommy Loughran, Mickey Walker, Benny Leonard, Al Singer, Rocky Graziano, Gene Tunney, Max Schmeling, Rocky Marciano, and Harry Greb, among myriad others. Rising stars and foreign threats were frequent topics. Heavyweight challenger Bob Pastor was singled out for attention in 1937, as was Tommy Farr, who went the distance in Joe Louis's first championship defense. Seen as a serious opponent for light-heavyweight champ Joey Maxim, former sailor and colorful contender Bob Murphy featured in a 1951 article, "Avast, Belay, Now Comes Murphy to Blow 'Em Down." Come-backing former middleweight champion Englishman Randy Turpin was closely scrutinized in September 1953. Many similar contributions followed. "How Good is Liston?" asked an article in October 1963, after Sonny Boy had demolished Patterson in less than three minutes for the second time, and in May 1970, Carroll wondered if hard-hitting Reuben Olivares was the "best bantam of all."

Some of Carroll's best works focused on the achievements and storied histories of specific national and ethnic groups. From Germans and Italians, through Jews and Irishmen, to British and Filipino fighters, African and Central

European boxers, and more, Carroll gave everyone their just due. African American boxers, the focus of articles such as "Sepian Sockers Supreme" or "Negro Ring Achievements Unequalled," featured prominently. As compelling were his accounts of the fistic fame enjoyed by different US states and neighborhoods. Starting with New York, Carroll worked his way through New Jersey, California, New York again, Jersey fighters for the second time, Hometown Prides, Philadelphia, California, Texas, and Louisiana.

Carroll's writing also looked at the different weight divisions and at every imaginable aspect of the fight scene. Mixed up with "Bantams in Favour," "Featherweight Class Tops," "Welters Busiest Class," and "Middleweights Rule the Roost," among others, were articles on training methods, secrets of hitting, different fighting styles, humorous poems mildly mocking sporting foibles, the "fistic follies" and "silly symphonies" of the year just passed, fighting or sitting tight, the role of managers, the impact of TV, one fight too many, boxing playboys, fickle fate, and southpaw favorites. All of them were executed with wonderful clarity and exceptional erudition. Nor did he avert his gaze from the violence at boxing's core. "Do Fans Make Brutality?" asked Carroll in July 1962, shortly after welterweight champion Benny Paret was killed in the ring. The last article he wrote was published in *The Ring*'s November 1972 issue. Fittingly, it was called "Marciano, Pep Brilliant Stars of Italian Descent in Our American Galaxy."

Professionally active in a time and place when racial stereotypes were pervasive, Carroll's work was notable not only for its range but also for its balance. Described in his midfifties by *Ebony* magazine as a "greying, genial New Yorker" and by Dan Daniel as "a man of unruffled temper," Carroll invariably brought these qualities to bear in his writing.[8] His greatest single written work was his *The American Black Man and Boxing* series. Spread over seven issues of *The Ring* between October 1969 and April 1970, these articles covered the history of black boxers' contributions to the sport and the meanings of this for American society. Unlike Fleischer's own narrowly conceived study written thirty years earlier, Carroll was at pains to look beyond the confines of the square circle and place black boxers in a wider societal context.

The Ring itself understood that the series was something special. Exceptionally, the first of Carroll's articles was prefaced by an explanation of the forthcoming series' significance. "Demands made on many American colleges to set up courses in the history of the American Negro, and his achievements in literature, commerce, invention, entertainment, the professions and boxing have met with widespread responses," the magazine explained to its readers.

"Approached on the subject of the Black Man and boxing, *The Ring* decided to make an admittedly tardy summation of the Negro's place in the Sour Science, from Bill Richmond to Joe Frazier and Jimmy Ellis." This was the start of a series dealing with black achievements in boxing, declared Boxing's Bible, "written and illustrated by the most competent man for the job, nationally famous cartoonist-writer, Ted Carroll."[9] "*The Ring* is certain," continued the editorial endorsement, "that as this series expands, it will offer interesting information and hitherto undisclosed revelations for all readers of this magazine." Dan Daniel, for one, was in no doubt that the series was worthy of preservation as a book. "It was a complete, painstaking job," he wrote, "full of evidence that he had researched his subject to the limit."[10]

Carroll's talent was such that he could master multiple illustrative styles. *The Ring* (June 1949)

OTHER WORK

In addition to his output for *The Ring*, Carroll also produced various works, mostly illustrative, for a range of projects and companies. According to the *Ebony* article, his first published cartoon appeared in the *New York Bulletin*. In

1935 and again the following year, he contributed a series of cartoons to the *Post Boxing Record Sports Annual*, published and edited by John J. Romano. With Carroll's name on the front cover of both editions, the 1936 issue was notable for including what was his first full-page illustration of Joe Louis, a fighter to whom Carroll devoted a lot of attention over the remainder of his life. The collections also provide multiple examples of his skill as a sporting artist, with his renderings of horse racing and professional cycling showing a particular flair for capturing action shots.

In April 1947, Carroll released his first major publication since returning from active service. It was a project he had been working on since before the war, he told a local newspaper. This was *Ring Career: Jack Dempsey; Joe Louis*, a pictorial account of the life and times of iconic heavyweight champions Jack Dempsey and Joe Louis. Containing a foreword by renowned New York journalist Dan Parker, *Ring Career* underscored Carroll's remarkable talents as both an illustrator and a writer. Demonstrating a mastery of the popular genre of comic-book panels, Carroll detailed the lives and careers of the two fighters acclaimed by many fans as the best heavyweights ever to win boxing's greatest prize. Up until Carroll completed *The American Black Man and Boxing* series some twenty years later, this illustrated book, containing more than four hundred individual drawings, was his only substantial work based solely on his own text and illustrations. Describing Carroll as possessing "a talent unsurpassed in the field of sports cartooning," Parker's glowing foreword insisted that the book represented the "pinnacle" of Carroll's professional career.[11] The 1959 feature in *Ebony* magazine speaks of Carroll working on another two books, one of which was a collection of sketches of New York City. It is unclear, however, whether these works were ever completed.

At the same time, Carroll took on a variety of projects for other companies and institutions in and around New York City. For many years, he did publicity illustrations for Madison Square Garden, enjoying a close personal acquaintance with Harry Markson, the senior executive in charge of the Garden's boxing operations from the late 1950s onward and, after 1968, its president. A capable painter as well as sketch artist, Carroll supplied illustrations and paintings of horse racing for Roosevelt Raceway, a popular motorway racetrack that was also home to horse races between 1940 and 1988. Toward the very end of his career, Carroll turned his attention to painting past equine "stars of the turf." A series of these paintings were displayed at the Aqueduct track, where, according to Daniel, they drew much favorable comment. Available for all to see at popular and crowded venues, these drawings and paintings by Carroll must have been enjoyed over the years by hundreds of thousands of sports fans.

Other media outlets also featured Carroll's works. These were always associated with sporting events, as he was notorious for turning down lucrative commercial art commissions in nonsports fields. As far as Carroll was concerned, they lacked the color and the excitement of sports: "He especially likes the personalities of the sports world," reported *Ebony* magazine.[12] By the late 1950s, Columbia Broadcasting System (CBS) News was buying dozens of cartoons from him each year for onward distribution to newspapers and magazines across the nation. Carroll would occasionally meet with Irv Kaze, a prominent CBS sports executive and radio host, often enough under the gaze of a Carroll cartoon hanging on a wall in the company's main headquarters. Such was Carroll's talent that he also supplied drawings for journalists working in New York City. From 1958, he furnished illustrations for the regular columns of Dan Parker, the *New York Mirror*'s hugely influential sports editor and

A distinctive aspect of Carroll's artistic style was his ability to capture movement and action. *The Ring* (June 1955)

columnist. They had known each other for many years, Parker writing the fore-word to Carroll's study of Dempsey and Louis and bringing his considerable weight to bear when Carroll was discriminated against in his professional ca-reer. Another of Carroll's close newspaper friends was Jimmy Cannon, the *New York Journal-American*'s famous sportswriter born, like Carroll, in the neigh-borhood of Greenwich Village.

PERSONAL LIFE

Carroll worked as a professional illustrator almost continuously from his early twenties onward. The only gap in this record, before illness made it impossible for him to carry on during the last months of his life in 1973, was caused by World War II. Drafted in late 1942 or early 1943, Carroll spent the next four years in the US military. Although Dan Parker remarked of Carroll that he "felt a sense of personal pride as I followed his rise from the rank of buck private to a first lieutenancy in the Air Corps," a rather different slant was provided by Dan Daniel.[13] Carroll, he observed, did not particularly enjoy his time in uniform.[14] That he nonetheless rose to the rank of first lieutenant suggests a keen sense of duty and responsibility, despite the fact that American forces were racially segregated for the duration.

Once in the armed forces, Carroll was unable to write and draw regularly for *The Ring*. After his final contribution in December 1942, he only published in-termittently over the next two years: in March, July, and November of 1943 and in May and June of 1944. After the latter date, Carroll wrote nothing more for the magazine until February 1947. Some of his older cartoons were occasion-ally reprinted, however, but only to illustrate the work of other contributors.

In his younger days, Carroll was regarded as an above-average athlete. He was good at basketball, spending time coaching local youngsters. In 1939, Carroll was helped by two sporting greats—former heavyweight champion James J. Braddock and baseball all-time star Joe Di Maggio, whom he particu-larly admired—to set up a basketball program at Greenwich Settlement House. As the Settlement House team coach, a serious-looking Carroll was photo-graphed with these two sports stars. Carroll's coaching success also had an im-pact on college and professional basketball, as he helped Frank McGuire launch his own successful coaching career.

A lifelong bachelor, Ted Carroll was said to have "numberless" friends and contacts. He enjoyed the respect and admiration of his professional contempo-raries in a hugely talented cohort of sketch artists and illustrators that included

Burris Jenkins Jr., Tom Paprocky, Willard Mullin, Rd Hughes, Tad Dorgan, and Bob Edgren. Carroll was particularly close to Jenkins and Paprocky, near-contemporaries and artists whom he greatly admired. One of his most cherished possessions was a large cartoon of himself drawn by Burris Jenkins Jr. Carroll returned the compliment, in his turn drawing one of Jenkins, captioned "World's greatest sports cartoonist." So close was the bond between Carroll and Jenkins Jr. that in 1942 the former organized a party in honor of his friend. Held in Harlem just before mass mobilization put a stop to similar gatherings of the great and the good, prominent among those invited were Joe Louis and Sugar Ray Robinson and the writer Dan Burley. A photograph subsequently published in *Ebony* magazine showed a beaming Carroll seated next to Sugar Ray, with Burris Jenkins and Joe Louis to his immediate left.

Inside the world of boxing, Carroll was on familiar terms with a number of notable figures in and around New York City. He counted Sugar Ray Robinson as a friend, spoke to Jack Johnson in Nat Fleischer's company, and conversed with Jack Dempsey and Benny Leonard on several occasions. He was a close acquaintance of Jimmy Bronson, an ex-manager and agent, and appears to have been in regular contact with Charley Rose, a larger-than-life Broadway character and fight personality, given the number of times Carroll directly quoted their conversations in his columns for *The Ring*. "I miss the guy terribly," said Harry Markson on learning of Carroll's death. "He was a rare man, a great artist."[15] Years previously, Markson had written to *Ebony* magazine, congratulating its staff on the feature they had published on Carroll, "Sports Cartoonist." "Quite apart from his considerable talents as a cartoonist, Mr Carroll has a vast knowledge of sports, both major and minor," wrote Markson, "He is also a good friend and I am happy to call him one."[16] On the staff of *The Ring* itself, Carroll's best friend was associate editor Dan Daniel, author of Carroll's 1973 obituary.

In a short but moving piece, Daniel wrote warmly and fondly of his relationship with Carroll, quirkily observing in passing that "all of his life Teddy wore bow ties." They had known each other long enough to have spent countless hours discussing "mostly not fights and fighters, but literature." A shared love of sport certainly came into it, though. Daniel knew that for Carroll, Joe Di Maggio was the "No.1 ballplayer"; Ken Strong of NYU and the New York Giants were his American football favorites; and Bob Pettit and Bob Cousy were his basketball heroes. But boxing was Carroll's absorbing interest. "Fighters are mostly meek men trying to make it the hard way," he mused in Daniel's company one day. "Meek men, but they are endowed with a world of courage. Fighting is the toughest dollar in sports."[17] Carroll thought the greatest pound-for-pound boxer had to be Sugar Ray Robinson, once welterweight title holder and five-times middleweight champion, though he believed that featherweight marvel Willie Pep was the cleverest.

When asked along with other members of *The Ring* staff in 1951 to name in successive issues the strangest punch, the most appealing camera shot, the most dramatic upset, the oddest incident, the funniest moment, forgotten men, and the most thrilling single round of boxing he had ever seen, Carroll came up with a connoisseur's offering. The strangest punch was yoga-devotee Lou Nova's "cosmic punch," which the challenger claimed would bring about Joe Louis's downfall. Baffled denizens of Jacobs Beach, that stretch of Broadway occupied by the fight mob, pronounced it "cosmetic," no punch at all as it turned out. The most appealing photograph was one taken in 1931 of Sam Langford and the original Joe Walcott, twenty-seven years after their famous 1904 bout. Still looking in pretty good shape, the old fighters had little to show for their long ring campaigns. Hard to look at the picture, Carroll felt, without regret that here were a couple of guys born just fifty years too soon.

The most dramatic upset for Carroll was light heavyweight sensation Jimmy Slattery's defeat by Dave Shade in 1925. Only nineteen, Slattery had twice beaten Jack Delaney, himself an outstanding fighter. Slattery was regarded then as Ray Robinson was later. Shade, by contrast, was a light-hitting welterweight served up to fatten Slattery's record. To the partisan crowd's amazement, Shade, fighting out of a crouch, twice nailed Slattery in the third round with a looping right, the second time putting him down and out. Carroll, who watched the contest from the bleachers, believed that no fight result ever surprised onlookers more. The oddest incident? When Jack Sharkey tried to leave the ring in a fit of pique after the referee allowed Primo Carnera to continue despite the Boston Gob's insistence that Da Preem had actually been counted out, only to be blocked from doing so by Johnny Buckley, his manager. Reading his eccentric fighter's mind, Buckley, a short fat man, saved Sharkey from disqualification by jumping onto the ring apron and turning him back. On Columbus Day, 1931, Sharkey was the eventual winner over fifteen rounds.

Carroll's choice of funniest moment could only have come from someone possessed of his wry humor and deep knowledge of boxing lore. Serving as a referee after his retirement, all-time great lightweight champion Battling Nelson, the "Durable Dane," brought his career as the third man in New York rings to an abrupt end when he refused the entreaties of a purple-faced state commissioner to break two fighters who round after round got themselves entangled in clinches, with "Bat" calmly watching from the ropes and doing nothing to restore action. "What d'ya mean 'break 'em'?" snapped the old champ. "When I was fightin' nobody ever broke me!" Nobody broke Bat, so Bat broke nobody.

World bantamweight and featherweight champion George Dixon was Carroll's forgotten man. A masterful boxer, a slashing hitter, and gamer than most, Canadian-born Dixon met the best fighters of the 1890s at weights between 105 and 130 pounds, winning the bantamweight crown away from home in London before he was twenty. After eight years as featherweight title holder, he finally lost in 1900 to Terry McGovern in New York.

As for the most thrilling round, Carroll opted for the sensational first and only round of the June 1927 bout between lightweights Ruby Goldstein and Sid Terris. "The bell had hardly rung before Goldstein crossed his deadly right and Terris was on the canvas. Sid was in bad shape, he took nine, and struggled to his feet," recalled Carroll. "When Sid finally arose, Ruby's eyes popped in amazement. He seemed astounded that Terris was back up there. He made a slight forward movement. Sid tossed his own right with every ounce of his power behind it." The greatest fight he ever saw, he told Dan Daniel, was the May 1936 match between lightweight champion Tony Canzoneri and former welterweight king Jimmy McLarnin. Canzoneri was almost stopped early on, Carroll recalled, "but he had the heart and he got the decision."[18]

While Joe Louis was always an exception to Carroll's marked preference for boxing's lighter divisions, one heavyweight for whom Carroll always had a soft spot was Floyd Patterson. Broadly sympathetic portraits over the years of "Freud" Patterson, starting with the second year of his professional career in 1954, culminated in a finely observed attempt in the December 1962 *Ring* to understand what made the by then ex–heavyweight champ tick. On the publicity staff at Patterson's training camp, he arranged for the famous novelist James Baldwin, commissioned by *Nugget* to write about the buildup to the big fight, to take a lengthy walk through the woods with the reclusive champion. Carroll himself obtained a close-up view of the fighter he described as a "nice fellow" but a "complex character, mysterious and remote."[19]

Seemingly against his better judgment, Carroll had earlier picked Patterson over Sonny Liston in their upcoming "battle of the century" scheduled for September 1962 in Chicago's Comiskey Stadium. Influenced more by his heart than his head, Carroll's choice was in good company. Nat Fleischer, Dan Daniel, Jack Hurley, Rocky Marciano, and Ingemar Johansson all went along with the reigning champion. Headed "Patterson Nervously, Wishfully," Carroll's opinion piece set out a powerful case for Liston, only to backtrack at the very end. "In Liston, Patterson faces the most formidable heavyweight since Marciano. Liston is a giant, a powerful puncher with either hand plus a pole-axing left jab. While slow and ponderous, he is not a slow thinker in the ring and most important, he seems immune to punishment. Liston never has been staggered by a blow and is not prone to cuts or bleeding. A mean man in action, he is sometimes given to anger which could react to his disadvantage."[20]

Detailed portraits were a regular feature of Carroll's work, with Floyd Patterson's quirky personality being the inspiration for this piece. *The Ring* (July 1969)

On the other hand, continued Carroll, "I consider Patterson a much better fighter than given credit for. Working in the champion's favour will be the relative lack of activity on Liston's part. The last real match in which Sonny engaged was the [Eddie] Machen affair in September 1960. Ring rust could add to his natural slowness. . . . With a choice born of nervous wishfulness, I look for Patterson, using his great speed, to stay out of danger by fast foot-work for the full fifteen rounds, scoring often enough with punches of sufficient force to stall Sonny's attack, while winning a close decision."

Not unlike Patterson himself, beneath Carroll's apparently calm exterior, the "happy and contented" appearance he presented to the outside world, there surged hidden currents. These surfaced only rarely. As "a long-time friend of the artist," Daniel disclosed in Carroll's obituary, "I feel certain that he was frustrated by limited opportunities and unattainable goals. Teddy was a Negro, and he felt that his colour discounted his ambitions."[21] Doubtless hurt and angered by the humiliation and pain inflicted by racial prejudice, Carroll was known to be "a man militant for the Negro."[22] Quite how and at what personal and professional cost Carroll navigated a world filled with slights at best and overt discrimination at worst cannot now be recovered. If the experiences and reactions of black sports stars Joe Louis, Jackie Robinson, and Jesse Owen, among others, are a matter of historical record, many more voices have been lost in private conversations behind closed doors. A handful of white friends and colleagues helped where they could. On Carroll's own telling, Dan Parker was the "man who has done most to rectify it [discrimination]."[23]

While the defining experience of Carroll's professional career was unquestionably his long association with *The Ring*, the relationship was nonetheless shot through with ambiguity. Quick to appreciate Carroll's extraordinary talent, editor and publisher Nat Fleischer gave the young cartoonist and columnist

Ted Carroll, pictured with Dan Parker, sports editor of the *New York Mirror*. *Ebony* magazine profile (December 1959), courtesy of the Ford Foundation, J. Paul Getty Trust, John D. and Catherine T. MacArthur Foundation, Andrew W. Mellon Foundation, and Smithsonian Institution

his big break in the mid-1930s. Yet Fleischer seemingly never countenanced Carroll's further recognition and advancement. Until 1954, Carroll was regularly included in lists of *Ring* staff experts; in December 1949, he was described as the magazine's "ace illustrator and scribe"; and in April 1952, he was acknowledged as "America's leading combination boxing cartoonist and writer."[24] But there it stopped. Aside from featuring in the contents page and the "Next Issue" column, he disappeared from view once the names of the expanded editorial staff, all of them white, were regularly published. In 1952, *The Ring*'s thirtieth anniversary was celebrated in a four-and-a-half-page spread, written by Fleischer and liberally illustrated by Carroll. Although writers who in the late 1920s and 1930s subsequently joined the initial staff of three were named, Carroll was not among them.

Fleischer's autobiographical *Fifty Years at Ringside*, as already noted, made no mention of Carroll, despite paying fulsome tribute to other colleagues, especially the cartoonist Tad Dorgan. In October 1963, when *The Ring* reached its five hundredth issue, this significant milestone was the subject of a lengthy article by Fleischer himself, "Publisher Nat Fleischer Grows Nostalgic as He

In celebration of *The Ring* reaching its fortieth anniversary, Carroll reminisced on some of boxing's greats during that time. *The Ring* (October 1962)

Wanders Down Good Old Memory Lane." "Under the capable guidance of Dan Daniel, Eddie Borden, Ike [brother of Tad] Dorgan and myself in the early days and Nat Loubet, Jersey Jones, Lew Eskin and the late Johnny Salak in the post-war years," he wrote, "*The Ring* grew into a truly great sports monthly."[25] Ted Carroll's name never came up, even though that very same issue carried a long and thoughtful article by him.

Nor was Carroll's race specified in the few instances when he was mentioned. Even the editorial preface to the first installment of the *American Black Man and Boxing* series merely stated that Carroll was the most qualified person for the job.[26] Despite the racially charged ferment of the times, Carroll's blackness was left unstated. Whether this was by commission or omission was left up in the air by *Ebony*'s profile of him. "Until recently only a few who employed his art knew he was a Negro," it commented, "though he never tried to suppress his racial identity."[27] What is clear is that Carroll, free of editorial interference to the extent that one can tell at this remove, never tempered his opinions to suit *The Ring*'s predominantly white readership. Although scrupulously fair in his treatment of whatever subject attracted his attention, Carroll was not one to pull his punches when celebrating black boxing achievements. As early as February and March 1937, back-to-back articles were devoted to African American fighters: "Negroes Who Starred in 1936" and "Coloured Boxers Make Progress."

The only discernible change over time was a shift in emphasis from the exploits of individuals to a greater acknowledgment of the social and political context in which they lived, particularly from the 1960s onward. Carroll's reservations about heavyweight king Jack Johnson's absolute disregard for white racial sensitivities and admiration for the nonthreatening public persona adopted for white consumption twenty years later by Joe Louis were increasingly challenged by the no-holds-barred assertion of black pride personified by Cassius Clay (soon to be Muhammad Ali). A bland observation made in 1959 to *Ebony* magazine that "socially, sports is the greatest factor helping the Negro to progress" had been replaced by a much sharper formulation a decade later.[28] Carroll's introduction to his *The American Black Man and Boxing* was unequivocal. "For better or worse, down through the years, the Black history most publicized and familiar to the mass American public has involved the Negro's exploits in the ring. . . . The reason for this is quite obvious. For many decades boxing afforded the only avenue of escape by the Black Man from the suffocating anonymity of repression imposed upon him by social conditions."[29] It may not be too great a stretch to deduce that Carroll's own stifling professional experiences were close to the surface at this point. What, asked essayist Springs Toledo in *Murderers' Row*, was "a bloody nose compared to the soul-searing pain of the black experience in America?"[30]

In the last ten or so years of his life, Ted Carroll worked alone from his home, a small sixth-floor walk-up apartment that he shared with a younger couple, on Harlem's Edgecombe Avenue. Carroll's final article for *The Ring* was published in the November 1972 issue. On his death in 1973, he was survived by his brother, John. Following the publication in April of his obituary, Carroll virtually disappeared from the record. A reader's letter published in *The Ring* for November 1974 invoked "so eminent an authority as the late Ted Carroll," but after that, there was nothing for almost forty years until his induction into the International Boxing Hall of Fame in 2013.[31]

He surely deserves better than this. *A Boxing Legacy* acknowledges and celebrates Carroll's extraordinary record of achievement as a sports cartoonist, illustrator, painter, and writer of the first rank. Amounting to thousands of illustrations and more than a million words, his work is a hugely important contribution to sports journalism. The body of this book pays long overdue tribute to an artist and author who illustrated the place of boxing in American society with quite remarkable skill and insight. With characteristic self-deprecation, Carroll once declared that "if my career, such as it is, can help make this a better country for all, it will have been well spent," bittersweet words spoken by a man held back by racism but true to his talent and the sport he loved.[32]

The following edited collection of Ted Carroll's contributions to *The Ring* is arranged under five headings:

1: Profiling the Greats

This section brings together Carroll's profiles of ring legends Joe Louis, Jack Dempsey, Rocky Marciano, Ray Robinson, Billy Conn, Harry Greb, Mickey Walker, and Cassius Clay/Muhammad Ali.

2: Here, There, and Everywhere

Carroll's writing was notable for its focus on and celebration of a variety of ethnic groups and fighters from every part of the world. Contributions included here cover Africa, Britain, Japan, Germany, Italy, and South America.

Writing in a time when Irish, Italian, and Jewish fighters remained prominent in professional boxing, Carroll's analysis of their myriad contributions provides genuinely fascinating commentary on an aspect of American boxing that has largely faded away.

3: African American Boxing

A key theme within Carroll's writing from start to finish was his willingness to engage with questions related to the role of black athletes in American boxing. In addition to earlier contributions, this section contains his celebrated seven-part series, *The American Black Man and Boxing*.

4: Brains vs. Brawn

The titles of the articles in this section say it all: "Puncher Always Has a Chance," "Stamina Is a Great Ring Asset," "Secrets of Hitting," "Age vs. Experience," "Every Fistic Great Has Style Nemesis," and "KOs Thrill but the Name of the Game Is Boxing and Buchanan Proves It."

5: Fighters and Fans

The final section presents a selection of Carroll's essays concerning the ups and downs of professional boxers. Containing material spanning almost thirty years, they engage with a variety of topics, including the role of managers and trainers, knowing when to stop, sex and boxing, and the part played by fight fans in encouraging brutal encounters in the ring.

The articles are reproduced as originally published with the exception of deletions made for the sake of space. These are indicated by ellipses in the text. The dates listed at the beginning of each section refer to the monthly issues of *The Ring* in which Carroll's articles and drawings were published.

As a further note on the text: Carroll's articles in *The Ring* were written over a thirty-five-year period, from 1937 until 1972. The terminology used was very much a product of its time and needs to be understood in that changing historical context.

1

PROFILING THE GREATS

Carroll's admiration for Joe Louis as a man was equaled only by his celebration of the Brown Bomber's fighting qualities. Comparing Louis with previous heavyweight champions, Carroll placed a high premium on the fact that by December 1947, Joe had put his crown on the line as many times during his reign as all of the title defenses put together between 1915 and 1937 by Jess Willard, Jack Dempsey, Gene Tunney, Max Schmeling, Jack Sharkey, Primo Carnera, Max Baer, and James J. Braddock. More than this, he insisted, Louis ducked no one along the way. He fought them all, from the courageous and durable Tommy Farr in his first defense of the title; to his rematch with Schmeling when he shattered the former champion in 2.04 of the first round; and beer-guzzling Tony Galento, whose murderous left hook briefly deposited the title-holder on the canvas. Arturo Godoy managed to go the distance in 1940 by crouching as low as he could, only to fall victim to a thunderous uppercut the second time around. The "Bum of the Month" series of 1941 ended with what was probably Louis's hardest defense, when Billy Conn's brilliant boxing gave the champ all the trouble and more that he could handle until the fateful thirteenth round. Louis's defense against Lou Nova got off to a slow start, as he waited for yoga-practicing, elephant-riding Nova's mysterious "dynamic stance" and "cosmic" punch to materialize, but ended dramatically when a bored Bomber decided he had seen enough and sent over a crushing right. In 1946, after Louis's discharge from the Army, knockout victories followed over Conn, for the second time, and Tami Mauriello, who managed to stagger the champion in the two minutes the bout lasted. They set the scene, at the time Carroll penned this profile, for Louis's upcoming title defense against the veteran Jersey Joe Walcott. Although Carroll insisted that Jersey Joe was a worthy challenger, no one else gave him much of a chance. The experts could not have been more wrong.

Toward the end of 1954, Rocky Marciano was just over two years into his reign as world heavyweight champion. He had defended his title on four occasions: a rematch against ex-champion Jersey Joe Walcott, who had promptly folded at the first solid punch to land on him; against New Yorker Roland La Starza, who several years previously had held Marciano to a disputed ten-round split decision but whose boxing skills could not stop "The Rock" from bludgeoning him to an eleventh-round defeat; and twice against former titleholder Ezzard Charles. The first match had gone the full fifteen-round distance, with Rocky a clear points winner, but the second ended abruptly when Marciano, in danger of being stopped because of a deep and bloody cut on his nose, put Charles down and out in the eighth round. These winning displays of raw power against men who were far better boxers than the crude "Brockton Blockbuster" caused ring enthusiasts to wonder just what type of fighter could handle the all-conquering champion, the question posed by Carroll in his December 1954 article.

Steeped in the past of every one of boxing's then eight weight divisions, from heavyweight to flyweight, some of Carroll's best writing was reserved for the lives and times of three outstanding middleweight champions: Mickey Walker, Ray Robinson, and Harry Greb. Walker, "The Toy Bulldog," was the subject of a lengthy piece in April 1961, which paid due regard to his dashing Three Musketeer D'Artagnan-like behavior out of the ring, while tracing his remarkable career from winning the welterweight title in 1922 to annexing the middleweight crown in 1926 and holding heavyweight contender and champion-to-be Jack Sharkey to a draw in 1931. Along the way, Mickey picked up Jack Kearns, erstwhile manager of the fabled "Manassa Mauler," as his pilot and drinking companion. One memorable occasion saw Walker, Kearns, and the rest of the fighter's entourage blow the entire purse from a successful overseas title defense in less than a week, too far gone until told that they were on the way to Paris and not Dublin, the destination originally selected for postfight celebrations.

In one of the last columns he wrote, in January 1972, Carroll asked if Harry Greb, "The Pittsburgh Windmill," was the "greatest for his pounds." Mickey Walker would have known the answer. Outpunched and outmaneuvered by Greb's swarming attack, Walker was only one of many Greb opponents to emerge looking like they had been put through a meat grinder. Holding the middleweight title between 1923 and 1926, Greb feared no man and chased every woman. After thrashing the hitherto undefeated Gene Tunney for the North American light heavyweight title in 1922, Greb repeatedly challenged heavyweight king Jack Dempsey to meet him in a title match. Thrown out of Dempsey's training camp for making the champ look foolish in sparring sessions, the 168-pound Greb had to content himself with taking on and beating the best bigger men around. A notoriously "dirty" fighter who repeatedly "thumbed" other boxers, Greb lived and died by the sword, expiring on the operating table when undergoing surgery to repair his remaining good eye.

Concluding that the fabulous "Pittsburgh Windmill" posed a challenge to any fighter deemed to be the best ever, Carroll had a decade earlier, in March 1962, nonetheless designated "Sugar" Ray Robinson as the greatest pound-for-pound boxer of all time. Former welterweight champ and five-time holder of the middleweight crown, Robinson was hailed by Madison Square Garden even while he was still active in the ring as the "All-Time Great Champion of Champions." Ray had everything, the pundits said: a left hook, a right cross, defensive skill, ring generalship, the will to win, courage, speed of hand and foot, split-second reflexes, and, lest it be forgotten, punching power. Garden matchmaker Teddy Brenner thought Sugar Ray was the "greatest one-punch hitter we've ever had." Middleweight title bouts saw him batter the previously indestructible "Bronx Bull," Jake La Motta, to a thirteenth-round standstill; leave Randy Turpin helpless against the ropes in their New York fight; twice shatter Bobo Olson; and KO tough Gene Fullmer, the only fighter ever to do so. One left hook was all it took. Two or three opponents aside, only Father Time beat Robbie. Carroll thought that marvelous Benny Leonard, lightweight champion between 1917 and 1925, came within a hair's breadth of matching Robinson's ring assets. All the other greats, from Jack Dempsey onward, including Joe Louis and triple champ Henry Armstrong, fell short in one respect or another. Sugar Ray, Carroll decided, was the best of them all. "If Sugar Ray does not meet all the qualifications of the perfect fighter, who does?"

Only light heavyweight Billy Conn, completely lacking Sugar Ray's firepower, came close to equaling his ring artistry. Like Harry Greb before him, the hard-boiled "Pittsburgh Kid" feared no one. Turning professional in 1935, well before his eighteenth birthday, Conn lost his first fight, never having boxed as an amateur. A quick study, within the next two years, he was beating the best middleweights around. Not yet twenty, in 1937 Billy pulled off the astonishing feat of taking on five men who later became middleweight champions, defeating four of them, losing to Solly Krieger, whom he outpointed the following year. In 1942, Conn added Tony Zale, the "Man of Steel" from Gary, Indiana, to his list of vanquished foes. Writing in August 1961, when the long-retired but wealthy "Pittsburgh Kid" thought nothing of staying in the $100-a-night Hampshire House during his New York jaunts, Carroll recalled wryly that what had bankrolled Billy's postwar investments in oil gushers was his $312,000 share of the gate drawn by his 1946 rematch with Louis. A weary shadow of a once-great boxer, Conn was counted out in the eighth round of a dismal encounter. But it is for his first fight five years earlier against the "Brown Bomber" that Conn is forever remembered. By jabbing and moving and occasionally mixing it up, Conn was ahead on some scorecards going into the thirteenth round, only to throw caution to the wind and run into a Louis right hand. "What's the point of being Irish," joked Conn, back in his dressing room after the fight, "if you can't be thick?"

Once thought of as a big Billy Conn, the former Cassius Clay, known as Muhammad Ali by the time *The Ring*'s July 1966 issue hit the newsstands, was fresh off a victory over Canada's rugged George Chuvalo. Ali had previously defended the heavyweight title he had taken from Sonny Liston in 1964, against Liston in a one-minute fiasco in Lewiston, Maine, and against Floyd Patterson in New York. Next up was cut-prone British and Empire champion Henry Cooper, whose left hook, "'Enry's 'Ammer," had dropped Clay in a 1963 bout. This was the moment, Carroll reasoned, to determine how the present champ would have done versus past heavyweight stars. When it is remembered that at the time of writing much of Ali's spectacular career still lay ahead of him, Carroll's appreciation of his potential greatness was finely considered. Could Ali take a punch? How hard could he hit? Nobody really knew in mid-1966. But then again, no one of Ali's size—210 pounds—had ever possessed such speed of hand and foot. Carroll thought that the taller, far faster Cassius Clay would have outpointed both Jack Johnson and Gene Tunney, for all that boxing doyen Nat Fleischer never wavered in his opinion that the "Galveston Giant" was the best heavyweight champion of all time. Ali himself dismissed his predecessors as either too small or too slow. Offsetting these ring handicaps was the fact that Dempsey, Louis, and Marciano were all murderous punchers. Carroll was persuaded that Ali's unorthodox habit of leaning back from punches would be fatal against Louis and that Dempsey's ripping left hooks to the body followed by a right in a blur of action would have made for a great fight while it lasted. A Marciano victory would have turned on "The Rock's" ability to trap Clay in a corner and then bludgeon him unmercifully, not impossible but hard to do against a bigger, faster, smarter opponent. Carroll anyway was convinced that the sharpshooting Ali would have cut Marciano, a bleeder, to pieces. High praise, when the best of Muhammed Ali was yet to come.

"Love matches are made in heaven, fight matches are made at Jack Dempsey's," so ran the advertisement for the old "Manassa Mauler's" long-established Broadway restaurant. "Come in, Fellows" began a welcoming advert for the establishment, going on to highlight "Here's where you'll meet the writers, the managers, the fighters. Mingle with those you know and those who know you." Nearly every day in the 1950s and 1960s, passers-by could spot Dempsey sitting at a window-side table surrounded by autograph seekers. His popularity undimmed by the passage of decades, Dempsey's seventieth birthday in 1965 bore witness to thousands of messages of congratulations, including one from vice president Hubert Humphrey. No fighter ever drew bigger gates in the days before TV and inflationary dollars. It was the tigerish Dempsey and promoter Tex Rickard who made boxing a million-dollar business. His ballyhooed fights against Georges Carpentier in 1921; Luis Firpo, the "Wild Bull of the Pampas," who sent Jack hurtling through the ring ropes before being hammered into submission in the second round; Jack Sharkey, who should have protected himself at all times—"What was I supposed to do, send him a telegram?," snarled Dempsey—and Gene Tunney, especially the controversial long count in the return match—all of them million-dollar-plus gates, reaching two and a half million dollars against Tunney in Chicago in 1927—are certainly part of the answer. But how to explain the old champion's enduring popularity, garnering thunderous applause well into the 1960s whenever he was introduced from the ring before title fights? Much of the answer, Carroll believed, could also be found in Dempsey's common touch, his willingness to sign autographs, probably more than anyone else, adding to an aura that intrigued and attracted the public.

December 1947	Joe, a Real Champ, Has Met 'Em All
December 1954	Marciano, the Human Blockbuster, Has Experts Wondering, What Style Would Stop Rocky?
April 1961	Mickey Walker: D'Artagnan of the Ring
August 1961	Billy Conn: The Collar Ad Hero
March 1962	Ray Robinson: The Greatest Champion Since 1922?
July 1966	How Would Clay Have Done Against Stars of Past?
September 1968	The Man in the Broadway Window: Matchless Dempsey
January 1972	Was Greb Really Best Fighter for His Pounds?

JOE, A REAL CHAMP, HAS MET 'EM ALL

Louis' Coming Fight with Walcott Stresses Fact
That He Has Met Every Man with a Claim

One of the quickest ways to start a long argument among ring fans is to ask "Who was the greatest heavyweight fighter of all time?" The support for Joe Louis is vast. Jack Dempsey has many a booster, and there are still a lot of people who think Jack Johnson would have baffled both.

It seems there should be a line of demarcation between the terms "great fighter" and "great champion." It's conceivable that a great boxer might be a poor champion due to unwillingness to meet tough challengers or other reasons; in fact there have been some such.

A great champion is one who bars no one and convincingly demonstrates his superiority over all contenders. While they both undoubtedly rate along with Louis as fighters, it is hard to see where either Dempsey, Johnson, or any other titleholder since John L. Sullivan rates with him as champion.

Joe's claim to superiority over all fighters past and present is open to debate, but his position as the outstanding boxing champion of them all should be undisputed.

With all respect for their abilities, the records of heavyweight champions of the past, during their respective reigns, look puny alongside the Brown Bomber's.

Louis has put his heavyweight title on the line no less than 23 times since winning it from James J. Braddock ten years ago! He has defended his championship more times than Jess Willard, Jack Dempsey, Gene Tunney, Max Schmeling, Jack Sharkey, Primo Carnera, Max Baer and James J. Braddock put together in a space of 22 years!

Every one of Louis' title fights was a perfectly legitimate risk, with no strings attached, with the fellow in the other corner having a fair and square shot at the crown.

In every case it would have been possible for any of the challengers to win the championship by eking out a decision.

During the four years in which he held the title, big Jess Willard defended it twice, Dempsey had his title on the line six times during his seven-year reign. Crowned champion in 1926, Gene Tunney engaged in two title bouts before calling it a day in 1928. Max Schmeling risked his laurels twice in a couple of years as a titleholder. Jack Sharkey was an ex-champion following his one and only defense of the title.

Surprise! Big Primo Carnera risked his crown three times in a year as heavyweight king. Max Baer won it in '34 and dropped it in his only defense in '35. James J. Braddock had Louis to contend with in his only bout as world champion, and that was that. That makes a total of 18 title bouts in all, taking place between 1915 and 1937!

Detractors, confronted with the cold figures revealing Louis' championship glory, usually come up with yowls regarding the calibre of Joe's opposition. No one ever has asserted that the majority of Joe's foes were supermen. But coming back to those inevitable comparisons with the preceding champions, the contenders of the Louis era stack up pretty well with challengers of bygone days.

Drifting back to Johnson we find that the Galveston Gallivanter, after winning the title from Tommy Burns on Dec. 26, 1908, in Sydney, Australia, engaged movie actor Victor McLaglen, Philadelphia Jack O'Brien, Tony Ross, Al Kaufman, Stanley Ketchel, Jim Flynn, Frank Moran, one A. Sproul, Jim Johnson and Jess Willard.

Of these, Stanley Ketchel was obviously the class [act], but he was a middleweight. Philadelphia Jack O'Brien was a good light-heavyweight, while all the others, with the possible exception of Willard, to whom Jack lost the title, would have been just good sparring partners for Louis.

In the years after Johnson, the following men competed unsuccessfully for the world's heavyweight championship—Frank Moran, Billy Miske, Bill Brennan, Georges Carpentier, Tommy Gibbons, Luis Firpo, Tom Heeney, Young Stribling, Tommy Loughran, and Paolino Uzcudun.

Dempsey, Tunney, Schmeling, Sharkey, Carnera, Baer, and Braddock won the title. Of these former champions, all but Dempsey and Tunney were flattened by the Bomber.

The first group contains the names of some notable light-heavyweights, few if any top line big men.

Here is the lineup of Louis victims since Joe became champion: Tommy Farr, Nathan Mann, Harry Thomas, Max Schmeling, John Henry Lewis, Jack Roper, Tony Galento, Bob Pastor, Arturo Godoy, Al McCoy, Red Burman, Gus Dorazio, Abe Simon, Johnny Paychek, Tony Musto, Buddy Baer, Billy Conn, Lou Nova and Tami Mauriello.

There never will be cities named after most of this crew, it must be admitted, but there is little difference in ability between them and the unsuccessful aspirants of the past. At least most of them were honest to goodness heavyweights.

Everyone agrees Louis has barred no one. Possibly the two most formidable contenders of the past 40 years never got a crack at the big shot, Harry Wills and Sam Langford. While there has been nobody around with the ability of either of these during Louis' decade as champ, the opinion is certain that Joe would have been at home had such a challenger come a-knocking at his door.

There have been many interesting tales and sidelights of Joe's 20-odd title bouts. The only challenger to escape a knockout at the hands of Louis was Tommy Farr. That was only because tough Tommy was never in there again with Joe after his route going stunt back in 1937.

Many credit Farr with the outstanding showing of all the Louis challengers. Bloodied and battered by the ramrod left Louis kept continually sticking him with, Farr showed great durability and courage that evening. So much so that he thought he won, and refused to shake hands with the champion when the verdict was announced.

Only other contender to hear the final gong with Louis was Arturo Godoy who turned his shot into a game of squat tag back in 1940 and lasted the 15 rounds. What happened to the Chilean the second time was something terrible to behold.

With all respect to Farr, it is the consensus of opinion that Billy Conn in his first attempt at the Polo Grounds on June 18, 1941, provided the only real threat to Louis among all the challengers.

Willie was doing so well going into the 13th round he figured the time had come to throw caution to the winds, a most unhappy decision for anybody to make while still in there with the Brown Bomber. Conn went from one extreme to the other in his two efforts against the champion, his first was a top performance, but the least said about his second, the better.

Louis' fight-a-month campaign back in 1941, an object of much disparagement at the time, served to demonstrate the chances a champion takes whenever the title is at stake. Facing 250-pound Buddy Baer in the May, 1941, offering, Joe found himself on his shoulder blades outside the ropes, with the big Bud just about six inches away from the title in the very first round. Had Joe tumbled out of the ring completely, anything could have happened, a new champion possibly.

Louis climbed back in to chop down the tall Californian but the fight served to prove any time the title is on the line, danger is present.

Galento may have been a joke to the public but no one was laughing, least of all Louis' adherents, when Tony landed that wild left that spun Joe into the ropes in the first, and dropped him in the third. The Galento brawl was the most exciting of all of Joe's 23 title matches.

The Jersey Gargantua was dangerous right up to the time Louis dumped him, a soggy shattered mass, onto the canvas in the fourth heat.

Jack Roper, whose bid for the crown lasted just two minutes against Louis back in 1939 was probably the oldest man to ever fight for the heavyweight championship. Old Jack, third of a trio of fighting brothers, was a member of the United States Marines back in 1919 and fought Louis just 20 years later! Roper will also go down in history for having offered the most intriguing alibi of all Louis' victims. Jack, the battle over, after first assuring the folks back in his old home town in Mississippi that he was all right, offered as the explanation for his rapid disposal the following profundity, "I shoulda zigged insteada zagged."

Most terrified of numerous jittery Louis contenders was Johnny Paychek. Poor John might have been facing the guillotine.

Of all his great ring triumphs, Joe's blasting of Schmeling in 2.04 of the first round on June 22, 1938, is pre-eminent. The fact is seldom commented upon, but the German failed to land one single punch the night he made his bid to become the first man to regain the world heavyweight championship.

The Schmeling triumph was also marked by the greatest crowd that yet has seen a Louis championship bout, 80,000.

The smallest turnout, 10,500, watched Louis dispose of muscle-bound engineer, Harry Thomas, in five rounds in the Chicago Stadium on April 1, 1938. This match also drew the smallest gate, $45,600.

There was more money in the house $1,952,564 for the second Conn fight than in any other Louis match.

For what was expected of him, Giant Abe Simon provided the most surprising opposition among the challengers. Joe tells you, "That ol' Simon did a nice job o' boxin' for such a big heavy man." And he did too, until Louis dynamite caught up with him in the thirteenth round out in Detroit back in 1940.

Red Burman was probably the most unafraid. Fourteen pounds lighter than the champion the Baltimore carrot top tore right in from the opening gong right up to the finishing left hook that caved him in, in the fifth and final stanza.

No fighter ever underwent as strange a routine of preparation for a title bout as did Lou Nova. Although the fact has been pretty well obscured, the Californian was the shortest priced, in the betting odds, of any Louis rival. All the others, with the exception of Schmeling, were such long shots most of the wagering concerned the distance they'd last with the Bomber.

Not so Nova. When he climbed into the ring to face Louis on Sept. 29, 1941, many fancied his chances coming as it did so soon after the close shave with Conn. Lou had done his training, if it could be called that, at the Rockland County estate of a character referred to by the press as the Omnipresent Oom, a disciple of the ancient Hindu practice of Yogi.

How much of it was ballyhoo and how much the real McCoy is a moot point, but shots of Nova squatting Hindu style at the feet of the Oom while getting an earful of the mystic's mumbo jumbo appeared throughout the country.

Nova rode elephants, muttered mysteriously of his "dynamic stance," and the "cosmic punch," which was to become famous and eagerly awaited, but was never to materialize.

Lou apparently succeeded in putting himself in some kind of haze for after five rounds of snail-paced action, a right that would have floored one of Nova's elephants got him out of there.

Louis has planted some horrendous haymakers on hapless challengers. Galento claimed to have never been knocked off his feet, but he hit the canvas with a crash that seemed to shake the Yankee Stadium in the second round after Joe made contact with a solid left hook. This was the sockdolager that caused great humorist "Bugs" Baer to coin this all time classic. "Joe hit Galento so hard they could have counted him out in the air."

A right hander spun 250-pound Buddy Baer completely around and deposited him upon the mat as though he had fallen out of the sky. Johnny Paychek sailed through the air on his way to fistic oblivion so powerful was the polthogue that propelled him.

The thunderbolt that stuck Nova finished Lou as a first-rate fighter.

Mauriello came close to turning in the great upset of all time last year but as soon as the champion righted himself, he swept tough Tami before him.

Since several of these were repeaters in title matches against Louis such as Conn, Godoy, Buddy Baer and Simon, Jersey Joe Walcott will be the 20th man to get a crack at the Bomber's crown.

While there is already an anvil chorus of low rating going on about his fitness as an opponent, this has been the case with all of Louis' foes. In the light of cold hard facts, six children or no, the man from Merchantville, N.J., is just about on a par with most of the heavyweight challengers of the past quarter century, champions excluded.

Few will deny that he rates with Fireman Jim Flynn, Bill Brennan, Tom Heeney, Buddy Baer, or Galento, all of whom made more or less commendable efforts against the champions they faced.

That he is the No. 1 contender should be obvious also. He dropped a couple of decisions in the past year or so, but reversed them in later contests. He defeated Joe Baksi, first in line until recently. Another noteworthy effort on his part was his win over Lee Q. Murray, a fellow nobody wants any part of. He punches hard enough to be dangerous and knows his way around the ring.

While Louis is an odds-on-favorite to retain his title, there are no more than four or five boxers in the entire history of pugilism who wouldn't have been rated as long shots against Louis, so this can hardly be held against him.

He's no callow youth but even the great Louis doesn't get any younger. Regardless of the showing he makes there is no disputing that he is the best man around to face Louis at this moment. There never have been too many great heavies around at any one time and there certainly have been a whole lot worse than Walcott.

Ted Carroll was a huge admirer of Joe Louis, both as a boxer and as a man. *The Ring* (December 1947)

MARCIANO, THE HUMAN BLOCKBUSTER, HAS EXPERTS WONDERING, WHAT STYLE WOULD STOP ROCKY?

Boxing circles wonder just what type of fighter is best equipped to handle all-conquering Rocky Marciano. Although the heavyweight champion is a slugger, pure and simple, it is becoming clearer every day that clever boxing alone is no antidote for the brand of pugilistic poison he dishes out.

If anything, the clever boxers like Roland LaStarza and Ezzard Charles did better in the bouts in which they traded socks with him than they did when they attempted to rely solely upon skill.

This is particularly true of Charles, who stood toe to toe with the Blockbuster back in June, without once being decked, but who was picking himself off the canvas in a hurry in his defensive-minded exhibition against the champion in September.

Marciano, one of the best of the heavyweight champions, is oddly enough, by far the most primitive in execution. Outside of a baffling awkwardness, there is nothing in his free-wheeling style comparable to the skilful bobbing and weaving of Dempsey or the rhythmic combination punching of Louis. Neither Louis nor Dempsey could be classed as members of the scientific school, but both were clever by comparison with rough-hewn Rocky.

It would seem logical to assume that the clever jab-and-step-around stuff would be the proper prescription for success against the mauling Marciano, but the record counteracts this conclusion. Harry Matthews, Jersey Joe Walcott, LaStarza and Charles, all rate as honor graduates of the school of scientific boxing, while Rocky is still in the kindergarten, yet all of them wound up on the canvas.

In a pre-battle interview, Charles advanced the theory that to back up against Marciano is suicide, then he promptly went out and proved his contention by doing just that on the night of Sept. 17.

With the Fancy Dans ruled out as presenting any problem for Marciano, it appears that we must look among the punchers and the sluggers for prospective trouble-makers for the rough champion from New England.

Marciano has beaten the cleverer men who have opposed him by the elemental system of firing punches until a good one landed. Since he has the stamina, determination and fortitude to keep swinging indefinitely, this plan of battle has been invincible up to now. With the possible exception of Jersey Joe, none of his victims has been able to dent his granite-like jaw, and he has not had to worry too much about lightning striking before getting his big blow home.

Since there is no hitter on the heavyweight horizon of, let us say, the power of Tony Galento, the Brockton Blockbuster does not have to worry too much about having his own block busted by any prospective rival.

This is fortunate for him. In days gone by, Dempsey could not afford to ignore Firpo's bludgeoning blows, nor could Louis take such hitters as Baer, Schmeling, and Galento, lightly. Nor have we rugged maulers of the type of Paolino, Johnny Risko, Tommy Farr, or Arturo Godoy, steel-chinned and oaken ribbed characters, who kept pressing forward continually, and sopped up punishment as though they enjoyed it.

It so happens that the contenders of recent years have been of defensive habit and Rocky has certainly proved he can handle that kind.

All the great men of years past have had their troubles with one particular style. Dempsey never solved the cuffing, unorthodox antics of Fat Willie Meehan. In three recorded meetings, he finished all even with Willie, one draw and a decision apiece.

Squatters who fought as though looking for something on the canvas befogged Joe Louis, from the beginning to the end of his long career. The likes of Tony Musto, got down as far as they could, while Joe fumbled for the key to kayoing a man who crouched. Arturo Godoy did the same thing and got away with it the first time he met the Brown Bomber. He not only went the route, one judge actually gave him the decision!

Gene Tunney, a master boxer himself, had his troubles with fighters who used similar tactics. The sorriest episode in Gene's once-beaten career came one night in Philadelphia, with cagy Jack Renault, who was just as cautious and canny as Tunney. The champion-to-be and Jack were given the heave-ho out of the ring, after a punchless 4 rounds in which both men lay back waiting to counter against leads which never came.

Gene was well aware of the problems imposed upon him by clever men, which accounted for his insistence on plodding Tom Heeney, as a farewell foe, in preference to flashy Jack Sharkey.

Inquiry among ring vets reveals unanimity of opinion, that above all else, a real punch is pre-requisite for any Marciano foe with a chance. Venerable Joe Woodman, presents this view thusly, "Rocky catches up with the boxers because they don't hurt him while he's coming on. I don't care how little he can box, a fellow with a punch has a good chance with Marciano."

At this point I reminded Woodman that most punchers don't take it any too well, themselves, and what happens when Marciano hits them?

"The same thing that happens when he hits the clever fellows, but let's see what happens if he gets hit first," came back Woodman.

Inspection of Rocky's record does show a surprising scarcity of punchers. Some analysts have offered the interesting speculation that rushing charges a la football would keep Marciano on his heels, thereby breaking up his attack which depends upon forward momentum for its effectiveness.

This supposition gets support from Trainer Teddy Bentham who has gained high ranking among boxing students and corner-men.

"Against Marciano, it's got to be do or die," he believes. "There's no future in lying back and waiting for the roof to fall in. I've noticed that as long as those guys threw punches along with Marciano, they lasted. When they stood off and boxed it ended all of a sudden."

"But Marciano has so much endurance, he tires out the other fellow," it was pointed out.

"The guys he tired out were all old guys. What's to stop a young guy who's in shape from lasting as long as he does?" Ted came back.

As might be expected the noisiest rebuttal to the now-accepted idea that good boxers are futile against the champion comes from Manager Bobby Gleason. Gleason isn't exactly a disinterested party, since his Nino Valdez is No. 1 contender for the heavyweight crown.

"What's all this about Marciano having an easy time with boxers! Don't forget there are two kinds of boxers, old boxers and young boxers. All the guys you mentioned were way older than Marciano, except maybe LaStarza," Gleason argued.

"Ted Lowery, a boxer, showed a long time ago, that a boxer whose legs hold out does all right with Marciano. My guy, Valdez, is a boxer, but his legs figure to stand up a whole lot better than a 40-year-old like Walcott.

"Dempsey beat all the clever guys too, till he came up against one who was younger than he was. That's the difference. Those old guys ran out of gas, Valdez is younger than Marciano and he won't get tired," declares Bobby.

Still, the ranks of those who call Marciano a standout among heavyweight champions continue to grow larger. These people swear that he is one of the great fighters of all time. Manager Lefty Rimini sums up this attitude neatly.

"Style, they're talking about styles beating Rocky. Old age is the only thing that's going to beat Marciano, same as Dempsey and Louis. He'll belt out those walk-in guys quicker than the smart guys he has to look for," he says.

"They're easier to hit solid. A puncher won't do too good either. The best puncher around today is Bob Satterfield. What would the odds be on him against Rocky, you could make your own! Rocky has the answer to all styles. He can take it and he can hit!" explains the astute former mentor of ex-contender Tami Mauriello.

Although he has been doing it only a comparatively short time, Marciano got a very late start in boxing and he cannot be expected to withstand the rigorous routine he subjects himself to both in training and in the ring for too many more years. There has long been a suspicion that the New Englander may be a wee bit older than wily Al Weill wants people to believe. If this is so the limitless stamina and strength which have made him one of the most formidable fighters of all time, may be on the wane even now. He is in his thirties and although he applies himself to his physical conditioning with fanatical zeal, his rugged style is not one which is adapted to a long career.

Maybe Father Time is the only one with the style to beat Rocky Marciano after all.

MICKEY WALKER: D'ARTAGNAN OF THE RING

One day back in the Twenties, old "Doc" Kearns, emerging from a West Coast movie house where he had just been thrilled by Douglas Fairbanks Sr.'s electric acting as the dashing D'Artagnan in his classic movie "The Three Musketeers", was struck with a sudden idea. Then as now a man of many ideas, Kearns at the moment charge-d-affairs of middleweight champ Mickey Walker, was at the time finding some difficulty making any advance with three heavyweight members of his stable of no particular talents.

A great one at substituting ballyhoo for ability, why not dub the three non-descripts "The Three Musketeers", he thought and where in the world could you find a more swashbuckling D'Artagnan than his own mighty Mickey? Contacting a Broadway song writing pal, the good Doctor had a song composed around the idea, got out lurid posters proclaiming his "Three Musketeers of the Ring" and their dashing leader, Mickey "D'Artagnan" Walker.

The identities of Kearns' musketeers have long since been swallowed in oblivion; Jim Jennings of the old N.Y. Graphic wise-cracked, "Kearns should have called them 'Mousketeers'", but the old Doctor could not have picked a more perfect ring prototype of Charles [sic Alexandre] Dumas' devastating D'Artagnan than Mickey Walker, both projected the image of the happy warrior in D'Artagnan's case a foilsman, in Walker's a fighter. In each was found a fantastic fusion of fury and form.

D'Artagnan, the peerless swordsman, dispatched his foes while laughing his way through life. Mickey Walker battered his opponents against a bacchanalian backdrop of the "Roaring Twenties" of which he was so much a part. The revelry and riotousness of these tempestuous times reverberated through his career in a fashion which would have delighted the heart of D'Artagnan himself.

Mickey, the D'Artagnan of Boxing

Mickey Walker was truly the D'Artagnan of the ring. A genuine hero not only to the Irish, who found in him the ideal combination of the fighting heart and the happy smile, but to the public at large who pedestalled him as a great idol of the Twenties.

Mickey Walker came out of Elizabeth, N.J. in the post-World War I era, a black-haired stocky, rip-roaring kid with the features of a bulldog, softened by a grin as wide as it was frequent. When the smiling little Irisher belted over his first seven opponents in a hurry, he was tossed in with one K.O. Phil Delmont, a shifty, terrific-hitting import from New York's East Side who in less than a round demonstrated the foolhardiness of the match with a quick kayo of the novice.

Showing a resiliency that was to be typical of his career Walker bounced back and in less than two years after this setback he had blasted his way into contention among the leading welterweights. By 1921 he was making trouble for such superior boxers as the master himself, champion Jack Britton, and wizard Dave Shade.

Mickey had some trouble however with one of the neighbor's children from his own home town, a stylish, refined fellow called "Gentleman George" Ward, whose smart boxing thwarted Mickey's slambang attack on two occasions in the early Twenties. Although he always made the going very rough for the clever ones, shifty tactics continued to befuddle him. A couple of dropped decisions to rugged Lou Bogash and cagy Jock Malone, caused eyebrows to be raised when it was announced that he was to be given a chance at Britton and the title in New York's old Madison Square Garden on November 1, 1922.

Not everyone considered him worthy of the shot, mindful of the Ward and Malone setbacks, but there was one conspicuous dissenter there. Old Dan Morgan, Britton's manager solemnly warned that his fighter was in for a rough evening, reminding the critics that clever Jack had his hands full the year before with this same Mickey Walker in a no-decision affair in Newark.

To the consternation of all, Walker won, but still the recognition as a great fighter which later years was to bring him, was withheld. Prevailing opinion was that Father Time, working against the aging Britton was more responsible for Walker's victory than the aggressive youngster himself.

Quickly Outgrew Welter Class

In those early days Walker was a serious-minded young man with an engaging personality lit up by his ear-reaching grin, and fighting had not yet been displaced by frolicking as his forte. As welterweight king, he defended his crown against once great lightweight Lew Tendler in 1924 and against persistent challenger Dave Shade in 1925.

For some reason Mickey's luck was never bad when the contest was close, and the verdict retaining his title against Shade caused plenty of controversy. But when the dust of disagreement churned up by Shade's voluble manager

Leo P. Flynn had settled, Mickey was still champion of the 147 pound class but finding it more and more difficult to make the class limit.

That same year he made a valiant try for the middleweight title against Harry Greb in the semi-final—yes, that's right—the "semi-final" of an all-star extravaganza staged by Humbert J. Fugazy on July 2, 1925. During most of the fight, a classic of the Twenties, Greb's gyrations and whirlwind punching had Walker battered and reeling. But suddenly catching fire in the fifteenth and final round, Mickey cornered the pin-wheeling Pittsburgher along the ropes and belabored him lustily for the last moments of the fight. His rousing finish thrilled the spectators in the prohibition era night clubs along Broadway, that same evening, he was hailed as a hero.

Greb, also hitting the hot spot circuit himself, is supposed to have crossed paths with Mickey later that night in the wee small hours, and both "feeling no pain," engaged in an abbreviated re-run of their earlier set-to on a Times Square street corner. This legend—probably apocryphal—is dear to the hearts of old time fight people, although evidence is strong it happened only as a figment of the late boxing writer Hype Igoe's imagination.

On May 20, 1926, a previous two-time foe, Pete Latzo won a decision over Walker, and along with it his welter title in Latzo's home town, Scranton, Pa. A month later, Walker met Joe Dundee, then considered the best of the welterweights and was stopped due mainly to a cut eye in the eighth round in Madison Square Garden.

Jack Kearns Comes into the Picture

By now Jack Bulger, Walker's first manager had passed on and dapper Jack Kearns had talked his way into the picture. The shrewd Kearns, suspecting that weight-making rather than any deficiency was the cause of Mickey's slump, warmed him up with a victory over old Foe, fading Jock Malone. Then by some piece of legerdemain, Jack inveigled astute Walk Miller into venturing into his Chicago lair and having his champion Tiger Flowers, defend his middleweight title against Walker. Chicago, then in the clutches of Al Capone, was a spot where Doc Kearns had never been known to get any of the worst of it.

The Walker-Flowers fight on December 3, 1926, proved no exception to Kearns' run of Chicago luck. Miller, who figuring that his Tiger would be so far superior to this over-sized, over-the-hill welterweight, was shocked when Walker's hand was raised at the finish and Mickey was now middleweight champion of the world. The same year he had been divested of his welter crown and was written off as all washed up! This was one of Doc Kearns' greatest coups and he profited from it to the fullest.

Miraculously Walker now enjoyed a rebirth of form. Fighting at a strong weight, not even the round-the-clock routine of merry making to which he adjusted himself in imitation of the fun-loving Kearns, had any effect on the new power and vitality which now coursed through his middleweight campaigning.

An overseas junket to London in which he stopped the well-regarded British champ Tommy Milligan brought such encomiums from the British as "the greatest American fighting machine since Sam Langford" in 1927. The peripatetic pace along pleasure's primrose path never slackened for Kearns and Walker while overseas.

Seized with a sudden yearning to view the ancestral environs of Ireland, the pair delegated eccentric hireling Walter "Good Time Charley" Friedman to arrange for a trip to the Emerald Isle. Friedman, with no such roots there, had other ideas about a likelier locale, and figuring that his ever-celebrating pals would never know the difference, the following morning bundled the party aboard ship and when half way across the English Channel, announced that Paris and not Dublin was their destination. Too late to do anything about it, the entourage proceeded on to Gay Paree where they did their best to make it even gayer.

Since Walker had found such rejuvenation at 160 pounds, Kearns decided to build him up still more and take on big fellows, a practice he deemed more lucrative than middleweight campaigning. As a 168 pounder fighting light heavies and heavies, Walker came to greatness while never yielding in his pursuit of life's pleasures. He engaged opposition from ten to forty pounds heavier. Regarded as through with his career in 1925, Mickey established himself from 1927 to 1933 as one of the most remarkable ringmen of all time.

Although two matches with Ace Hudkins plus the Milligan affair were his only middleweight title defenses during this period, he defeated such heavyweights as Johnny Risko, Paulino Uzcudun and King Levinsky, real bruisers and no pushovers at the time.

He battered light-heavyweights Mike McTigue, Leo Lomski, Maxey Rosenbloom, Charley Bellanger and George Manley.

He extended champ Tommy Loughran to the limit in a try at Tommy's lightheavy title in Chicago on March 28, 1929 in a bout in which he was guaranteed $50,000 if he lost but only $10,000 if he won.

He got another chance at the 175 pound title in 1933 when he chased Maxie Rosenbloom futilely for fifteen rounds in Madison Square Garden and dropped the decision.

When his handicap match against big Jack Sharkey was called a draw at Ebbets Field in Brooklyn on July 22, 1931, even the heavyweight title seemed within reach of the undersized terror. Max Schmeling, however, put an end to that. The German's powerful right hand was too much for Mickey, who made his usual valiant try but was a knockout victim on September 26, 1932.

Walker had relinquished his middleweight title in 1931, seeing no particular reason for continuing the ordeal of weight making with no big money matches available. His career was amazingly long, spanning some sixteen years and ranging from meeting the post World War I era expert boxers like Britton, Ward, Malone, Krug, Shade and others, through the Flowers-Greb period, and building up to heavyweight kings Sharkey and Schmeling. Mickey really fought 'em all!

Writer Paul Gallico, in a tribute to him in the twilight of his career, offered an interesting analysis of Mickey's durability. . . . "Why did Walker last so long? Because in addition to being a powerful slugger, he was a first class boxer and one of the most deceptive of fighters and hardest boxers to hit. He was a great blocker, with his big powerful arms, and many a lethal punch rolled off his shoulders, upper arms, neck and forearms. Added to this, he had a staunch chin set firmly on his neck and could sop up punches like a blotter . . . "

One of the most unimpressive of all good fighters in the gym, Walker was a changed man once the gong rang. In action he was colorful. He liked to bull his foe into the ropes where he would whale away with powerful hooks to head and body. A solid puncher it took a good boxer to last the limit with him when Mickey really turned the heat on at his peak.

Tagged the "Toy Bulldog" by the late Francis Albertanti many years ago, he was far from a plaything once the going got rough. Few could stand and trade punches with him, and as he showed in his second bout with Ace Hudkins when he turned boxer, he could do a pretty good job at that, too.

But above and beyond all this, there was a flair about him, a devil-may-care dash of D'Artagnan which made him one of the most popular fighters of his time. There were times outside the ring when the revelry of an after-fight celebration might spill over into a bit of truculence, but when this flurry had subsided, there was the same old Smiling Mickey—everybody's friend.

Like the rest of the heroes, he fought too long. The last entry in the record book against his name is a "KO by" but that is the inevitable fate of all ring heroes.

Today he is surprisingly unmarked, his appearance always drawing wonderment that "such a little guy could fight and beat heavyweights". He smiles as readily as of yore, although the huge fortune he earned in the ring has long since been strewn along the happy highway of the gay life he chose.

He has earned some reputation as a primitive painter, in recent years. The color of his past lending some of its quality to his paintings. His paintings have been on exhibition in New York and in Hollywood and in his new field, he has met with considerable success.

BILLY CONN: THE COLLAR AD HERO

Since fight people are no less impressed by affluence than the rest of us, long retired Billy Conn is the object of considerable attention when he shows up in town to add to a big fight ballyhoo these days. A bit bulgy and balding, but still attractive, the old Pittsburgh "collar ad"—his opinions given added lustre by reputed wealth—is eagerly sought out by press and sundry others in search of pre-contest comment. Never one to hold back any ideas he may have on anything, Conn given importance by his past high ring stature and his present high solvency, has over the past decade blossomed into a kind of Barney Baruch of the Boxing business. Apparently enjoying his new status as one of Pugilism's elder statesmen, Billy usually blows into town a week or so before the big battle, emphasizes his financial well-being by engaging quarters in the fanciest hostelry—in New York it's the posh hundred dollars a day Hampshire House—and is now available for interviews.

Time and oil wealth have lubricated the one-time rough edges of the hardboiled kid from East Liberty, Pa. into the conservative smoothness that marks the successful business man. The tough talk of his fighting days has been tempered by modulated accents, the challenge of the old Conn smile replaced by the charm of self-assurance and economic sufficiency.

Conn is kinder in his comments about contemporary fighters today than he was a decade ago which is in line with the general moderation in everything that now distinguishes him. He still sees possibilities of Patterson developing into an outstanding heavyweight champion, gives Paul Pender credit for knowing what boxing is all about, and calls young welter king Emile Griffith one of the sharpest young boxers to come along in many years. On the subject of clever boxing no one is more qualified to be listened to than Billy Conn; he was one of the greatest boxers of all time. Completely lacking in any real fire power, he nonetheless compiled one of the best records in the book; relying entirely upon skill, heart and a deceptive ruggedness.

In a division which has had its full quota of quality fighters, he was one of the best light heavyweight champions of them all.

Few boxers ever had a more trying apprenticeship in the ring. Never an amateur, he was so continually mixed up in street corner and alley scraps, there was no place for him to go but into the ring, and since by his own admission, working had no appeal for him; it had to be for money.

From the beginning he feared no man. According to the record book he lost his first fight, a four rounder, in 1935. A complete novice he went along tangling with local talent in and around Pittsburgh, gaining experience which most boxers today find in the Golden Gloves. According to Conn himself, he didn't become what he calls a real fighter until he hooked up with another promising Pittsburgh boy, Honeyboy Jones. The pair met four times; in the last two set-tos Conn established clear superiority and the good looking eighteen year old was on his way.

Battle-tested capable Fritzie Zivic spotted him weight and gave him a hard time of it, but Conn, staging one of the stretch finishes which were to feature his efforts in later years, edged out a bitter decision over Fritzie on Dec. 8, 1936.

In 1937 Billy Conn, not yet twenty years of age, performed a most remarkable feat. He engaged in 7 bouts that year opposing 5 men who became middleweight champions! He defeated Babe Risko, Vince Dundee, Teddy Yarosz and Young Corbett, all former titleholders, and lost to Corbett and champion-to-be Solly Krieger.

Strangely enough the lone man he faced who was not a champion was the one he credits for making him the outstanding ringman he turned out to be. "I don't care what anybody says, but Oscar Rankins hurt me more than any man I ever fought. There was something about that guy, he never stopped forcing you and he'd tear your belly apart with body punches; he was a red headed guy and there must have been some Irish in him too," grinned Conn. "When they raised my hand at the end of that fight, I was ready for any man in the world."

In 1938 he evened the score with Solly Krieger—"another mighty tough bird who never got the credit he deserved. The fight between Krieger and Rankins in Pittsburgh was the best fight ever seen anywhere for my dough."—he says. But Billy dropped a decision to Teddy Yarosz which still rankles him to this day;—"he held, ran, and grabbed and they gave him the decision!"

For some reason his home town was slow warming up to Conn despite his outstanding success—"What do you expect, from Pittsburgh," he once said, "they had the greatest fighter in the world fighting out of there for years—Harry Greb—and they never really gave him the support he deserved."

So, like many another prophet without honor in his own home town, Conn had to make it big elsewhere and this is exactly what happened. Coming into New York to meet Fred Apostoli after beating Krieger, he was on the betting short-end but at the conclusion of ten bitterly contested rounds in the Garden, on Jan. 6, 1939, the Pittsburgher was declared the winner. There were some dissenters, so a month later Conn repeated over the Californian by a wider margin this time. Apostoli at that time was verging on greatness as a middleweight boxer, and Conn does not minimize his own achievement when he insists that Fred Apostoli was the best "all-around" fighter he ever met.

"Sure, there were the big punchers and the cuties, but Apostoli could do everything in there. He was a wonder when he fought me," is Conn's encomium to the Coast fighter.

Conn had beaten five middleweight kings without winning that title. Now weight and maturity were advancing him into the heavier class. As a light heavyweight Conn came to glory in the ring. To gain his championship he was called upon to defeat the smart, powerful, and dangerous hitting southpaw Melio Bettina, a trick he turned twice, winning the New York State version of the light heavyweight crown in the Garden on July 13, 1939 and defending this fractional title successfully against this hard-to-lick lefthander in Pittsburgh on Sept. 25 of the same year. His acceptance as champion became universal when he had to go all out to beat the N.B.A. nominee highly capable Gus Lesnevich in the Garden on Nov. 17, 1940. As he always did, he gave a defeated foe another chance, and repeated against the stubbornly resisting Gus in Detroit the following June.

With the 175 pounders thoroughly subdued, Conn publicly challenged Joe Louis; solidifying his deft with victories over heavyweights Bob Pastor and Lee Savold. While the Pastor fight, winding up in a flurry of foul claims by the New Yorker, shrilly amplified by his manager, waspish Jimmy Johnston, triggered a feud between Johnston and Conn which sizzled for months afterwards, Conn's exhibition against Lee Savold—then an unusually promising big fellow—was one of Billy's banner performances.

Canny Mike Jacobs and collaborators then set the "build-up" boom in motion, and by June of 1941 when Conn and Louis climbed into the ring, it had become the most eagerly awaited meeting of the decade. Conn did not disappoint the 55,000 customers who laid 450,000 depression dollars on the line to bet their money's worth from the brilliant boxing Billy, and the mighty blasting Bomber. Unshaken by his lack of a punch against the dread dynamics of the great Louis, Conn by some accounts came into the thirteenth round with a lead on points. This, however, became purely academic when a Louis barrage which many contemporaries charged to Conn's bravado in attempting to trade punches instead of pursuing a defensive pattern, penetrated his cleverness, and ended a gallant bid with just twelve seconds of the round remaining. Scaling 174 pounds to Louis' 199½, Conn was widely hailed for his performance, and rightly so.

During the training period Conn had suffered the distraction of a vendetta which completely obscured the Johnston jibes, a clash of personalities between himself and hard-bitten former ballplayer "Greenfield Jimmy" Smith, a rough customer whose prospects of becoming Conn's father-in-law disturbed him no little. This had culminated into a conflict which made headlines coast to coast.

Feuds were never alien to the good-looking Conn whose handsome features once sent a covey of training-camp visiting schoolteachers into dismay "that such a good-looking boy should have to be fighting Joe Louis". Conn's looks belied his temper on occasions, although usually pleasant, his tongue could be as sharp as his boxing: he was one of the last of the "Talking" fighters. Like clever Jim Corbett years before him he would often taunt his opponents while active in the ring: but at his peak Billy did not need caustic conversation to help his case.

He mastered the knack of arm blocking to a degree that left his features completely unmarked after years of battling. His left hook, while not numbing was like a whip lash as he raked his rivals with blinding swiftness. Few light heavies took a punch as well, his ruggedness was not revealed by his build, he did not rely upon leg speed to the extent that Jimmy Slattery and others of that school did, but when he made a move, it meant something and the moves were quick. He was as game as they come; and had the competitive spirit to get up steam as a tough bout progressed and out-finish the other fellow with a burst of action. There have been few better "stretch performers" than this clever, combative former champion.

Before entering the army, middleweight champion Tony Zale was little more than a workout for him in what turned out to be his unrecognized farewell as a first-class fighter on Feb. 13, 1942; with World War II raging he was called up soon after.

What happened to Billy Conn in the years of his army service has proven mystifying to fight people ever since. Only twenty-nine at the time he was separated from service it could hardly have been age. Upon his and Louis' return to civilian life arrangements were speedily concluded for the much-heralded return bout. High above the chorus of anticipation over the pending contest soloed the somber warning of Gene Tunney, that Conn was finished as a fighter. "The fight will be a farce," predicted the one-time champion, "Conn has been a playboy, he is through!"

Unfortunately, Gene who neither before nor since had ever been hailed as a soothsayer, was only too right in this instance. Although Louis himself showed traces of ring rust, the flitting, flashing, phantom boxer that had been Billy Conn was clearly a casualty of World War II; in its place a weary shadow of a once great boxer offered but token resistance to a lumbering Louis before being counted out in the eighth round on June 19, 1946 in New York's Yankee

Stadium, to the vast discomfiture of a crowd of 45,000 which had paid up to a hundred dollars a ticket.

His performance notwithstanding, Conn collected a staggering $312,958 as his share of the near two million dollar "gate". Happily, from all appearances and unlike so many other fighters, he put this golconda to good use with oil well investments which turned out to be gushers from all reports. Because of this windfall he is free of the worries that have plagued so many others, notably his eminent rival, Louis: whom he is said to have once contacted with the idea of advising Joe on some oil dealings. For his present affluence more power to him, he was a truly great boxer at his pinnacle whose final effort should be disregarded in any summation of his standing as one of the best of them all.

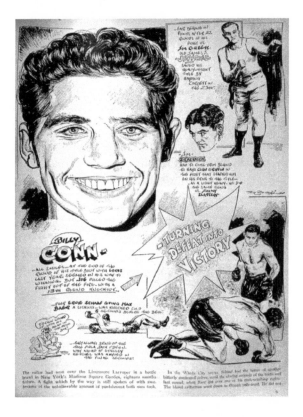

Equipped with an encyclopedic knowledge of the sweet science, Carroll's work featured multiple subjects. *The Ring* (November 1942)

RAY ROBINSON: THE GREATEST CHAMPION SINCE 1922?

Twenty-one years after his first professional fight in the huge New York Arena, Madison Sq. Garden placards advertising his match with young Denny Moyer describe Sugar Ray Robinson as the "All-Time Great Champion of Champions". While the cynical may label this lavish encomium nothing more than the same old box office "hypo", there has been a surprisingly large amount of agreement with this sweeping statement, remarkable since personality-wise Sugar Ray has been something less than adored in his bailiwick. Leading the chorus of "yeas" to this contention has been Garden Boxing Director Harry Markson, who, all commercial considerations aside, has long held that if Sugar Ray does not meet all the qualifications of the perfect fighter, who does?; and goes on to give solid support to the Garden's showcard claim with this logic, as reported in Milton Gross' sports column in the New York Post, " . . . during the height of his career, Sugar Ray didn't lack a single attribute which the great fighters need. He had a left hook, a right cross, defensive skill, the will to win, ring generalship, speed of hand and foot, courage, a sense of pacing, a variety of punches, the ability to size up an opponent after a round or two, split second reflexes, magnificent legs, and the ability to reach superior heights when the situation required it. Some keener students of boxing than I may have discovered a flaw, but I didn't see it, and if Robinson had any, where and when did they show?"

As complete as this size-up is, Mr. Markson's matchmaker Teddy Brenner, bolsters it with some added observations on Robinson. "People are inclined to overlook," he declares, "that along with his great skill, Sugar Ray was the greatest one punch hitter we've ever had. Was there ever a tougher fellow than Gene Fullmer? I don't think so; Ray got him out of there with one left hook, and that was a guy who'd seldom been off his feet before, let alone knocked out. Steve Beloise took a good punch, Sugar Costner looked like a coming champ, if you think Bobo Olsen wasn't a good fighter look at his record when he was young; well, Ray took them all out with just one shot. Many a guy was around at the finish of a fight with Robinson just because Ray felt like sharpening up his boxing that particular evening."

In the forty years since the first copy of The Ring appeared many fighting men have flashed across the fistic firmament, and Robinson's credentials as detailed in behalf of his being the super-star of them all is naturally vulnerable to counter-claims in favor of certain others.

Certainly, one of the most valid of these contenders, for the superior status of greatest fighter of the past four decades, is the peerless Benny Leonard.

Although the undefeated lightweight champion did most of his boxing in the previous decade, winning the championship in 1917, he was still in his prime during the early years of this magazine's existence, and can be included among those eligible for top ranking during the past two score of years.

There is every evidence that Leonard possessed all the ring assets of a Robinson, combining beautiful "ballet-like" boxing skill with powerful punching. Invincible as a lightweight champion, some critical whispers have come down through the years that the great Benny rarely made the weight limit, and much of his reputation was gained in contests with smaller men. Whether or not this was the case, Leonard in frequent forays into the welterweight class demonstrated a decisive ability to handle men in the heavier division with ease and dispatch, which seems to take care of that disparagement.

Jack Dempsey, likewise won the world's heavyweight championship in a prior era, beating Jess Willard in 1919 in what has been called his most devastating performance, but he again—like Leonard—was still a mighty fighting machine in the early Twenties, and the dominating figure in boxing during most of the early days of "The Ring". Back in 1950 a consensus of sports writers voted Dempsey the greatest fighter of the half century, since that year Robinson has embellished his reputation with the most successful comeback of any fighter in history, and Rocky Marciano came to ring glory. Any rundown of Dempsey's ring talents, has become repetitious. His tigerish attack, steel chinned ruggedness, and savage punching have been so consistently lauded over the years, they have become traditional in ring annals.

Still, strongly mitigating against according him pre-eminence among the fighting men of the past forty years, is the cold fact that he never faced the most formidable challenger of this time, Harry Wills. While this may have been through no fault of his own, it happens to be true that during the period ranging from 1919 when the Manassa Mauler was crowned champion until and including 1924, the pantherish Wills was clearly best of what opposition there was available.

Within this time Dempsey faced Carpentier, Miske, Brennan, Gibbons and Firpo, during the same period only Fred Fulton could be induced to meet Wills among the leading heavies, and he proved no match for the Brown Panther.

Yet, Dempsey was the man who made boxing a million dollar business, his colorfully ferocious style of fighting fascinated the public, turning the glove game into a golconda during the post-World War I period. To many he remains the "champion of champions" to this very day.

Gene Tunney, eventual conqueror of Dempsey, finds his fistic as well as his fiscal prestige advancing with each passing year. Whether this is due to the aphorism voiced by fight manager-philosopher Eddie Walker, years ago that, "Money makes anybody greater," or the growing realization that Tunney may have had the style to beat Dempsey at any time is a matter of opinion. At any rate, more and more students of ring affairs are coming around to old-time Tunney-attaché Jimmy Bronson's idea that Tunney quit fighting short of his peak, and could have gone on to gain ranking in a class by himself. Praise for Gene came from an unusual—but competent—quarter some time ago when astute George Gainford, after first admitting little personal affection for Tunney, conceded that in his opinion, of all the heavyweight champions familiar to him Tunney would have been the best bet to beat Rocky Marciano. "I don't care too much for Tunney," admitted big George, "but he had the style, the brains, the stamina and condition to give Rocky Marciano more trouble than any of the other champs."

While it may be somewhat difficult to award Tunney top position on the strength of two defenses of his title—against Dempsey and Tom Heeney—there is no disputing his right to be acclaimed the outstanding boxer of the century for post-career achievement in the business world.

Among fighters active since 1922, Joe Louis belongs in his own category. Joe was a social force; he changed the thinking of a nation. Today Negro athletes in all sports revel in a freedom of participation which was unknown before his time. While there have been other factors operative in this sociological upheaval, the career of Joe Louis contributed mightily to this new enlightenment; no single individual was more responsible for the breakdown of long-standing barriers. Notably, the "color line" in organized baseball, where both Branch Rickey and Jackie Robinson freely admit that the example of Joe Louis made their task so much easier.

While possessing his share of human imperfections, the public accounted them minor as it paid homage to Louis for his unswervingly genteel behaviour, commendable war service, and amazing record as world's champion. Louis' financial affairs, in reverse ratio to the esteem brought Tunney by success, have tended to obscure his great feats in the ring in the minds of the present generation.

Children of his heyday grew to manhood knowing no other world's heavyweight champion; he held the title longer than anyone else, eleven years, defended it more times than anyone else, 26, and took on all comers. A facet of his career startling in its merit, is Louis' stunt of knocking out two ex-heavyweight champions Primo Carnera and Max Baer in 1935, less than two years after he fought his first professional fight!

As a two-handed power hitter he was in a class by himself—a sparmate once called his left jab as powerful as a good puncher's right cross—not for nothing was he called the "Brown Bomber." Yet he had a flaw which he never fully overcame, he could be hit with a right hand, but for this there would have been little question as to his rating as the peer of all heavyweight champions. In spite of this weakness, this stature is still accorded him by many, writer Jimmy Cannon being the most vocal in this assertion.

His unfortunate comeback, attempted against the well-meaning advice of his friends, is invariably discounted by fistic appraisers.

Only one champion in the history of the modern ring has a record clear of defeat, that is Rocky Marciano, and that is sufficient to make his consideration as the top performer logical, if not unanimous. Marciano accomplished what he did in the face of formidable handicaps, a very late start, and a natural ungainliness, both of which he overcame by the most intense dedication to fighting ever displayed by anyone; with an assist from manager Al Weill in a most cannily contrived campaign of opponent selection.

No fighter was ever more meticulously matched than the "Brockton Blockbuster" while on his way up. This, plus the fact, that trainer Charlie Goldman had the good sense not to impair Rocky's power by diluting it with anything remotely resembling ring finesse or refinement. His awkwardness eventually complemented his numbing punches, with an unorthodox defense, this, coupled with boundless stamina, courage, determination, strength, and incredible condition paid off with a history of 49 fights with 45 knockouts, minus any loss or draw.

Most of the belittlement of Marciano's unbeaten record centers on the ages of his most noted foes. Critics point out that Lee Savold, Louis, Archie Moore, Jersey Joe Walcott and Ezzard Charles were verging on middle age, their best years just a memory, when the New Englander got around to them. This, however, was no fault of Rocky's, who never said "No" to any challenger.

So much for the bigger pretenders to pre-eminence among fighters of the past forty years. Besides Leonard—Harry Greb, Mickey Walker, Henry Armstrong, and Willie Pep are prominent nominees for this stratospheric status.

Former fighter and present historian Packey O'Gatty recalls that Harry Greb once toured with burlesque shows, billed as "The Marvel of the Ring." No fighter ever deserved the description more. Although he was most impressive as a light-heavyweight, Greb could make the middleweight limit handily, and if considered as such, is a solid contender for the title "Greatest Fighter of the past Forty Years." In fourteen years in the ring Greb fought more than 250 times against opponents in every class from welterweight to heavyweight. He feared nobody, a whirlwind fighter, he set a terrific pace from bell to bell, often with little regard for the Marquis of Queensbury. Inside of a year—although only a middleweight—he beat heavyweight contender Tommy Gibbons, handed Gene Tunney his only defeat winning the American light heavyweight title in the process, then "windmilled" Tommy Loughran all over the old Madison Sq. Garden ring in defense of it. The match in which he lost the U.S. crown to Tunney on Dec. 10, 1923, caused wide dissatisfaction with the decision going to Gene.

It is doubtful that any middleweight, Sugar Ray included, could have duplicated these feats against heavier men of such calibre. Greb was such a phenomenal fighter, his challenge to Dempsey was taken seriously, many still claiming Jack Doc Kearns, Dempsey's pilot, feared the "Pittsburgh Windmill."

Mickey Walker, no bigger than Greb, like him showed an astonishing ability to compete against bigger men. Winner of both the welter and middleweight championships, the "Toy Bulldog" never weighing any more than 170lbs. and only 5 feet 7 inches tall, defeated heavies of the calibre of Paolino Uzcudun, Johnny Risko and King Levinsky—no setups at the time he met them—and boxed a draw with big Jack Sharkey. One wonders if Sugar Ray could have played the part of David against these ring Goliaths with such success.

Still, both Greb and Walker ran into plenty of trouble against men their own size. Mike McTigue, Jeff Smith, Tiger Flowers, welterweight Soldier Bartfield, Mike Gibbons and Mike O'Dowd, repeatedly fought Greb on at least even terms, Walker never established any clear superiority over middleweight Dave Shade, few agreed with the decision that deprived Flowers of his title when he met Mickey, and Ace Hudkins and Joe Dundee were other small men who proved tough problems for Mickey.

The late Hype Igoe once wrote that at his peak "Hammering Henry" Armstrong would have beaten anybody at or around his weight. Armstrong's attack was unstoppable, maintained old Hypus, and his whirlwind offense would have blasted through the cleverest of defenses. Two years ago, sportswriter Jimmy Powers in the N.Y. Daily News, attempted to prove that Armstrong was the greatest Negro fighter of all time—no small honor—by analyzing his career in comparison with others. Outside the realm of conjecture and looming large on the factual horizon are the three world's championships won and held by Henry Armstrong simultaneously, in the featherweight, lightweight and welterweight classes, an achievement unequalled by any boxer since the sport began and one doubtlessly beyond the reach of any fighter of the future.

Sugar Ray has been quoted as naming Willie Pep the greatest boxer of his time, puissant praise from one master to another. Certainly, at his best and before his serious airplane accident, wispy Willie has mastered techniques of clever boxing rarely seen before or since. Performing with blinding speed and coordination, Pep at times seemed to be moving in two directions at once as his lightning like thrusts at his opponents came from everywhere. Endowed with inhuman quickness of eye and reflex, Willie, before his style became tainted by unbecoming tactics, and tarnished by the passing of time, was the epitome of boxing brilliance at its best.

Some detractors have deprecated the quality of his opposition, but he outclassed the field by such overwhelming margins, it was obvious that at any period in ring history he would have been a wonder.

Worthy of inclusion in the minds of many no doubt as candidates for top fighter since 1922 are such idols as Tony Canzoneri, Jimmy McLarnin and flyweight Pancho Villa. Canzoneri, champion in two divisions, featherweight and lightweight, great boxer, sharp hitter and valiant warrior was indeed a wonderful fighter but was plagued with inconsistency throughout his career, losing often to fighters whom a great boxer such as he should have handled easily. Harry Dublinsky, Johnny Jadick, Wesley Ramey, Andre Routis, Chuck Woods and Sammy Fuller, all Canzoneri victors, were good fighters but not of the class to have beaten an aspirant for top honours of the past forty years.

Jimmy McLarnin, likewise a great public hero, conqueror of thirteen champions in classes from flyweight to welterweight, combined power punching with shrewd boxing and heart to a remarkable degree, but the weight edges Jimmy enjoyed were too frequent to permit him a pre-eminent position.

Villa, greatest of the oriental fighters, was a genuine pugilistic prodigy who not only won the flyweight championship, but buzz-sawed his way through the ranks of the best bantamweights of his time. But he could not beat Frankie Genaro, who had the answer to his rapid-fire punching.

Billy Conn performed miracles with cleverness alone, in Conn's case reinforced with a deceptive ruggedness, but lacking a punch he failed in comparison with Jack Delaney for instance, on a par with him for skill and at the time also possessing a knockout wallop.

The late Jess McMahon, long time sports promoter, always insisted that had Cuban Kid Chocolate, best of the Latin-American fighters, taken proper care of himself he would have become the best little man of all time.

Horse races are not the only things created by differences of opinion, and fight people, aficionados, and Ring readers are both welcome and entitled to their own designations as the greatest fighter of the past forty years. They can if they choose use Sugar Ray Robinson as the model in comparing their candidates. They will find him hard to beat.

Giving the question considerable thought throughout his career, Carroll ultimately settled on Ray Robinson as his choice for the Greatest of All Time. *The Ring* (July 1950)

HOW WOULD CLAY HAVE DONE AGAINST STARS OF PAST?

An Analysis of Cassius' Chances in Some Mythical Embroglios

In line with his new "humility", the war cry of Cassius Clay, "I am the greatest", does not ring as loud and clear as it once did. But let no man believe that his unfamiliar restraint on the champion's part betokens a lessening of confidence.

Although the volume has been muted Muhammad is no less definite in his opinion that no heavyweight champion of the past could have beaten him. Clay capsules his critique of all the one-time kings in one simple sentence. "They were all either too slow or too small!"

Harkening back just a few short years to the time of Sonny Liston, when many fistic observers went overboard on the "invincibility" of the since deflated Big Bear, critics have become wary of tabbing the outstanding champions of other days as inferior to Clay. Still, it is becoming obvious that compared to titleholders of yore, Muhammad Ali has a lot going for him.

Everyone concedes that no man his size ever possessed such speed of hand and foot. But it is equally evident that the better champions of the past had assets of their own which Clay hasn't shown.

The first and most important of these is punch. Cassius hasn't flashed firepower comparable to that of such blasters as Joe Louis, Rocky Marciano and Jack Dempsey. Max Baer, Max Schmeling, Jersey Joe Walcott, even Ingemar Johannson and Floyd Patterson packed more power than Clay has shown thus far.

Clay is quick to point out that Louis, for all his greatness, was slow on his feet. It is true that Joe was no fancy Dan for footwork but the old Brown Bomber could unleash lightning-fast punch combinations with devastating effect.

In his younger days, Louis had one of the fastest right hands ever seen in the ring. It boomed out of his slow-moving gait with the speed and suddenness of a striking rattler. Joe was also capable of following it up with a double left hook to body and head with great rapidity. Against a foe such as Louis, Clay would have undoubtedly tried to use his leg speed to its utmost with a lot of dancing about as he did with Liston.

He would succeed in making Louis look cumbersome and plodding for a time, but Clay's defensive technique relies greatly upon leaning backwards out of range of his opponent's blows. Against a right hand of Louis's speed and power, this would have been a highly dangerous maneuver and the current champion would have been flirting with disaster every time he tried it.

Clay does not give the impression of extreme ruggedness, and just one of Joe's right-hand bombs finding the target could have meant curtains for Cassius. On the credit side for Muhammad, it should be recalled that Billy Conn, a boxer of the Clay stripe, and only a light heavyweight, at that—gave Louis trouble before falling in a late round. Bob Pastor, a crafty boxer, survived ten rounds with Louis.

It is possible to conceive of Clay getting a decision over Louis in a bout lasting the full fifteen rounds. But it is not so easy to imagine his going that distance without getting tagged by Louis's fast hands somewhere along the way. When that happened, it could mean the end of everything right then and there for Muhammad Ali.

There are those who saw in Clay's adept handling of George Chuvalo a similar dose for Rocky Marciano had fate ever brought the undefeated retired champion into the ring against Muhammad Ali. Both Rocky and the rugged Canadian are charter members of the old-time school of sluggers. But there are important differences between the two, all of them in Marciano's favor.

First there is the matter of punch. Chuvalo isn't the same class with the Brockton Blockbuster in this vital department. In the matter of defense, Chuvalo stood up straight against Clay. Rocky fought in a crouch which would have made him a much more difficult target than the upright Canadian.

Although Rocky wasn't clever, he still was the type of foe "you had to look for", in the words of Ray Robinson. He fought close to the ground, his head barricaded by his heavy forearms and elbows. Clean shots at him were not easy to get.

Clay insists Rocky would have been easy for him because he was too small, his arms were too short, and he was too slow. This may be true but Cassius forgets that there are ropes around the ring. Chuvalo did his best work when he jammed the elusive champion into them.

At trapping a rival against the ropes, or in a corner, and then bludgeoning him mercilessly Rocky Marciano was in a class by himself. Rocky would have staked his victory hopes against Cassius on such tactics. Whether such demolition methods would have succeeded against the bigger, faster and smarter Clay is anyone's guess. The opinion here is that Rocky, who was a bleeder, might have been too hampered by cuts by the sharpshooting Clay to get the full mileage out of his blasting attack.

Of the mythical opponents here discussed Jack Dempsey is the only one in a class with Clay for both hand and foot speed. Clay dismisses the Manassa Mauler as too little. There would have been besides a height advantage, a thirty-pound disparity in Clay's favour.

At his peak Dempsey was quick as a cat on his feet. He was not called the Tiger Man for nothing. He would rip a left hook to the body and to the head, followed by a right in a blur of fast action. He relied so much upon his offense as a defense that the great middleweight Harry Greb challenged him frequently because, as Greb put it, "Dempsey checks his brains in the dressing room".

The crafty Tunney proved there was something to Greb's analysis. Clay is a thinking fighter. His comments on boxing and boxers prove that. Against Dempsey he would have had all the advantage of cleverness that Tunney possessed.

On the other hand, he would have been spotting Jack—as in the cases of Marciano and Louis—punching power, and this never can be discounted, especially among the heavyweights.

Regardless of result Dempsey and Clay would have made a great fight, bringing together a high octane rapid-fire offense against an equally fast moving defense.

While Clay's chin is not exactly suspect, no one knows how rugged he really is. Against Englishman Henry Cooper he was down and in shaky condition at the bell ending the fourth round.

Liston, the only other hitter he has faced, never landed a worthwhile blow in their two fiascos. Until the matter of Clay's ruggedness has been settled more to the satisfaction of the afficionados it is still somewhat premature to rate him as a probable victor over blasters such as Dempsey, Louis and Marciano despite the distinct advantages in speed and skill he would have had over them.

In answer to a query as to how he thought he would have fared against Jack Johnson after viewing an old film of this all-time master in action, Cassius Clay said, "Johnson was a talker. He keeps talking in the ring all the time."

A mythical match between the loquacious lad from Louisville and the garrulous giant from Galveston would have settled the all-time conversational championship with the ropes. In this Cassius would have had to be favored. He has been quoted as refusing to play the role of Johnson in a movie because of the old champion's interracial marriages and what he would have had to say to Johnson on this subject probably would have topped any rejoinder the glib Johnson could have voiced. Cassius might even have angered Johnson to such a pass that Jack's fabled poise and skill would have been affected allowing Muhammad Ali to find openings in his airtight defense.

Although time is decimating their ranks, adherents of Johnson as the best of them all remain unswerving. They base their superlative assessments of the Texan in his impenetrable defense.

"Johnson would have caught Clay jabs like Willie Mays catches a baseball," declaims the indestructible octogenarian Charlie Rose, a relic of the Johnson era. He may well have done so, but how much landing of punches could he have done from his flat-footed stance against the stepping, mobile Clay?

A fight between Clay and Johnson can hardly be visualized as an exciting affair. Cassius, taller, and with a vast edge in legwork, could well have sprinted his way to a 15 round verdict over the blocking, countering Johnson, who preferred the kind of foes who came to him, thereby setting themselves up for his swift retaliatory counters.

Much the same analysis could be made of a match between Clay and Gene Tunney had these two been contemporaries. After Johnson and Jim Corbett, Tunney usually gets the call as the cleverest boxer among the heavyweight kings. Like most boxers Gene was more at home as a counter fighter but he was also adept at the left jab and right cross one-two, with the trailing right packing considerable power. Like Dempsey and Marciano, he would have been conceding to the present champion height and weight. Gene stepped about smartly in action but Clay's unusual fleetness gives him an edge here.

A Clay-Tunney match would never figure to set the crowd roaring but would have provided an interesting duel of skill. In such a contest Cassius, as the bigger and faster of the two, would have to be given the edge in the odds.

Comparisons such as these between Cassius Clay and champions of the past are intriguing but are not without danger to the comparer since, as in the drab denouement of Sonny Liston, the future may make such analyses seem ridiculous.

Were Henry Cooper to land a lucky one or Doug Jones get the official nod over Clay next time, a conjectural piece like this would become a mere flight of fancy.

On the other hand, no one has beaten Cassius Clay. Only one man has ever come close in the bouts he has had since turning pro. Nor does anyone figure to do so in the near future.

With a situation such as this all that is left is speculation on how well the fast stepping, fast punching present kingpin would have done with the giants of the past.

THE MAN IN THE BROADWAY WINDOW: MATCHLESS DEMPSEY

New York's Annual Summer Festival is under way to the blare of tourist-tempting trumpets sounding forth the wonders of the great metropolis. The ballyhooers have plenty to blow about. Visitors have the opportunity to indulge themselves in an endless round of museums, historic spots, shimmering skyscrapers, theatres, Fifth Avenue, Lincoln Center, the downtown financial district, the five-cent Staten Island ferry ride, the circular New Garden, Greenwich and East Village, and countless other features which native New Yorkers seldom get around to seeing but tourists always discover.

On New York's famous Broadway, long-time lure of the hinterlander, the lights are still bright and the crowds still large. But the tinsel of the famed thoroughfare has taken on a tawdriness, and a good deal of its glitter has become phony. It retains a good part of its fascination and among its still-redeeming features is the glimpse it affords of one of sport's most fabled figures, Jack Dempsey.

Almost daily, around lunch and dinner time, passer-byes take time out to stare at the old Manassa Mauler ensconced at a window-side table, usually surrounded by autograph seekers. Although his once coal-black hair is grey-spattered, Dempsey looks many years younger than his age of 73. His perennial appearance through the window of his Broadway restaurant has become one of the brighter spots on New York's once Great White Way. Visiting firemen can always tell the neighbours back home they got a good look at a guy the old folks have been telling them about for a long time.

So, if the summer festival publicizers want to include a look at one of the most famous of all heavyweight champions in their prospectus, here is the suggestion free for the asking—if they haven't done so already.

In strong contrast to the fates of most of the cafes and eating places run by fighters, Jack Dempsey's restaurant has proved as durable as the old champion himself.

Jack's original spot occupied a corner in midtown New York on 8th Avenue at West 50th Street, opposite old Madison Square Garden. It was the brainchild of the late Max Waxman, then handling Dempsey's business, in 1939.

A few years later the site shifted Eastward to Broadway where, through the years, with Jack framed in the window, it has become a must-see for Broadway strollers.

According to Jack Amiel—noted as the owner of long-shot Kentucky Derby winner, Count Turf—and successor to Waxman and the Amron brothers as Jack's charge d'affaires, the restaurant assures Jack financial stability.

To this solvency is added income from the real estate in New York and personal appearances. Stipends for these engagements cover a wide range, dependent upon the size of the city and seating capacity. Where a worthwhile cause is involved, terms usually differ from those required from an out and out commercial proposition.

Many years ago, Jack made the mistake of endorsing a liquor but this was speedily abandoned when the injury to his professional image became apparent.

Jack's charisma is as long lasting as his restaurant and his youthful look. Sugar Ray Robinson has been in the habit of waiting for a late introduction at important bouts and then blanketing everybody with a big burst of crowd applause. At the recent Tiger-Foster light heavyweight championship, Sugar's welcome was as vociferous as ever, but for the first time in a long while, it was topped when Dempsey climbed into the ring behind Robinson, after being introduced.

One of the surest ways to start an argument is to call Dempsey the greatest of all heavyweight champions. Middle-agers who grew to manhood knowing no other champion but Joe Louis during the Brown Bomber's long eleven-year reign, are slow to accept this. And there is surprising support among the New Breed unfamiliar with both Louis and Dempsey for the controversial Cassius Clay (Muhammad Ali).

Veterans like Ring editor Nat Fleischer and Charley Rose stand firm for Jack Johnson. The "Greatest of All Time" dilemma is a question beyond settlement, but there is no dispute about who put boxing in the big money.

Jack Dempsey was the man who made the ring game a million-dollar business. Considering the kind of cash he put in the till, he should have been called Dollar-Sign Dempsey: $1,888,000 with Carpentier at Boyle's Thirty Acres in Jersey City in 1921; $1,270,000 with Firpo in the Polo Grounds in 1923; $1,895,733 with Tunney in Philadelphia's Municipal Stadium in 1926; $1,075,000 with Sharkey in Yankee Stadium in 1927, and $2,658,660 with Tunney in Chicago in 1927! Even by today's stratospheric fiscal barometer these figures are fantastic!

They were compiled in the days when bread was ten cents a loaf, twenty dollars a week was a good salary, and twenty-five dollars bought an excellent suit of clothes!

What was the secret of Dempsey's incredible drawing power? The Garden took a bath when it presented his conqueror, Tunney, against Heeney in 1928. There have been great and colorful fighters, both before and after Dempsey, but none has approached the plus two and a half million dollar gate he drew with Tunney in Chicago in 1927.

Dempsey's earnings from all sources: boxing, appearances, business ventures, refereeing and movies exceeds ten million dollars. In 1916 Dempsey wound up with 16 dollars, for boxing Wild Burt Kenny at the old Harlem Sporting Club in New York. Ten years later he got $717,000 for boxing Gene Tunney in Philadelphia. In his first fight in New York Dempsey faced Andre Anderson, managed by the late Jimmy Johnston. Johnston kept exhorting his man to fight harder. Finally Anderson turned to the manager and said, "Do you think I'm crazy? It's tough enough in here now. If I make this guy mad I'm liable to get killed!" In 1931 and 1932, under the management of Leonard Sachs, Dempsey made a barnstorming tour in which he faced 98 opponents in bouts limited to four rounds in cities from coast to coast. The junket turned out to be a real bonanza, the biggest touch being a four-round "no-decision" go with King Levinsky in Chicago on Feb. 18, 1932 for which he received $79,000. Other "names" of the period who met the Manassa Mauler on the tour, were Babe Hunt, Art Lasky, Charley Retzlaff, Jack Roper, K.O. Christner, Bearcat Wright, and Charley Bellanger.

Harry Wills, destined never to face Dempsey in the ring, always spoke well of the old champion. Harry's favorite tale about Dempsey concerned Dempsey's refusal to allow long-time sparmate Big Bill Tate to suffer any discrimination which he could prevent. Dempsey's actual "discoverer"—it has been claimed— was John Tholmer, old-time Negro boxing figure from New Orleans, who died 5 years ago at the great age of 99. Tholmer, who boxed Wills in 1912, first saw Dempsey's possibilities in Salt Lake City when he was known as Kid Blackie, touted him to boxing man Jack Price, who took him East to New York for three bouts.

When Dempsey won the championship from Willard in 1919 no weights were made public, but he is said to have been outweighed 58 pounds, 187 to 245. When one-time sparmate George Godfrey died destitute on the Pacific Coast in 1948 Dempsey footed the bill for the funeral of the "Dark Shadow of Lieperville". When Dempsey reached the age of 70 in 1965 among the thousands of messages of congratulations was one from Vice President Hubert Humphrey. No heavyweight champion ever used smaller men than Dempsey did for sparring partners. Among them were such stars as welterweights Jock

Malone and Panama Joe Gans, and middleweights Dave Shade and Allentown Joe Gans.

During a serious illness in 1939 Dempsey received more than 27,000 messages of cheer. He is in his tenth year of happy marriage to the former Deanna Pietelli. Famous movie star Estelle Taylor, whom he wed in 1925, and ex-showgirl Hannah Williams, married to Jack in 1933 were the former Mrs. Dempseys. Performing on a stage tour in 1922 he played the famous old New York Hippodrome. Movies of his life were stymied in the past by the demands of one-time manager, the late Jack Kearns, and the bitterness of Jess Willard, from whom he won the title.

Jack's two daughters by Hannah Williams have made him a happy five-time grandfather. He loves the pasteboards, card playing is his favorite pastime. His career gave former Postmaster General James A. Farley's climb to political fame its initial impetus, owing to the famous Dempsey-Wills controversy. In 1926 Farley, supporting Wills, barred the Dempsey-Tunney fight from New York. Dempsey's last refereeing stint in New York took place thirty-three years ago,

For Carroll, former heavyweight champion Jack Dempsey possessed an unmatched hold on the attention and curiosity of the public. *The Ring* (September 1968)

the third McLarnin-Ross welter title fight. Often called the Tiger-Man in his fighting days, Dempsey's current endorsement of a cat food on a TV commercial is, according to The Ring's Nat Loubet, a case of going from a "growl to a mee-yowl".

The years have had a little effect on the nervous cat-like quickness of his movements. A far-ranging nomad in his younger days he has been a New York resident for more than thirty years. Octogenarian old-time sports scribe, Ned Brown is rounding out more than a quarter century of association—publicity wise—with Dempsey. Jack has probably signed more autographs than any living individual, and no one has done so more willingly.

In the foregoing sentence lies much of the answer to the old champion's mystique. The Dempsey incandescence, catalyst of the million-dollar gate, radiating through a Broadway window still attracts and intrigues the public.

WAS GREB REALLY BEST FIGHTER FOR HIS POUNDS?

The volcanic celebration which erupted in the city of Pittsburgh following the World Series triumph of the Pirates caused reverberations countrywide. Probably no individual received this orgiastic frenzy with the mingled emotions of Billy Conn in his comfortable home in a Pittsburgh suburb.

As one of the best boxers of modern times, the good-looking light heavyweight made the lack of enthusiasm and appreciation on the part of Pittsburghers his pet peeve. "Before I was 20 years old," he would complain, "I had beaten five middleweight champions but I had to come to New York and whip Fred Apostoli before they gave me a tumble back home."

"They had the greatest fighter ever born and fighting in Pittsburgh, and they never even realized it."

The fighter Conn had in mind was Harry Greb.

Were Greb alive today he could well understand the feelings of baseball star Roberto Clemente, whose Latin-accented lamentations over being ignored until the recent World Series echo Billy Conn's criticisms of long ago.

The glare of the national spotlight has never penetrated the haze of Pittsburgh. Many would undoubtedly call Conn's high assessment of Greb extreme. But when one reviews the exploits of "The Pittsburgh Windmill," a phenomenon emerges.

Harry Greb was a middleweight who won the world championship from Johnny Wilson in 1923. But prior to this he had won the American light heavyweight championship—highly esteemed at that period—by handing Gene Tunney his sole defeat, in 1922. Greb defied the world, taking on as many heavyweights and light heavies as men his own size. Greb's philosophy was well expressed in this "Xmas Greetings" appearing in the Jan. 1925 issue of The Ring like this;

SEASON'S GREETINGS FROM HARRY GREB.

ANXIOUS TO DEFEND HIS LAURELS AGAINST ANY MAN WHO IS A LIKELY CONTENDER. WILL BOX LIGHT HEAVIES AND HEAVIES AS FAST AS THEY TOE THE MARK. IN ALL HIS YEARS OF CAMPAIGNING GREB HAS BARRED NO MAN, BLACK OR WHITE! WILLING TO GO THERE ON SHORT NOTICE. WRITE OR WRITE YOUR BEST TERMS. . . . FIRST COME, FIRST SERVED IS THE GREB MOTTO. SIGNED . . . HARRY GREB

WORLD MIDDLEWEIGHT CHAMPION

Greb wasn't kidding about the "short notice". He was always ready for anybody. In a fighting span of 13 years, he went to the post 290 times. Like most of the bouts of his era, many of Greb's contests were "no decision", which makes his greatness hard to tabulate.

But a run through of the outstanding names over whom he won decisions substantiates his standing among boxers as unsurpassed. Gene Tunney, Mickey Walker, Tommy Loughran, Billy Miske, Tom Gibbons, Jack Renault, Bill Brennan, Jimmy Slattery, Battling Levinsky, Mike McTigue, Jeff Smith, Kid Norfolk, Maxie Rosenbloom, Mike Gibbons, Charley Weinert, Frank Klaus, Willie Meehan, Jack Dillon, Bob Moha, Gunboat Smith, Bartley Madden, Eddie McGoorty, Ted Moore, Allentown Joe Gans and Augie Ratner comprise a list of Greb victims which takes in "Hall of Fame" middleweights, world champion light heavyweights and formidable heavyweights.

For a man with a notorious fondness for night life and female company, Greb's durability was as remarkable as his record. He made his first ring appearance in the old City Hall in Pittsburgh in 1913, winning the middleweight title after ten years of windmilling his way through all types of opposition. Greb's campaigning was as ceaseless as his style of boxing. In 1919 he fought 44 times.

Greb hit his peak in 1922 when, within a period of a few months, he defeated the great middleweight Jeff Smith, decisioned heavyweight contender Tom Gibbons; defeated Tunney for the U.S. 175 pound championship; and defended it successfully against Tommy Loughran.

Loughran, who engaged Greb four times later, credited much of his fistic education to Greb, whom he described as "a bundle of tricky moves who never got tired."

In a time when the color line was resorted to by many boxers Harry Greb ignored this unsporting racialism.

When Tunney and Gibbons turned down Leo P. Flynn's "Black Thunderbolt," Kid Norfolk, Greb stepped in against this highly competent light heavyweight. Their Pittsburgh encounter in 1921 cost both men dearly as they suffered eye injuries which had severe consequences. Greb, in 1926, volunteered as the first champion to defend his title against a Negro fighter since 1908.

A decision given to Mike McTigue over Tiger Flowers aroused such a public blast that New York Commission, headed by James A. Farley, reacted by exerting pressure in behalf of Flowers' getting a title chance. Flowers' prominence had been largely due to Greb's willingness to meet him in the small town of Fremont, Ohio in 1924.

Greb was a rarity of those times, a racial liberal who believed in "giving a colored guy a chance to make a buck". An unheralded Deep Southerner at the time, Flowers' performance against Greb catapulted him into the national spotlight.

Politically sensitive, the far-sighted Farley who espoused the case of Harry Wills in the Jack Dempsey controversy, prevailed upon Greb to meet Flowers, who became the first American Black champion since Jack Johnson in 1910 by winning the decision over Greb in Madison Sq. Garden in 1926.

The margin between the two men had been very close, not wide enough for a Negro fighter to win an important match, ordinarily, in those days, but the Deacon's prayers were answered. The men met again, with the edge equally slim, and again Flowers was called the winner.

The one great flaw in Greb's career was the accusation of thumbing frequently levelled against him. Walk Miller, Flowers' manager, circulated the take that his Tiger, a devout man, always prayed before and after each bout with Greb that the Pittsburgher's tactics not be held against him at the Final Judgement.

Whatever the validity of that fable, more likely reasons for Greb's loss were difficulty making the 160 pound limit, and fondness for feminine associations, at times.

Gene Tunney was lucky to escape defeat in his second go with Greb, in which Gene regained the U.S. title. Cries of "Robbery" resounded among Greb's followers and Harry himself, usually not given to complaint, insisted "I was jobbed!"

His volatile manager Reddy Mason charged Billy Gibson with having been instrumental in this New York ploy.

Greb and Tunney met four times, in all. In their final meeting the fast-improving Tunney, bigger and stronger, proved too much for the great middleweight. Gene figured body punching was the antidote for Greb's gyrations and Harry took quite a pounding in their St. Paul meeting in 1925. Greb gained some solace from the defeat when he picked short-ender Tunney to defeat Dempsey, and wagered accordingly.

During Dempsey's reign as champion, he had been the frequent target of challenges by Greb, basing his bravado on a gym workout between himself and the Manassa Mauler.

He defined the heavyweight champion with this analysis, "Dempsey is a tough guy, but he checks his brains in the dressing room. He can't get away with that against a fast man like me it would be a different story."

To amplify the challenge, Greb offered to meet the giant Harry Wills, leading heavyweight contender, and he meant it. Tex Rickard, Dempsey and Jack Kearns, aware that there might be something to Greb's argument, succeeded in laughing off the middleweight's defiance.

Nice looking, but a tough kid, at his beginnings, Greb thought nothing of hopping a freight to a nearby city and offering his services to the local promoter. An amiable, pleasant mannered chap in his later stages, he intermingled life's pleasures with his ceaseless trouping in the ring, including tours with burlesque shows in which he was billed as "The Marvel of the Ring."

His freewheeling lifestyle sometimes led to "newspaper decision" losses to inferior fighters but with something at stake he would recess his roistering with an arduous training routine. His preparation for his famous match against the welterweight champion Mickey Walker for his middleweight crown is a case in point, and its outcome a tribute to the greatness of Harry Greb, as recounted in the Police Gazette:

> Harry Greb surprised the wise fellows when he weighed in at 159 lbs. and was strong at the weight. Prior to the bout there had been plenty of talk along Tin Ear Alley to the effect that Harry, the middleweight champion, had been training of Anti-Volstead stuff (bootleg liquor) also that he had neglected his conditioning work at Atlantic City and furthermore, that he would be weak as a kitten at the middleweight poundage.

Greb tossed those phony rumors into the discard by putting up one of the best fights of his career. Combined with his untiring stamina and versatility of attack was a calculating boxing skill that amazed all beholders.

He not only punished Mickey Walker badly throughout their fifteen rounds but he maintained a perfect defense against Walker's desperate lunges. Mickey weighing 158, was tough but he soon found himself pitted against an even tougher antagonist, for Greb wasn't afraid of anything that walks or talks.

Greb proved his great fighting qualities in this bout. Moreover, he won many friends by fighting cleanly throughout. In past appearances Harry has not been too close an observer of ring etiquette, but he pulled nothing shady against Walker. Furthermore, Greb uncorked quite a punch, it astonished his fondest admirers.

For years legend had it that Greb and Walker, following a night of hilarity, engaged in a re-run of their epic battle on a Broadway streetcorner in New York but it has since been established that this mythical encounter was dreamed up by the late Francis Albertanti.

Greb's liking for the ladies—which was reciprocal—was as widely reputed as his remarkable ring record and this natural fondness had tragic results.

Forced to undergo an operation to save his right eye—the left eye was rumored to be without vision—Greb decided to make himself more attractive with a simultaneous nose-fixing job. Retinal operations, long drawn out at best and even more protracted in those times plus facial surgery collapsed Greb's hitherto iron constitution, caught up with the erosion of hyper-activity in the ring and on the primrose path.

The great boxer expired on the operating table at the age of 32 on Oct. 22, 1926.

Was Harry Greb a greater fighter than Sugar Ray Robinson? Ring afficionados of this period find it hard to conceive of a more marvelous ringman than the ultra-talented boxer-puncher Sugar Ray, but it is equally hard to imagine Robinson doing most of his campaigning against light heavies and heavyweights as did the fabulous Pittsburgh Windmill.

At any rate Harry Greb stands as a challenge to any other designee as "the greatest boxer of all time".

2

HERE, THERE, AND EVERYWHERE

In March 1940, when Carroll wrote about his hometown, New York was the capital of the boxing world, for all that Chicago insisted that the second Dempsey-Tunney battle cemented its claim to the title. Spoiled for choice, fight fans flocked to any number of boxing clubs and smaller auditoriums such as the Bronx Coliseum and the White Plains Armory, never mind Madison Square Garden itself. Neighborhood rivalries filled halls and spawned smooth boxing champions like featherweight Petey Scalzo and crowd-pleasing punchers such as lightweight Al "Bummy" Davis, who wrote *finis* to Tony Canzoneri's career.

Running Gotham a close second was Philadelphia, the "City of Brotherly Love"—except in the ring. As a fight venue, Philly hosted some notable heavyweight title bouts, including the first Dempsey vs. Tunney battle and Rocky Marciano's winning shot in September 1952 against Jersey Joe Walcott. Ring immortals Stanley Ketchel and Sam Langford fought there in 1910, as did welterweight champ Sugar Ray Robinson in a brilliant display against challenger Kid Gavilan in 1949. Given this boxing tradition, it was little wonder that Philadelphia produced so many outstanding fighters. From the perspective of January 1969 when Carroll's article was published, it was a list that included Joe Frazier, still a year away from being universally recognized as heavyweight champ.

Boston and New England's "Fighting Irish" had been hard to beat since the days of John L. Sullivan and his smaller namesakes, the twins Jack and Mike. As Carroll's April 1956 column appreciated, the value of an Irish moniker at the box office in the absence of Celtic ancestry was understood by the "Boston Gob," heavyweight king Jack Sharkey, real name Paul Zukauskas, and many others.

Although Jewish fighters sometimes changed their names, the first and most famous of them all did not. Daniel Mendoza, the most scientific boxer of his time, was much admired by Britain's King George III. A list compiled by

Carroll in the October 1971 issue of *The Ring* comprised twenty-six boxers of Jewish extraction who in the first half of the twentieth century had been claimants or recognized as world champions. These ranged from heavyweight Max Baer, through superlative lightweight Benny Leonard, to flyweight Corporal Izzy Schwartz. Boxers who stuck to their own names were usually foreign invaders.

Carroll returned to this subject in September 1965 when writing about Italians past and present in boxing history. The "Ambling Alp," Primo Carnera, wasn't the first Italian invader of American shores, but he was the man who most definitely put Italy on the boxing map. Firmly in the clutches of mobsters Owney Madden and Big Bill Duffy, Carnera won the heavyweight crown in mysterious circumstances from Jack Sharkey in June 1933, before losing it a year later in a farcical bout with Max Baer. Other Italian title challengers over the years included Tiberio Mitri (middleweight), Paolo Rosi (lightweight), Dulio Loi (junior welterweight), and Giulio Rinaldi (light heavyweight). They were about to be followed, so Carroll had heard, by Nino Benvenuti, who would take the middleweight title from Emile Griffith in 1967.

South Americans had featured prominently in an article penned by Carroll as far back as October 1939. Still fresh in popular memory was Argentinian heavyweight Luis Firpo, "The Wild Bull of the Pampas," only for another South American heavyweight to loom large on the horizon, Arturo Godoy of Chile. When he came to Carroll's attention, Godoy had just outmauled tough Tony Galento. The following year, up against Joe Louis, he surprised everyone by holding the champ to a split fifteen-round decision.

The only other challenger to take the Brown Bomber the distance before America entered World War II was Britain's Tommy Farr in 1937. Fourteen years on, so Carroll thought, British boxing prestige was booming. There were four likely challengers for world honors: newly crowned British, Empire, and European heavyweight champion Jack Gardner; light heavyweight Don Cockell; middleweight Randy Turpin; and welterweight Eddie Thomas. For once, Carroll's crystal ball failed him almost completely. While Turpin unexpectedly upset a jaded Ray Robinson in a London title bout immediately following an undemanding European jaunt by the Sugarman, the other three all fell by the wayside. In 1955, the burly Cockell, having far outgrown the cruiserweight division, as the British called it, tried his luck against Rocky Marciano. His gallant losing effort in San Francisco left Britain as far away from boxing's greatest prize as it had been ever since James J. Jeffries wrested the crown from Cornishman Bob Fitzsimmons in 1899.

Not so in Germany, where former heavyweight champion Max Schmeling was still a national hero forty years after winning the title in 1930. The only man to be declared world champion "while squatting on the canvas bleating 'Foul,'" as Carroll put it in a September 1970 article, Schmeling successfully defended his title before being controversially outpointed by Jack Sharkey in a return match two years later. Seemingly all washed-up after defeats by Max Baer and Steve Hamas, the "Black Uhlan" came back with a bang to KO previously unde-feated Joe Louis. This feat alone guaranteed Max a special place in Boxing's Hall of Fame. Celebrated in Berlin by Germany's Nazi rulers, Schmeling failed to live up to the regime's racial hype by lasting less than one round when challenging the "Brown Bomber" for the championship—and for his pains was unceremo-niously conscripted into the German Army at the outbreak of war in 1939. His latter-day equivalent was Karl Mildenberger, a skilled southpaw well known to stateside audiences for his determined effort against Muhammad Ali in 1966. Another familiar name in the 1950s and early 1960s was middleweight (later light heavyweight) Gustav "Bubi" Scholtz, who fought successfully in Madison Square Garden. His light heavy title challenge in 1962 was turned back, how-ever, by Philadelphia's skillful boxing master, Harold Johnson.

Where "Bubi" Scholtz ventured, Africa had been forty years earlier. In 1922, Battling Siki of Senegal won the world light heavyweight championship, knocking out France's Georges Carpentier in the sixth round. A war hero who had been awarded the highest French military honors, Siki was strong and cou-rageous in equal measure. The possessor of an iron chin, he was as quick on his feet as he was reluctant to train. Fond of strolling Paris boulevards with a lion cub on a leash, a lady on his arm, and a bottle to hand, Siki not entirely sur-prisingly lost his title in 1923 fighting an Irishman, Mike McTigue, in Dublin on St. Patrick's Day. Siki soon afterward decamped to America where tragedy followed farce. Too many beatings inside and outside the ring, too much brandy, and one drunken altercation too many after yet another racist slur cul-minated in Siki's murder just before Christmas 1925. He had been shot from behind. Carroll's sympathies were clearly aroused by the fate of the "Singular Senegalese." Written against the backdrop of African decolonization, his January 1963 column went on to laud Nigerian boxers; former featherweight title holder Hogan "Kid" Bassey; and then current World Boxing Association, soon-to-be undisputed world, middleweight king homburg-hatted Dick Tiger.

By the 1950s and 1960s, Japan too had emerged as a major force in box-ing's lighter divisions. Intrigued by the fact that the latest issue of *The Ring* listed ten Japanese fighters among the world's rated boxers in the flyweight, bantamweight, featherweight, junior lightweight, and lightweight divisions, Carroll took a long look in August 1969 at the history of boxing in Japan. He liked what he saw. Introduced in 1905 by a visiting American who had come to study jiujitsu, boxing was initially confined to the amateur ranks. The professional sport enjoyed limited success in the 1920s and 1930s, only really taking off after World War II, in part due to the extended stay of US occupation forces. An exhibition tour in 1951 by Joe Louis was a huge success. Japan's first world champion was Yoshio Shirai, winner of the flyweight title in 1952. After him came Fighting Harada, arguably Japan's greatest fighter, certainly at the time Carroll was writing. Harada won the world flyweight championship in 1962 and later seized the world bantamweight crown from Brazil's highly rated Eder Jofre, successfully defending it four times. Other notable boxers included Yoshiaka Numata, world junior lightweight champion in 1967, and Hiroyuki Ebihara, whose startling first-round victory in 1963 over Thailand's Pone Kingpetch made him the third Japanese holder of the world flyweight title.

———————

October 1939	South America in Pugilism
March 1940	New York Stars
July 1951	British Prestige Booms
April 1956	The Fighting Irish
January 1963	Men of Africa!
September 1965	The Italians, Past and Present, Hold Special Niche in Boxing History
January 1969	Philly's Fight History Features Greats Galore
August 1969	Japanese Boxing, Born in 1905, Has Enjoyed Spectacular Success
September 1970	Der Mox, Once Champion, Still Germany's No. 1 Idol
October 1971	Jewish Fighters Have Achieved Fame beyond Their Limited Numbers

SOUTH AMERICA IN PUGILISM

No sport has made such rapid strides among the South and Central Americans as has boxing. Considering the length of time that the game has been popular among the Latin-Americans, their progress in fisticuffs has been remarkable. Although South and Central America have yet to produce a world's champion, many first-rate boxers have been developed in those sections.

The man who came closest to being the first South American to win a world's championship as well as the first from that continent to gain international recognition as a boxer was Luis Angel Firpo, the one-time hero of the Argentine Republic.

Luis Firpo's achievements were so spectacular and his financial rewards so satisfactory, that the boxing game was given a great impetus among Latin-Americans. The fact that a native of Argentina had come so close to dethroning one of the greatest pugilistic champions of all time, Jack Dempsey, inspired the younger generation of South Americans to attempt to win gold and glory in the ring.

Firpo made his great bid for fame in the Dempsey bout in 1923. Shortly after, the first South American boxing invaders set sail for the lucrative shores of the U.S.A. Among these forerunners of the present crop of crack South American boxers was a slender, wide shouldered young man from Chile, Luis Vincentini, a lightweight. Vincentini had been the amateur champion of his native land in 1920, turned professional and had won the lightweight championship of all South America without much trouble.

He was touted as a great right-hand puncher with an impressive knockout record, when he arrived in the United States in 1923. As a hitter, Vincentini soon showed he was what he was supposed to be. He scored three successive knockouts over fair opposition and then set sail for the lightweight leaders. He beat Pal Moran, lost a close decision to the irrepressible Johnny Dundee and then scored his most brilliant triumph when he stopped rugged Rocky Kansas in Brooklyn, N.Y., on July 14, 1924, in eleven rounds.

This fine victory made the Chilean something of a sensation in America for a time, but Vincentini while a great hitter was not quite capable of coping with fast clever boxers. He always gave a good account of himself but dropped decisions to Jack Bernstein, Kansas and Sid Terris later that year. Although his title bid failed, he excited North American fight fans and attracted much attention to the potentialities of the fighters from the other half of the hemisphere. . . .

The next South American to create a stir in the United States was Justo Suarez of Buenos Aires, who looked most promising of all when he first arrived in the United States back in 1929. The unfortunate Suarez, whose career and life came to an untimely end, was undoubtedly the greatest prospect ever sent out from South America in his class. Undefeated as an amateur, unbeatable as a professional in the early part of his career, Suarez seemed to be a cinch to take the title in his first bouts in North America.

Back in South America, he was unbeaten, had defeated both the Venturi brothers, kayoing Enrico, and winning a decision over Vittorio. He had stopped the crack Americans, Lou Paluso and Babe Herman in a round apiece and beat Hilario Marinez in twelve. He reached New York in 1930 heralded as the greatest fighter ever produced in South America and for a time he looked it.

Suarez was given Joe Glick, no soft one as a starter, and he beat the New Yorker handily. Justo trounced Herman Perlick, and then created a sensation by stopping the capable Bruce Flowers. He continued to impress, beating the feared left hook artist, Ray Miller, and then beat the great Louis Kid Kaplan.

The Argentinian was acclaimed the outstanding challenger for the title following these victories over such outstanding American fighters. Returning home after this brilliant campaign, Suarez bowled right along, stopping Loayza in three rounds in Buenos Aires.

In action he was a rip tearing, rather awkward Mittman, who tossed punches from all angles, a damaging hitter, he wore his men down by his powerful persistent attack and then finished them.

Returning to America, only Billy Petrolle stood between him and a clear path to the lightweight title. Suarez met Petrolle in Madison Square Garden on May 25, 1931, and that fight ended his bid for ring glory. The old Fargo Express was badly battered by the South American at times during the battle, but the American flailed away at the Argentinian's body, and in the ninth round the weary Suarez collapsed from Petrolle's barrage of body blows.

Whether the beating he assimilated in the Petrolle bout, or the ravages of the disease that took his life recently curtailed Suarez' career, will never be known. From that time on he was but a shadow of the brawling battler he had formerly been and soon passed out of the title picture.

At one time the angular Argentinian, Vittorio Campolo, looked as if he was headed somewhere. The gangling gaucho had a long lopping right-hand punch that he reached out with no apparent effort that reduced many of his opponents to a state of wreckage. Alas, like many another T.N.T. fisted young man, the rangy heavyweight's ability to take it was far from equal to his power to deal out punishment.

He pulverized old Hard Rock Tom Heeney one summer evening in 1929 at Ebbets Field, Brooklyn, N.Y., but American fight fans refused to take him seriously after Phil Scott outfumbled him for one of his rare American victories the same year.

In spite of that, Campolo did fight his way to a match with Jack Sharkey which somehow never came off after all articles had been signed and sealed. In 1931, little Tommy Loughran befuddled gawky Vittorio completely in winning a decision over him, but the American fight public wearily cried enough, after punchless Primo Carnera knocked out Campolo in two exciting rounds on November 29, 1931. Campolo was gifted with the punch but possessed few of the other attributes necessary for a top-notch boxer.

While on the subject of heavyweights, possibly the best big man ever developed in Latin-America is the contemporary Arturo Godoy. This barrel-chested Chilean can't punch like Firpo or Campolo, but for all around ability he is apparently the superior of the Wild Bull of the Pampas or the towering Argentine.

The mighty muscled, rough-housing native of Iquigue, is probably the only man alive to give brawling Tony Galento more than he could handle at Tony's own pet pastime of "anything goes" mauling. Arturo turned the trick twice, once in New York's Hippodrome and the second time in the preliminary to the Louis-Braddock fight in Chicago. This should give Godoy a clear title to the free-for-all title at least, as in both these mix-ups the referee permitted the lads to make up their rules as they went along.

However, Godoy is more than a mere rough-houser, he is a fighter of genuine merit. Of his ability to take a punch, Dan Parker, witty New York columnist, said, "Galento's wallop caused Arturo Godoy no more concern than the bite of a Chilean mosquito," and while not a deadly hitter, he is a punishing puncher.

He campaigned successfully in America, kayoing Jack Roper and Otis Thomas and fighting draws with Maurice Strickland and Roscoe Toles. He lost to Toles and Nathan Mann and twice beat Galento.

Since his return to his homeland, he has convinced Luis Firpo that the ring is no place for a forty-five year old former fighter. Godoy won the South American heavyweight title from Alberto Lovell, but lost his last bout to Valentin Campolo, following his recent marriage. Rugged and game, he is high on the list of potential opponents for Joe Louis this coming winter.

This survey of South Americans would not be complete without some mention of the Chilean, Quentin Romero-Rojas, who came to this country shortly after Firpo. While Romero-Rojas never gained the front rank of heavyweight contenders, he was good enough to stop Jack Sharkey in Boston back in 1924, and campaigned in America for many years with varying success.

The republic of Venezuela, in the midst of a sports boom at the moment, proudly presents Simon Chavez as the latest addition to the ranks of South America's socking sons. Chavez is apparently a boxer of championship qualities. He first attracted attention some years ago by beating Kid Chocolate, and proved to be no false alarm when he defeated the American world's champion, Joey Archibald, last month. Described as a second edition of Henry Armstrong, Chavez is a lightning-fisted scrapper who should be a sensation in the United States. He has been boxing for some years. He split decisions with Sixto Escobar in 1932. He has also campaigned in England where he lost to Ginger Foran in 1935 in twelve rounds, but at the present time is showing better form than ever. . . .

South America has been distinguished by many a fine fighter in the past and there are prospects of even greater ones coming to the front in the future.

NEW YORK STARS

Old time politicians used to claim on election eves, that as "Maine goes so goes the nation," until the 1936 poll made a joke of this ancient axiom. In the world of pugilism, the saying has been that "as New York goes so goes the boxing business." Unlike the first political bromide the pugilistic proverb still holds true. Of course, everyone concedes that New York is the capital of Fistiana, whatever Chicago claimants may have to say about the second Dempsey-Tunney fight and that three million dollar gate. Because of the big town's place in the realm of fisticuffs, a flourishing fight business in the metropolis usually means that the boxing game is in a healthy state everywhere else.

New York fight fans are called upon to support a bevy of boxing clubs, and so far they have been flocking into the neighbourhood arenas, in encouraging numbers since the opening of the winter season. Fight followers climaxed a successful fall indoor season around New York when they jammed the Garden to the rafters, last December 15th, to witness a champion-less card of up-and-coming talent. As in every sport, personalities make the turnstiles click and a crop of crowd-pulling boxers have popped up in and around the big city.

This accounts for the interest in boxing around New York even in times as troublesome and tense as these and it seems to be a healthy sign. Number one man on the New York scene as a pepper-upper of boxing is the youthful Al Davis, who seems to be the answer to the promoters' prayer. Jewish, a puncher, and a colorful individual, the tawny haired toughie from Brooklyn's Ghetto looks like the greatest New York drawing card since the Goldstein-Terris era.

The December card in New York's Madison Square Garden was glutted with good talent, but most keen observers are inclined to credit young Mr. Davis with attracting most of that $47,000 into the coffers of Michael Jacobs and the Garden corporation. It is quite possible that this young man who is still in his teens may go on to set an all-time record as an indoor-boxing attraction.

In five "shots" in New York's mammoth arena, the Brooklyn brawler has drawn $121,900 into the till and less than two years ago he was an obscure preliminary performer in the small metropolitan fight clubs. New Yorkers paid $31,000 to see him write finis to the career of the war worn Mickey Farber and $15,000 for his battles with Eddie Brink and Bernie Friedkin.

Like Louis, McLarnin, Dempsey, and Leonard, the little Brownsville Bummie, as the boys call him, seems to have been touched with a golden wand.

Besides his demonstrated drawing powers, Davis has the ability to go with it. He likes to fight, is a savage competitor, and first and foremost he can hit!

However, so far as sheer ability goes, nearly everyone agrees, even as predicted in THE RING a year ago, that little Pete Scalzo is the ranking performer among the present-day New York boxers. Too good for his own good, the smooth boxing Petey, who can also stiffen a rival with a punch when he cares to let one go, is the outstanding world featherweight.

Scalzo hails from a predominantly Irish neighbourhood which oddly enough produced two great Italian champions, Johnny Dundee and Frankie Genaro, both one-time neighbors of Scalzo's on New York's roaring West Side, also known as Hell's Kitchen.

Scalzo, who has already flattened the present champion, Joey Archibald, would be a heavy choice to repeat and become the third protégé of Foxy Peter Reilly's to mount the featherweight throne if he could only get the chance to duplicate the stunt. . . .

Acting as an incubator for New York fistic talent, the Bronx Coliseum, and the White Plains Armory have had a great deal to do with the boom in boxing in the big city. Hardly a week passes that either of those thriving organizations does not turn away customers clamoring for admittance. Jimmy Bronson at the Coliseum and Joe McKenna at White Plains have done wonders for boxing. Outstanding among the gifted youngsters who have been holding forth in these pugilistic nurseries is the spidery Steve Belloise, brother of the celebrated Mike.

The fight game hasn't produced two champions in a single family since the Dundees of Baltimore, Joe and Vince, but if the hard hitting and clever Steve, whose pals call him Gink, can hold the pace he's setting, the Belloise family may also enjoy that distinction. Belloise hasn't come up to the ranking performers yet but the way he has been mowing down the tougher tyros, promises well for his future.

At this writing the Bronx boy has compiled a winning streak of 20 straight and the end doesn't seem to be in sight. Canny George Hughes who steered brother Mike to the title, is taking his time with the spindly Steve.

Not all the boys who are exciting the New York fight public are native New Yorkers. A young importation from the Middle West, Lenny Mancini, has had the good folk of Brooklyn talking to themselves all winter. This young man who blew in unheralded knocked the customers right out of their chairs with a string of the most spectacular knockouts ever seen in New York's Broadway Arena, over tough local opposition. He recently came a cropper against the seasoned Johnny Rinaldi of the Bronx, but was as sensational losing as winning, arising from a first round knockout to stage a thrilling comeback that narrowly missed evening things up.

Carrying the banners of the fighting Irish in New York's pugilistic parade, and also holding forth at the teeming White Plains club, we find a young man who at last seems to be cashing in on his latent possibilities, Eddie Dunne. This one-time pupil of the great Benny Leonard, now handled by Chris Dundee, has long possessed all the necessary qualifications of a ranking Mittman, but in the past has shown little resistance to punishment. Those days seem to be over now, for somewhere along the line the red thatched Irishman seems to have picked up the ruggedness so essential to a first-class boxer. Always a talented boxer and sharp hitter, Dunne turned in his best effort to date when he topped unbeaten up to then, Vinnie Vines, no mean prospect himself last month.

An Irish boxer is always a godsend to the gate and if Dunne is really on his way, the New York promoters will have something to cheer about.

Fourteen thousand customers jammed Jimmy Bronson's Bronx Coliseum one December evening recently to see a couple of local rivals, Joey Iannotti and Curley St. Angelo go to it. Nobody regretted coming after seeing the miniature war the lads put up. Iannotti was the winner thereby preserving his undefeated record but there was glory for both.

Neighborhood feuds such as these are what help keep New York the capital of the pugilistic profession. Iannotti and St. Angelo are the type of ambitious youngsters who supply the spark of competition that makes boxing the biggest sport in the biggest town.

Conspicuous among the many other metropolitan prides who do more than their share in keeping New Yorkers boxing conscious, are such as Paul De Bello, Tony Marteliano, and Walter Franklin. De Bello became embroiled in what looked like one of the greatest lightweight fights in years when he tangled with the veteran Johnny Bellus at the Coliseum on Dec. 27. Both men had hit the deck and were in the middle of one of the greatest slugfests seen at the club in some time, when their heads collided. DeBello suffered worse, and this caused the fight to be stopped and the victory awarded Bellus. Although it goes down in the record books as a kayo scored against the Italian, he lost little prestige with those who witnessed the scrap.

Marteliano, a busy two-fisted warrior, compiled a long winning streak before running into a slump last summer. The squat 135 pounder has rebounded from the kayo he suffered at the hands of Julie Kogan some months ago. He turned in a slashing victory over Primo Flores, the tough Puerto Rican last month, and is headed up the ladder again. Of the bruising club fighting class Marteliano is of the type designed to lure the customers. . . .

A New Yorker himself, Carroll devoted column space to detailing the collective achievements of various cities and regions of the United States. *The Ring* (April 1952)

BRITISH PRESTIGE BOOMS

Not in a long time have British boxers rated the high spots in world standing that is theirs at present. Austerity or no, the lads from the tight little isle are closing in on the international title holders from all directions. With middleweight Randy Turpin flattening all comers right and left, and welterweight Eddie Thomas a formidable threat to win Sugar Ray Robinson's vacated welterweight crown, British boxing may be approaching its highest point in decades.

True there has never been a time in the past half-century that at least one Briton wasn't knocking on a title holder's door in some division, but at this present moment there are four likely aspirants for world-wide honours.

While not overly impressive in his most recent outing against Jo Weidin, who proved a flop over here, Jack Gardner, Empire and European heavyweight king, is still a youngster with definite prospects. With the great Joe Louis just a memory shambling along a comeback trail there is hope now for almost any strong young fellow in the unlimited class. Not that Champion Ezzard Charles is not a competent performer, but title dreams among the heavyweights are no longer the near-impossibilities they were when Louis ruled the roost.

This present situation makes Gardner, along with Rex Layne, whose style we are informed he follows, as much a threat to Charles as anyone else you can name.

Gardner, a mustachioed mauler who came off a chicken farm in Market Harborough, England, to stop war-worn Bruce Woodcock in ten rounds last November, added the European heavyweight title to the Empire crown he won from Woodcock when he beat Austrian Weidin on March 27 of this year.

Overseas informants declare that the 24-year-old Gardner is still very much in the development stage with many rough spots to be ironed out.

With the exception of such prehistoric warriors as Savold, Walcott and Louis, this criticism also goes for most of the American heavyweights. So, Gardner is at no disadvantage there.

Both the record book and eyewitnesses agree that Welshman Eddie Thomas should be favorably considered in any comparison with the other welter title pretenders. Much of his opposition is unfamiliar to Americans but nobody is beating him. No blockbuster, he is touted as a bona fide boxer of the Welsh school of Jem Driscoll, Wilde and Freddy Welsh. All three understood the art of self-defense as have few others. They believed boxing to be a game of skill and they made it so. Over here we are well aware of the boxing abilities of Billy

The boxing achievements of various countries also drew regular comment from Ted Carroll, with British prospects his topic of choice here.
The Ring (July 1951)

Graham. So is Kid Gavilan, who in two razor edge encounters with the New York boxer had to be satisfied with an even break in two verdicts.

Open-minded observers insist that there was nothing close about the contest between Graham and Thomas in London on February 7, 1949. In a sparring match between two master boxing technicians, the wily Welshman from all reports proved master of more tricks and maneuvers than his American foe.

Thomas, who recently added the European title to his list by beating the antediluvian Italian Kid Frattini in London, is in a good spot. All boxing bodies are in complete agreement that there can be no universally recognized world's welterweight champion until Eddie Thomas is disposed of one way or another. This view has the complete endorsement of this magazine.

Thomas has only lost two fights since beginning to box in 1926 [*sic* 1946]. One of these was the result of a cut eye. The other, a decision loss to Gwyn Williams was reversed in a later meeting.

Most sensational of the British big four by all odds is middleweight hope Randy Turpin. Still, by a twist of fortune, he must be accorded the slimmest chance of winning the title in his class. This is only because the present title holder happens to be the greatest fighter in the world today, Sugar Ray Robinson. At almost any other time the Englishman would be a red hot favorite to become world's champion. Off his recent performances he is the "hottest" fighter in his class right now.

At this writing his last four bouts have been knockout victories. Included among his victims was the durable Dutchman, Luc Van Dam, who stirred up considerable trouble for the peerless Sugar Ray himself in Robinson's triumphant trek across the Continent last winter.

Ray himself rated Van Dam the best man he met in his overseas campaign. Sugar called him a smart boxer, who really knew his way around the ring. It took the Sugar four heats to dispose of Van Dam and his manner of doing it touched off a rhubarb.

Americans, remembering the Robinson affair, were impressed when Turpin had Van Dam out of there in just 48 seconds on February 27 of this year. The boy must have something to do that, they reasoned.

Since then, he has stopped Billy Brown, American boxer, who went the limit with Robinson, although Brown's showing irked disgruntled Britons.

Jean Stock is another recent victim of Turpin's. Stock went out in five. He had previously handed Turpin one of his two losses, a five-round kayo in London, back in '48.

Turpin is described as a youngster who started out believing that the only necessary requirement for ring success is a wallop. Following losses to former British champ Albert Finch and Stock, he discovered that such was not the case, and that some kind of defense was needed in a hurry.

Under the tutelage of brother Dick, a better than fair middleweight himself and a former British champion, he's learned his lessons well. . . .

Sugar Ray shows little signs of ring decay but he can't go on forever. Turpin is only 23, some seven years younger than the present champion. Father Time is in the English boy's side corner and that can mean everything. This may not be Turpin's year, but who can tell about the next one or the next? Two years from now he will still be only 25 and possibly an even better boxer than he is now.

British boxers have always favored the middleweight division. Some exceptional middleweights have come out of the island kingdom. Such a one was Jock McAvoy, who kayoed the American champion, Babe Risko, in jig time but outgrew the class before he could get a title match. Len Harvey was another, but he could never solve the puzzling style of American Vince Dundee. Tommy Milligan was good, too. He actually fought for the world's title, but had the ill fortune to run into Mickey Walker, one of the greatest. The same thing went for Ted Moore, who also got a chance to win the world's crown, but drew the great Harry Greb as defending champion. Frank Moody and Jack Hood were other good Britishers but neither ever fought for the crown.

Don Cockell, recent holder of the British and European light-heavyweight titles and recent winner over tough American heavy Freddie Beshore, has been coming like a house afire of late. The youthful Londoner, although he has never set foot in the States, is described as using what Continentals call the typical American style of milling—rough, bruising, body belting, and continual aggressiveness.

Since Beshore is no Fancy Dan himself, the Englishman must be a rough customer to handle the rugged heavyweight as easily as he did.

He is obviously a factor to be reckoned with in what the British call the cruiserweight division.

Not in many years have British boxers been held in such high estate. This is remarkable in view of the lower standard of living placed upon the hardy islanders by the austerity program.

Britons are Europe's best in the four most important weight classes—welter, middle, light-heavy and heavyweight. All these topliners are quite young with their best years ahead of them. Thomas, the oldest, is not yet 25.

Freddie Mills, light-heavyweight champ, was the most recent British world's champion, but fights with men much larger than himself curtailed the career of this dangerous and durable gamester. This taste of possessing a world title holder has whetted the British appetite.

With four live contenders shooting at world titles, at least one of them is a good bet to come through and the British lion with much reason to feel proud, has plenty to roar about.

THE FIGHTING IRISH

From the time of John L. Sullivan, New England has been the stronghold of the Irish. Latest Celtic to arouse interest is Bobby Murphy.

Whenever the character of John L. Sullivan is depicted in play or movie, the portrayal never fails to include a thick Irish brogue. The few remaining old-sters who recall the legendary Boston Strong Boy—venerable Joe Woodman is one of them—attest that liberties are being taken with reality here, and that old John L, his Hibernian heritage notwithstanding, actually spoke with a New England accent not unlike Rocky Marciano's.

Be that as it may, the Irish aura about boxing in New England has been as persistent as the imagined accent attributed to the ancient Hero of the Hub. With many of the best of the New Englanders, Irish nomenclature has had to suffice for Celtic Ancestry, as in the cases of ex-heavyweight king, Lithuanian Jack Sharkey (Cucoskay), one-time crack Jewish featherweight Red Chapman (Kaplan), the late great light heavyweight French Canuck Jack Delaney (Chapdelaine), and Italian bantams Andy—from Boston—and Terry—from Providence—Martin (both named Martino) among others.

Recent publicity showered upon young Bob Murphy from Brighton, Massachusetts, brings to mind that there is active in New England an honest to goodness Irisher trying to keep the old John L. tradition from being lost. A few years ago, it was Tommy Collins, a tissue paper thin featherweight, whose toothpick arms packed surprising power and who kayoed Willie Pep, but, alas, was just as fragile as he looked when it came to absorbing punishment. Tommy gained a left-handed fame which no doubt will cause him to be remembered when many champions have been forgotten. This stems from the ten knock-down affair with Jimmy Carter, then lightweight champion back in 1953, whom he shouldn't have been matched with in the first place. This so horrified a countrywide television audience, its repercussions were felt in the halls of Congress, with most of the blame being directed at Referee Tommy Rawson. Rawson allowed the one-sided spectacle, known as the Boston Massacre, to continue to such a point that for days following there was an irate aftermath demanding he be prosecuted.

John L. was a heavyweight and in the long years since he claimed the title no Irish heavyweight out of New England has come any closer to the crown than Jim Maloney who wasn't a bad fighter at all. Jim was a good boxer and he could punch, but townsman—by way of Binghamton, N.Y.—Jack Sharkey has a hex on his New England rival: Maloney won a decision over the erratic ex-sailor the first time they met but in three meetings after that Jim finished a poor second. The last of these bouts, reckoned too big for the boys' home bailiwick of Boston was transported to New York's Yankee Stadium back in 1927. They did $232,000 worth of business, in a fight which was to provide a foe for recently deposed champion Jack Dempsey with the winner to meet champ Gene Tunney. Sharkey kayoed Jim in five heats and went on to a controversial loss against Dempsey that same summer.

Maloney bounced right back the following year, 1928, and didn't lose a bout, licking among others, tough Johnny Risko and cagy Jack Renault. Incidentally, among Maloney's lesser victims that year was the present Massachusetts boxing boss, Henry Lamar, a college bred heavyweight, who was in over his head against Maloney and was belted out in three stanzas.

Maloney's ring fortunes deteriorated rapidly after 1928, but he still had enough left in 1930 to upset the Carnera applecart with a ten-round decision over the Giant Primo in Boston.

The value of an Irish name at the box office was never better demonstrated than by Maloney, who a few months before the Sharkey match notched a record $200,000 house with Jack Delaney in Madison Sq. Garden, a mark which has withstood the assaults of time and such mitt magnets as Joe Louis, McLarnin, Armstrong, Baer, Graziano, etc., in the 29 years that have passed. Maloney beat Delaney that night.

Maloney was managed by florid faced Dan Carroll, an ex-cop, now passed on, a stereotype of the Boston Irishman, whose St. Patrick Day cards were received by all those with Irish names in the boxing business, regardless of whether the monikers were spurious or the real McCoy.

Dropping down in the weight scale to the bantam weights, ring students of long standing are agreed that Boston has had few better all-round ring artists than Jimmy Walsh, a one-time bantam title claimant.

Walsh, a boxing wizard, was in his heyday during the early years of this century. He enjoyed great success against the best little men of his time excepting Abe Attell, who was a bit too much for him. Walsh lost three times to the former featherweight king in 1906 and 1907.

The Twin Sullivans, Jack and Mike were among the best of the Brother Acts in boxing history. These balding namesakes of the great John L. were scientific boxers of the old school. Jack, the heavier, was also considered the better of the two, but both of them rated high among the fighters of a half century or so ago. They were natives of Cambridge, Mass.

The various accomplishments of the Irish in boxing were a regular focal point for Carroll. *The Ring* (April 1950)

Old time welterweight Honey Melody [*sic*], with a name more suited to the musical comedy stage than the ring, belied his fancy nickname when he swung into action. He was good enough to win a couple of decisions over the original Joe Walcott, quite a trick even though the fearsome Barbados Demon had seen his best days when he got around to meeting Melody.

New Englander Eddie Shevlin had a cultured style of boxing. Fantastically clever, the best welters of the Twenties had their troubles solving Eddie's canny defense. One of the few to defeat Dave Shade, Shevlin found time between bouts to instruct Dartmouth students in the manly art of self defense.

Pat McCarthy of Boston met a lot of good heavies in his time, but the top ranks were a little beyond the reach of Pat. The same thing went for Tom Kirby, a good puncher and boxer, who never quite reached the heights predicted for him after a sensational amateur career.

Andy Callahan, a good southpaw lightweight and a real contender during his fighting days met a hero's end on a World War II battlefield.

Oldsters perk up at mention of Matty Baldwin, a rough and ready lightweight, active just before World War I, who made quite a hit in bouts in New York City. Young Donahue was another Celtic standout from up New England way. After becoming quite a card in New England, some 50 years ago, Young Kloby was exposed as owning the legal moniker of Tommy Corcoran. One can't help wondering why such an apt fighting name as Corcoran should have been converted into Kloby but there must have been a reason.

The New England states have had some wonderful fighters of non-Irish origin, Willie Pep, Rocky Marciano, Louis 'Kid' Kaplan, Bat Battalino, Delaney, Sharkey, and the recently passed on Sam Langford, but the great John L. set the fighting New England tradition and it is fitting that this St Patrick's day sees young Bob Murphy attempting to carry it on.

MEN OF AFRICA!

Battling Siki—A Saga of Sadness, Hogan Kid Bassey and Dick Tiger— Opposites of the Battling Senegalese

In some respects the story of Battling Siki has strong similarity to the struggles of the emerging nations of Africa, the "Dark Continent" from which he sprung. In both cases the adaptation to "western" ways of life had complex and—for Siki—tragic results. As the years go by, retrospection is gradually replacing the ridicule and rejection which was Battling Siki's lot thirty seven years ago, with the compassion and understanding which is the due of a pathetic individual who, in his contact with our "civilization" was more "sinned against than sinning".

Certainly the law of the jungle suffers little by comparison with that of a "civilization" which only half-hearted attempts to bring before the bar of justice, the slayers of the "jungle boy". Battling Siki found no even balance in the civilized scales of justice, in the final analysis they were loaded against this African in an alien world.

The world first became conscious of the existence of Battling Siki— also known as Louis Phal—when a flash came over the wires that Georges Carpentier, the "Orchid Man", had lost his world's lightheavyweight championship to an obscure Senegalese, Battling Siki, in Paris by a sixth round knockout on Sept. 24, 1922.

Various rumors have clouded this fight to the effect that certain "pre-arrangements" had been made whereby Siki was to play merely a "supporting role" to a "smash hit" performance by the "idol of France". However, things got completely out of control when Siki merely grinned when Carpentier's famous right hand knockout punch bounced harmlessly off his iron chin, and he responded with a savage onslaught which floored and then kayoed the fragile, fading Frenchman.

Off his European record Siki was no soft touch. Since his return from World War I, he had lost but two of more than fifty fights, defeating along the way Rene De Vos, the great Belgian middleweight; Hans Breitenstraeter, the German heavyweight champion; and Erminio Spalla, winner of the World War I Armed Forces heavyweight championship, who later fought Gene Tunney.

"Gorgeous Georges" undoubtedly taking his opponent too lightly and running into unexpected trouble, did his cause no favor by obvious butting, finally resorting to his time worn claim of "foul" when counted out by Referee Henri

Bernstein. The Parisians, annoyed at Carpentier's fouling, would have none of his complaint, and Siki was declared the new light heavyweight champion of the world.

Siki's next moves after winning the title were those which both before and since have been followed by champions everywhere, particularly in a city so given to gaiety as Paris. They were simply geared to getting the utmost enjoyment out of his sudden emergence as a world celebrity and ring champion.

Unfortunately in his case, not even the liberal French capital was quite ready for such a display as the Senegalese staged, with the wine flowing freely and female companions fluttering around nightly on the gay boulevards and in the boites of the French metropolis. As if this wasn't enough, Siki's own sense of the sensational, whetted by publicity-prompted suggestions by French fight people, conjured up the gimmick of a lion cub for a pet for the flamboyant new ring hero. Thus, pictures of Siki strolling the Paris thoroughfares, lion on a leash, completed the image of the untamed and uninhibited African indigene which was to follow him to the end.

When Siki, after firing his managers whom he accused of having shortchanged him in purse distribution in numerous instances, signed on his own to meet Irish born, U.S. bred Mike McTigue, for his lightheavyweight title in Dublin, Ireland, St. Patrick's Day, March 17, 1923, the world was convinced of Battling Siki's eccentricity, and from that time on he was known as the "Singular Senegalese".

As was freely predicted, Siki lost the decision to the cagy, smart boxing McTigue, but the tolerant Irish, although the land was then in a "time of troubles", had few cheers for the safety-first tactics of McTigue and much sympathy for Siki who was afforded all the kind treatment due a fellow human being while he was in Ireland, which was not always the case elsewhere.

Arriving back in Paris following the loss of his title to McTigue, Siki seemingly little upset, resumed his rounds of celebrating, fought and won a couple of fights, was hauled into court for wearing his old army uniform illegally and flung the proceeds of his fights far and wide in flurries of frenetic free handedness.

He became involved in other incidents, the most embarrassing of which was the appearance of one Miss Gertrude Amphler, a Dutch girl, who in support of her assertion that she was Mmm. Battling Siki, produced Battling Siki Jr. as evidence.

These involvements plus a growing dissatisfaction with a succession of managers, decided Siki on a visit of the United States. . . . Arriving in the States on September 1, 1923, the Senegalese placed himself under the management of Bob Levy, a U.S. Customs Inspector.

Bob Levy was a very fine man, honest to the point of unnaturalness, kindly and sincere. His appearance meshed with his paternal personality to a degree where few human beings projected the "father image" so markedly.

Now, Siki was no fool. He arrived here able to speak English, no mean attainment for a visitor of his background, but to the fatherly Levy from the time they first laid eyes on each other, Battling Siki remained a child, one to be pampered and indulged as a fond parent would a favorite offspring.

Siki, of course quickly realized this. He would pat the manager's balding head, and his pet name for him, "Papa Bob", quickly became famous in boxing circles everywhere. It is doubtful that any manager and fighter ever had an affection for each other equalling that of Battling Siki and "Papa Bob" Levy. Opinion has been strong among fight people for many years that with a manager of lesser virtue, but more severity, there would have been quite a difference in the American career of Battling Siki, whom they all agree had many assets as a fighter, including an iron chin, magnificent physique, quickness of hand and foot, incredible gameness and great strength. But he needed a strong taskmaster to force him to consolidate those qualities into fighting machinery by disciplined training and condition.

Upon being contacted for his ideas on this point of view, Harry Levy, surviving brother of Bob, and a long-time fight figure in his own right had a vigorous response.

"Nonsense," he said indignantly, "the people who say that, never knew the real Siki. Believe me, there never was a more loveable guy! No one could be mean to Siki or make him do what he didn't want to.

"Nobody ever got a rougher break over here either! They called him a wild man, a savage, a 'jungle boy'. I can name you fifty guys all around at the same time, who carried on worse than Battling Siki ever did, and that takes in lots of the same writers who wrote those crazy things!"

His voice raising now, thoroughly angered, Levy went on: "Did the people who made fun of him ever tell anybody how many languages he could speak? What about his war record? Did they ever mention the poor kids who would follow him on the street because they knew he couldn't stand to see poor people without giving them something? My brother managed him and I knew him and I would take Battling Siki over most of the people I have met in my time, and I'm over 75 years old."

There is something to Harry Levy's strong defense. Siki's visit to the U.S. coincided with the wild and wooly goings-on of the "Roaring Twenties". He was certainly no great exception to the general temper of the turbulent times. Mickey Walker, recounting this era and his own escapades in his recent book, makes Siki appear just one of many ruckus-raisers who epitomized that delirious decade; baseball player Babe Ruth and actor John Barrymore being two notable examples who come to mind.

For his first fight in the U.S. Siki was certainly handed no set-up. Kid Norfolk, shunned by both Tom Gibbons and Gene Tunney as an opponent and considered by many the best light heavyweight active at that period, faced Siki in his American debut on November 20, 1923. Siki lost but acquitted himself well against an unusually capable foe, in old Madison Square Garden.

Still Battling Siki had two grave weaknesses. He had an overindulgent fondness for brandy, and he could not keep money in his pocket. Handed $1000 of the sizeable $17,000 Norfolk purse, to keep him happy, with the rest put aside for him, he immediately repaired to New York's Harlem and by next morning had distributed every cent to residents of the area.

Equally serious from a professional standpoint was his unreliability in conditioning himself which prevented his getting the utmost return from his great natural gifts in the ring. Against nondescript opposition in small cities, he did well enough but proved unsuccessful against major opposition in this country.

He took a brutal beating from hard punching Paul Berlenbach in the old Garden on March 13, 1925. It was a savage cave-man struggle in which his lack of proper preparation subjected Siki to a sickening bludgeoning from the powerful New Yorker before the referee finally stopped the bout in the tenth round, far beyond the limit it would have been permitted to last today.

Siki possessed an unearthly immunity to pain and fear. He seemed impervious to suffering in the ring and his utter fearlessness was best demonstrated in World War I. In four years of the bitterest front line service, his gallantry in action brought him the French Croix De Guerre, the Legion of Honour, and the Medaille Militaire, France's highest honors.

Of all boxing champions Battling Siki was far and away the greatest hero.

Taken South by Levy on two occasions—a questionable move at best—he tangled with the segregation laws of this era in Memphis, then returned from that city to New York wedded to a Miss Lillian Werner. He received sympathetic treatment from U.S. immigration authorities, when French officials, voicing bigamous threats because of his prior and undissolved marriage in

Europe, showed a reluctance in re-admitting him into the country. He then declared his intention of becoming an American citizen.

Siki had a habit harmless of itself, but inadaptable to the racial climate of the time. When he felt like a drink, which was often—he would drop into the first place available, more often than not these places were located in the section in which he lived, New York's "Hell's Kitchen"—a neighborhood of legendary toughness.

Objections to his presence or any type of insulting remark, brought speedy redress from the fearless Siki, regardless of the odds. It was this practice which closed the chapter on Battling Siki. Completely ignoring the provocation for his actions, reports of the time painted Siki a "bar room brawler" when under the influence, an inaccurate depiction which disregarded wholly the reason behind his belligerency.

The night of December 15, 1925 a policeman patrolling a New York west side beat, saw a man lying face down on the curb. He turned the body over.

It was Battling Siki. He was dead.

Two bullets in the back had been "civilization's" farewell to the "Jungle Boy".

Although a suspect was apprehended—who in a signed statement implicated several others and charged the shooting to a lunchroom fracas in which Siki, having apparently bested several attackers was trailed and cowardly shot—the case was allowed to peter out after a few months.

Acidly commented the New York Daily News . . . "the white man's law failed to avenge the boy from Africa's jungles."

Although Siki's fighting record was far from impressive over here, it was directly opposite the estimate of him by three noted opponents, McTigue, Berlenbach and Norfolk. "The gamest and toughest man I ever met" was the unanimous appraisal of all three.

Thirty-five years after Siki won a world title, the Nigerian Hogan 'Kid' Bassey became the second "below the Sahara" African to win a world's championship, defeating Cherif Hamia for the featherweight title in Paris on June 24, 1957.

British bred Bassey was a far cry from the uninhibited Senegalese Siki. Cultured and formal in every way he was given to such statements as this summation of Willie Pep's ring trickeries. "I would say, sir, that Mr. Pep has most unusual ideas about the rules" was his refined rejoinder to a query regarding Wispy Willie's oft-criticized tactics.

Again, unlike Siki who believed in fighting to the death, if necessary, the genteel Bassey could see no point in continuing a struggle with no prospect of victory especially where eye injuries were possible. He was satisfied to "resign" in his corner, against present champion Davey Moore, which would have been unthinkable to the lion-hearted Siki.

The current fistic light of the "Dark Continent" Dick Tiger, WBA world middleweight champ, is a larger size replica of Bassey, a dignified, Homburg-hatted, conservative type, gentle speaking Nigerian. Few foreign fighters have made a better impression over here for dignity and decorum.

He—like Bassey—appears the other extreme of Siki. But then the western world and its reaction to native Africans, is far advanced from the ridicule and rebuffs that greeted poor Battling Siki. . . .

THE ITALIANS, PAST AND PRESENT, HOLD SPECIAL NICHE IN BOXING HISTORY

Taking a cue, no doubt, from the best-selling book, "The Italians", being so warmly received in America, Italy's fifth and sixth ranking middleweights, Nino Benvenuti and Sandro Mazzinghi are reportedly contemplating stateside invasions. Their hesitancy in heading this way has been understandable, considering the greenness of the grass in their own backyards. At home, the lads not only pack the fans in wherever they appear but also have the advantage of a highly partisan atmosphere.

In days gone by, fighting sons of Italy have seldom failed to challenge USA competition, where they often found Americans of Italian ancestry first in line as opponents. Such a circumstance faced the formidable Italian and European lightweight King of the thirties, Cleto Locatelli, who, upon arrival in the United States, found himself tossed in with America's outstanding lightweight, Tony Canzoneri. Against an opponent of such quality, Locatelli's American debut, on Nov. 15, 1933 in Madison Square Garden, turned out to be a losing one. But Canzoneri did not have an easy time with the invader, who proved to be a smart, game and rugged adversary.

Locatelli's showing was strong enough to earn him another shot in the big arena less than a month after the Canzoneri meeting. This time the black-haired Italian showed his true mettle by outscoring whirlwind Jack "Kid" Berg whom he had previously beaten in Europe. Back in the Garden against Canzoneri on Feb. 2, 1934, Cleto made it close once more but the decision went to the American. Locatelli, the gentlemanly type outside the ring, had only one comment to make after his second bitterly contested setback at the hands of Canzoneri, "Canzoneri is a lot better fighter than I thought he was."

Locatelli had arrived here with a long and impressive record of victories over the best lightweights in England and the continent behind him, beginning in 1927. By 1935 he was beginning to show some signs of ring erosion but he gave U.S. fans a good idea of the kind of fighter he was in his prime by waging an unbeaten campaign in the States in 1935. From April to December, he scored eight straight victories. Among his victims were such capable U.S. boxers as Eddie Cool, Izzy Jannazzo, Steve Halaiko, and Harry Dublinsky. In his 1934 showings over here Cleto had won over hard-hitting Benny Bass and Frankie Klick.

The year following Locatelli's win splurge, another Italian lightweight of classy calibre, Enrico Venturi, turned up in the United States claiming the

European lightweight title. Venturi, whose career pre-dated Locatelli's, going back to 1925, had turned up fighting in the small clubs around New York under the wing of Leo P. Flynn back in 1929 as a young featherweight. Heavier, seven years older, and smarter, he swept through a slew of second flight lightweights in 1936 with 13 consecutive triumphs plus a draw with Lou Ambers, before finally losing a twelve-round decision to Pedro Montanez, then a reigning sensation, in Madison Sq. Garden on Feb. 20, 1937.

In action, Venturi was a swift-moving boxer with fast hands and a keen ring brain. Like most of the Italians who came over he could not be accused of picking soft spots. On Jan. 12, 1938 in the Garden, he met Henry Armstrong, who had knocked out his last twenty opponents! Venturi turned out to be kayo victim No. 21, when his claim of foul was disallowed in the sixth round.

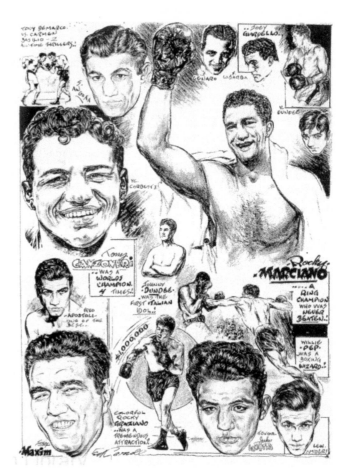

Boxing's Italian fraternity was another favorite of Carroll, prompting several comment pieces over his career. *The Ring* (January 1972)

By coincidence, an Italian lightweight, Aldo Spoldi, had been the last man to go the ten-round distance with Armstrong before Henry took on his extended kayo streak. This occurred in the Garden on March 19, 1937. Spoldi, tabbed as an early knockout victim, astounded everyone by lasting the limit by doing what one radio commentator of the time called "gamely retreating."

After coming here in 1935, Spoldi never returned to Italy to live, remaining active until 1944. His is the name most familiar to American fight fans among the Italian lightweights.

Of the trio of Locatelli, Venturi and Spoldi, Aldo proved by far the most popular personally, with his ready smile and likable disposition. Both the others affected an aloof continental air which did not find ready rapport with most statesiders. Aldo fought much too long, remaining active when his physical resources had been completely spent. At his best he was a dangerous hitter who, win or lose, could be counted on to give the fans value received.

The Italian lightweight trio previously mentioned were little more than children when the first of Italy's invaders performed in the United States. He was Erminio Spalla, the first Italian to gain any sort of fame in the ring, after he won an inter-allied tournament following World War I. However, Spalla was indifferently successful in Europe. Gene Tunney was the only American foe of note he met in the States. This match was fought as a preliminary to the Harry Greb-Ted Moore middleweight championship contest in the old Polo Grounds on June 25, 1924. When the fight was stopped in the seventh round and Tunney called the winner, Spalla protested vigorously, seizing Tunney about the waist and lifting him high in the air as evidence of his ability to continue. This was not one of Gene's better efforts and many of those present thought the referee's action in halting matters was premature.

Spalla was first, and the Italian lightweights were good, but giant Primo Carnera was the man who put Italy on the boxing map.

Carnera is often referred to as the most "exploited" fighter of all time. A lot depends on the definition of "exploited" as to the validity of this assertion. If by exploitation, one means publicity as outsized as his gargantuan frame, this is correct. Few visitors to these shores of any description were more extravagantly advertised than the one-time barefoot bumpkin from the hills of Sequals.

Arriving here in tow of Walter "Good time Charley" Friedman, a ballyhoo artist of vast imagination and eccentricity, Carnera was entrusted to the good graces of prohibition bigwigs Big Bill Duffy and Owney Madden, both of whom have now gone to glory. They machinated a barnstorming trek of the country by the giant which, whatever its other aspects, made the big fellow world famous. Along with this, Friedman fostered a frenetic flurry of Barnum-like tales about his mammoth charge. "Good time Charley" called Carnera's appetite so vast, it cost $30 a day at depression prices to feed him; his feet so large one of his overpriced brogans was placed on display in a Broadway store.

His physical dimensions were drastically exaggerated. He came into the city from overseas preceded by carloads of publicity and his reception here was hysterically thunderous as crowds followed him on the streets. The whole idea being the creation of a new Goliath come back to earth.

Carnera won the championship from Jack Sharkey in a baffling bout in June 1933. His campaign was crowned with success and sunny Italy now claimed a heavyweight champion of the world. Whatever the feelings about him in America, Italians, from Il Duce down, paid him high homage when he returned to his native land to defend his title against Paolino Uzcudun four months later. Carnera's ability has, in the long years since, become one of the most controversial of boxing topics. But Italians found nothing wrong with his performance against the much smaller Basque, whom he outclassed all the way.

Tommy Loughran found an 80-pound weight difference too much for him to contend with in Miami in 1934 against the Giant, who had little trouble with Tommy. But Max Baer's big right hand had Primo doing a yo-yo act with the canvas later that year, thus terminating his reign as world's champion.

Few men have been wept over as object lessons of man's inhumanity to man more than Primo Carnera, but the sob stories always neglect the fact that his "exploiters" did make him a world champion and world famous.

This fame gained in the ring, he turned into gold in the grappling game. On the strength of his reputation as a former world's heavyweight champion in a ten year post-war wrestling career, he recouped the fortunes lost in the hurly burly of both Nazi and Allied occupation in Italy. He is today a wealthy man with little to worry about as he basks in the sunny affluence of his California home.

The example of Carnera initiated an exodus of Italian giants to these shores. These Pachydermal paisanos, Roberto Roberti, Arthur DeKuh, Ricardo Bertazolla and Salvatore Ruggirello had little to recommend them save size. Roberti, for whom the late Jack Fugazy had high hopes, could never get his feet untangled when tagged on the chin. DeKuh looked most promising of all but was rushed prematurely into a match with Boston's Jim Maloney and petered out after that debacle. Ruggirello was a tremendous puncher, but had a way of losing interest if unable to take out his man in short order. All of them became familiar failures to the aficionados of the early Thirties in this country.

Carnera was the first Italian to fight for a world championship in this country. Since his time, Dulio Loi dropped the synthetic junior welterweight championship to Carlos Ortiz in San Francisco in 1960. Loi, one of the better Italian mittmen of the past thirty years, regained this tepid title from Ortiz three months later in Milan and never returned to the U.S.

Light heavyweight Giulio Rinaldi's try for Archie Moore's title on June 10, 1961, was so disappointing to both the large Madison Sq. Garden crowd and himself that he wept upon the sympathetic Archie's shoulder after the ageless marvel had befuddled him through a lacklustre 15 rounds.

In 1950, blond Tiberio Mitri, a sharply contrasting fair North Italian type to the swarthy, ebony-thatched, lowlanders familiar to American audiences, did better, but he was not quite good enough to handle tough Jake LaMotta. Before a rabidly partisan Garden crowd rooting against the native New Yorker, he lost out in his try to take Jake's middleweight title.

Italian born Paolo Rosi, a long time Bronx resident and now a U.S. citizen, was doing very well against Joe Brown, with old Joe's lightweight title on the line until a cut eye caused a cessation of hostilities in the ninth round back on June 3, 1959 in Washington D.C. Rosi campaigned in the U.S. so long he eventually lost his identity as an Italian, being pinned with the appellation "The Bronx Baldhead."

The visit of handsome Enzo Fiermonte, a promising middleweight to this country a generation ago took a peculiar turn. Enzo's wavy hair and classic profile had such a romantic impact among the ladies over here that he wound up wedded to a millionairess. He later became caught up in the Hollywood social swirl, ballooned into a heavyweight, met speedy disaster against a nondescript opponent and eventually vanished from the scene. Enzo was too good looking for his own good.

Veteran fight people recall featherweight Vittorio Tamagnini, light heavy Nando Tassi; welterweight brother of Enrico, Vittorio Venturi; middleweight Oddone Piazza; welterweight Saverio Turiello, who remained over here and became a bistro Boniface, collapsible heavyweight Gino Buonovino and bantamweight Kid Francis (Bonagura) with varying emotions.

For the first time in decades there is no Italian-born fighter of merit campaigning in the States. The Minelli brothers, Aldo and Livio, were the most recent Roman imports to have extended stays on these shores.

Either Benvenuti or Mazzinghi, both to the present talent depleted American highly touted, would be welcome additions [to the] fistic market.

PHILLY'S FIGHT HISTORY FEATURES GREATS GALORE

When the gentle Quakers founded Philadelphia back in Colonial times, they hardly could have foreseen that pugilism was to find such a welcome and enduring haven in the 'City of Brotherly Love.' As the site of the signing of the Declaration of Independence on that fateful July 4th, 1776, the city's place in history is forever secure. But notwithstanding the difference in importance, Philadelphia's spot in boxing's history is equally eminent.

The ring game has flourished there since the turn of the century, minus the spells of illegality which have interrupted boxing activity in places like New York and Chicago.

If one individual could be singled out most as responsible for Philadelphia's boxing durability it would have to be Herman "Muggsy" Taylor. The octogenarian promoter, still active after more than a half century of labor, became noted for the "All Star" extravaganzas he put on in Philly in partnership with Bobby Gunnis back in World War I.

In the long years since, either solo, or in alliance with outside collaborators, "Muggsy" has held his position in the front rank of entrepreneurs. His most recent offering, in conjunction with Madison Square Garden, the Emile Griffith-Gypsy Joe Harris bout on August 4 in Philly, was a rousing success both artistically and financially.

The largest crowd to see a boxing match anywhere in the world—102,000 people—turned out for a Philadelphia presentation, the second Dempsey-Tunney fight at Municipal Stadium on September 23, 1926.

All of the greats of the past half century have appeared in Philadelphia in every division from flyweight to heavyweight. For many years, boxing was so popular in Philadelphia, that holiday fights—often on Christmas Day—were solid attractions.

In the great days of vaudeville, sing-and-dance men scored heavily singing, "Tell them what I did to Philadelphia Jack O'Brien, but don't tell them what he did to me."

With a boxing tradition as strong as this, it's not surprising that the long and imposing list of fine Philadelphia fighters contains the names of outstanding champions.

In Joe Frazier, Quakertown has a superlative heavyweight who is recognized as world champion not only in his state of Pennsylvania, but in New York, Massachusetts, Maine and Rhode Island, as well. Other Philly titleholders whose recognition was more complete were:

Light heavyweights: Battling Levinsky, Tommy Loughran, Harold Johnson
  and Philadelphia Jack O'Brien.
Middleweight: Joey Giardello.
Junior welterweight: Johnny Jadick.
Lightweight: Bob Montgomery.
Featherweight: Benny Bass.
Flyweight: Midget Wolgast.

Giardello was Brooklyn-born, but started his career in Philadelphia, did most of his boxing there and was identified with the city throughout his career.

Philly's four light heavyweight champions were all unusually clever men: genuine ring scientists who were masters of the art. Tommy Loughran was referred to as the "Phantom of Philly."

At the age of 40, Harold Johnson remains one of the most skilled operatives in the ring.

Two of Philadelphia's greatest fighters, lefty Lew Tendler and old Jack Blackburn, never became champions. Tendler had the misfortune to be a contemporary of the great Benny Leonard, whom he met twice. He is invariably regarded as the best of the left-handed boxers and the superior of many more fortunate ones who became champions.

Blackburn, who was to become famous as the teacher of Joe Louis, was a rangy fellow who weighed only about 150 pounds but thought nothing of meeting and beating men 50 pounds heavier.

According to that venerable authority, Charlie Rose, Blackburn was one of the greatest boxers of all time. He was a protégé of the late Billy McCarney, himself a Philadelphian and a fistic celebrity in his own right.

Since the end of the Second World War, Philadelphia fighters have endured the frowns rather than the smiles of fortune where ring titles were involved. Gil Turner was one of the best fighters ever produced in Philly, and one of the greatest of what the British call "value-for-money" fighters yet seen in the ring.

He faced Kid Gavilan for the welterweight title in Philly in 1952, as an undefeated challenger who had swept all before him. But it was his tough luck to have the Cuban Hawk turn in one of his greatest fights. The men fought a blistering pace for 10 rounds before Gavilan halted the Philadelphian in the 11th in one of the most stirring championship matches yet held. Win or lose, Gil Turner never disappointed the fans. All his matches were classics of sustained action.

Philly's most brilliant prospects included Sugar Hart, a sleek welterweight who showed such talent as an amateur that he was considered a cinch to become a champion. But the good-looking flossy dressing Sugar was too sweet to the ladies. This short circuited a most promising career.

Lightweight Len Matthews was another Philadelphia comer of recent vintage who fell by the wayside, as did Jimmy Soo, part Chinese lightweight who could both box and punch, but whose chin was pure china.

Thirty-odd years ago big Jack Gross looked like a genuine Jewish heavyweight hope, but he proved unable to solve the clever style of neighboring light heavyweight Tommy Loughran. Philly heavies Gus Dorazio and Al Ettore were tough nuts until they tangled with Joe Louis.

Many of the ring's greatest men engaged in crucial bouts in Quakertown. In 1918 Jack Dempsey dazzled a Philly crowd by swarming all over clever Battling Levinsky and then knocking him out in three rounds.

Rocky Marciano had to come from behind before winning the heavyweight title from Jersey Joe Walcott in the 13th round in Philly in 1952. Benny Leonard turned in a classic performance knocking out featherweight champion Johnny Kilbane there in three rounds in 1917.

Gene Tunney had an unhappy experience in the city. His bout with Jack Renault was halted and declared "no contest" in the fourth round because of lack of action back in 1923. Tony Canzoneri was a great fighter but Philadelphia's Johnny Jadick had his number. He twice defeated Canzoneri, winning the junior welterweight championship from Tony in 1932.

Sugar Ray Robinson had some great moments in Philly rings. He knocked out Bobo Olson there in 1950 and turned in one of his most sparkling performances against Kid Gavilan there in 1949. In 1936 Jersey Joe Walcott knocked out Phil Johnson and 14 years later he knocked out Phil's son Harold in a Philly ring.

Many observers thought Ezzard Charles had regained his title from heavyweight Jersey Joe Walcott in Philadelphia in 1952 but the judging officials thought otherwise. Back in the long ago—1907—Jack Johnson knocked out old Bob Fitzsimmons in two rounds in Philly. A couple of ring immortals, Stanley Ketchel and Sam Langford fought six no-decision rounds there in 1910.

The ill luck which has trailed Philadelphia's better prospects struck again recently when welterweight Gypsy Joe Harris, a loser of only one bout, to Emile Griffith, saw his career come to an untimely end because of an eye injury.

Other names to remember in Philly fight annals are southpaw featherweight Danny Kramer; Unk Russell, old time lightweight protégé of Billy McCarney; lightweights Bobby Barrett, Nate Goldman and Johnny Mealey; lightweight Wesley Mouzon; featherweight Harry Blitman, a southpaw who defeated Tony Canzoneri; baseball-named lightweights Ty Cobb and Babe Ruth, a couple of Italian lads who took the names of diamond heroes and did well by them; Brooklyn-born lightweight Joe Tiplitz, who kayoed George K.O. Chaney; Philadelphia Pal Moore a featherweight who beat the great Welshman, Jem Driscoll; the oddly titled Louisiana, a Jewish lightweight; bantamweight Battling Murray; lightweight Harry Kid Brown; middleweight Vincent Forgione; featherweight Lew Massey; one-time featherweight contender Percy Bassett and Stan "Kitten" Hayward, who recently defeated Emile Griffith.

Much ring history had been made by the fighting sons of the "City of Brotherly Love."

JAPANESE BOXING, BORN IN 1905,
HAS ENJOYED SPECTACULAR SUCCESS

The latest issue of Ring Magazine lists ten Japanese fighters among the world's rated boxers: Lightweights, Jaguar Kakizawa; Junior Lightweights, Champion Hiroshi Kobayashi, Yoshiaka Numata, Rokuro Ishiyama; Featherweights, WBA Champion Shozo Saijyo, Fighting Harada; Bantamweight, Takao Sakurai; Flyweights Hiroyuki Ebihara and Yoshiaki Matsumoto.

Of these named Fighting Harada is a double former champion and probably the most internationally noted of them all. Harada won the world's flyweight championship by beating Thailand's Pone Kingpetch in 1962 and lost it back to him the following year.

Harada came back to win the world's bantamweight title from Brazil's highly rated Eder Jofre in 1965. He defended it successfully against four international challengers including Jofre, before relinquishing it to Australia's Lionel Rose early in 1968.

Hiroyuki Ebihara brought the flyweight title back to Japan by defeating Kingpetch in 1963 only to lose it back to the tenacious Thailander in 1964. Yoshiaka Numata defeated the veteran Filipino, Flash Elorde, for the junior lightweight title in 1967 and lost it to fellow countryman Kobayashi the same year.

Shozo Sajiyo was declared featherweight champion by the WBA after defeating Raul Rajos in California last year. Ebihara also fought for the flyweight crown in 1966 as did unlisted Katsuyoshi Takayama the same year.

Japan's first world boxing champion was Tokyo born Yoshio Shirai, a tiny, baby-faced buzzsaw who won the flyweight title from Filipino Dado Marino in Tokyo in 1952. Shirai, following an amateur career, and service in the Japanese Army in World War II, was picked up by Dr. A.R. Cahn, a civilian worker for the Army during the early days of the U.S. occupation.

Shirai, who was a fine little scrapper, did practically all his fighting in Tokyo, winning the championship in the Japanese capital and defending it successfully 4 times against Marino, Tanny Campo, Terry Allen, and Leo Espinosa before losing it to Argentina's Pascual Perez in Tokyo late in 1954.

According to the most reliable records, boxing was introduced into the Land of the Rising Sun in 1905 by A.M. Loughrey, a U.S. athlete there for the purpose of studying jiujitsu. Once initiated into the intricacies of the Manly Art the Japanese proved highly receptive to the sport, both as spectators and participants.

For many years competition was confined to amateurs. In 1909 the first Japanese fighters, Young Oyama, a lightweight, and Young Togo, a flyweight appeared in California where J.J. "Moose" Taussig, a prominent promoter of those days on the coast, interested himself in the Orientals.

The professional side of boxing received its first impetus in Japan during a tour of the country by U.S. fighters Spider Roache, a featherweight, and Young Ketchel, a welterweight. The Japanese were especially impressed by the littler Roache's speed and dexterity and the budding boxers of the country set out to emulate his style.

Amateur boxing was still favored in Japan and it was not until July 1922 that the first professional boxing show was staged there, on a Sunday.

Yujiro Watanabe figured prominently in popularizing professional boxing in Japan in the nineteen twenties. In the States "Moose" Taussig, who never lost his interest in the Japanese, was instrumental in the importation of their earliest boxing representatives into this country.

Included among these invaders were S. Otshu, a bantamweight; Tobuchi Kowata, a welter; Fukuo Kimura, another bantam; Einei Hattori, a bantam; Yoshio Nattori and Suco Kirakawa, a lightweight.

The best of the first Japanese pros, according to legend, was Tsumeo Horiguchi, a Waseda collegian, who was called "The Piston" because of his rapid fire precision punching.

Kanao Nakamura, a rugged southpaw Taussig protégé, who campaigned on the Coast, became a writer when he finished his career in the ring.

The pioneer Japanese battlers, while showing plenty of spirit, heart, and willingness found contendership status hard to attain. The first to establish himself as a solid challenger for a title was Korean born Joe Tei Ken, raised in Japan. Tei Ken began his boxing career there and was referred to as Japanese throughout his career.

Arriving in California in the early thirties he fought under the management of Charley Cook, a well-known boxing man. He did well enough to be rated among the leading bantamweight contenders by the Ring in 1933.

One of his most notable victories was scored over the capable French boxer Eugene Huat. Tei Ken gained such worldwide recognition in the bantam and featherweight divisions, that upon his return to Japan in 1937, he was accorded a hero's welcome in Tokyo and presented to the Emperor.

The feats of Joe Louis also had an energizing effect upon boxing in Japan. The Brown Bomber's triumphs were received with general rejoicing in the tense climate of pre-Pearl Harbor Japan. When Louis toured the country in 1951, giving exhibitions in aid of a fund for children, he was royally welcomed.

Westerners are inclined to view the fighter-manager relationship in Japan as almost tantamount to foster parentage in this country. If means permit it, training quarters are in or adjacent to the manager's house. The boxer lives and takes his meals there, living a life not unlike that of an adopted son in a household. Contracts are complicated, difficult to break and attempts to make managerial changes are usually looked upon as unsportsmanlike and in bad form.

Despite an amateur boxing background reaching back to the early years of this century Japanese boxers have found Olympic championships elusive. Takeo Sakurai, who won the Olympic bantamweight championship in Tokyo in 1964, when Japan was host to the games, is the only Japanese to enter the charmed circle of Olympic winners. Olympic decisions being what they are, success in these contests is quite dependent on luck. The best the Japanese could do in the Mexico City Olympics last year was a semi-finalist in the bantam class, Eliji Moriok. Paul Fujii, Hawaiian born of Japanese extraction, caused a ripple of interest in the States because of his Hawaiian background, when he won the junior welterweight title in 1967 by beating Sandro Lopopolo. He lost it to Argentina's Nicolino Loche last year.

Although junior lightweight kingpin Kobayashi is Japan's only current world champion, fistic Orientalists are especially high on the young featherweight WBA titleholder, Shozo Saijyo.

In terms of achievement, Fighting Harada, a double champion who presently is ranked No. 4 among the world's featherweights, must be granted top honors among the busy little nippers from Nippon.

A Japanese sports historian, S. Nakata, has been a respected source of boxing history there since the sport was introduced into the country 64 years ago. The pace of Japanese progress in boxing has been greatly accelerated in the score of years since the Second World War due, in considerable degree, to the long tenure of U.S. forces there. . . .

DER MOX, ONCE CHAMPION, STILL GERMANY'S NO. 1 IDOL

Luis Firpo in the Argentine and Georges Carpentier in France had their German prototype in Max Schmeling. Ever since the sport took hold in that country, during post World War I American and British occupation, boxing there has centered around the big fellows.

The nation's first heavyweight champion, Hans Breitenstraeter, attracted some attention on the continent but never ventured overseas or attained world class.

Schmeling's appearance on the scene as a promising light heavyweight in the early twenties, and his subsequent winning of the heavyweight championship in the early thirties, gave the boxing picture in Germany a heavyweight frame which has persisted through the years. This concentration on the bigger men has limited the Teutonic world title roster to Schmeling, solo.

The former heavyweight king is also the only German fighter who might properly be called a national hero. The Germans, one of the less demonstrative of the nationalities, have rarely reached the levels of enthusiasm over their ringmen common to the French, Italians, or Mexicans, for example. With but one world champion to pedestal, a German Boxing Hall of Fame is largely confined to those who demonstrated their abilities to handle international competition.

These would include, besides Schmeling, Walter Neusel, Franz Diener, Karl Mildenberger and Hein ten Hoff, heavyweights; Adolph Heuser, Bubi Scholz and Max Dickmann, lightheavyweights; and Erich Seeling, middleweight.

For world-wide renown, none of this group belongs in the same paragraph with Schmeling who, besides being the only German champion, was one of the most controversial figures in boxing history.

The disputation which dogged his footsteps for so many years is at complete odds with his personality, which is that of a courtly, continental gentleman. The man from Hamburg was caught in a whirlpool of events which kept his career at an uneven keel through his heyday.

The heaviest of his burdens was the Hitler regime, but even prior to the Nazi takeover, complications—mainly managerial—plagued the German champion. Schmeling no sooner had stepped off the gangplank in New York on his first U.S. visit in 1928 when he was tagged The German Dempsey by some near-sighted nicknamer. This precipitated a mad stampede by American fight managers after the job of U.S. representative for the German heavyweight champion who was then handled by German Arthur Von Bulow.

This free-for-all took in Charley Rose, who got to Von Bulow first; Pete Reilly, Humbert J. Fugazy, Joe Jacobs and Billy McCarney. Ring Magazine Editor Nat Fleischer spotted Schmeling in Europe and got a signed agreement from this likely prospect.

When the smoke cleared, Von Bulow was still in the saddle with Charley Rose a minor shareholder and Jacobs hovering menacingly about. Jacobs eventually outmaneuvered everyone by winding up in control of the fighter, with German Max Machon going along for the ride.

For frugality, Max Schmeling ran Luis Angel Firpo a close second and, like the Wild Bull, he had trouble reconciling his thriftiness with the managerial cut of 33⅓ percent. This had been at the bottom of his managerial mixups.

Schmeling soon established his contendership for the heavyweight title with victories over tough Johnny Risko and rugged Paolino Uzcudun. Jack Sharkey posed the final obstacle in his path toward retired Gene Tunney's vacated title. In this match, one of the most controversial of the decade, Schmeling was declared the world heavyweight champion while squatting on the canvas bleating "Foul."

Manager Joe Jacobs generally gets credit for yelling the German into the title. He got considerable assistance from the noted Hearst newspaper editor Arthur Brisbane that evening back in 1930 in New York. Brisbane, a man of authoritarian presence, erupted from his seat as the German lay on the floor and in a tone fraught with foreboding charged referee Jim Crowley to "Give Schmeling the fight or I'll kill boxing in this state!"

The manner of his triumph left much to be desired, but a year later, in Cleveland, Schmeling proved he was of championship class with one of his best performances, against W.L. (Young) Stribling.

Stribling was an excellent fighter, with nothing at stake. But with a championship on the line he would become strangely futile. With Strib floored by Schmeling in the 15th round, the bout was stopped by referee George Blake with just two seconds remaining.

Often called the Black Uhlan by U.S. sportswriters, Max found the dark shadow of controversy complementing this nom-de-guerre.

Schmeling lost his championship to Jack Sharkey in Madison Square Garden Bowl in Long Island City. Long vanished from the metropolitan landscape, this sprawling wooden arena was haunted by one of the most potent hoodoos in sports history. No champion ever defended his laurels successfully there.

Schmeling was no exception, although the decision which dethroned him was widely disputed as most onlookers thought he had a substantial edge at the finish of the 15-rounder.

Later that same year 1932, Schmeling came up with another good showing when he stopped overambitious Mickey Walker in Brooklyn. Walker was a great middleweight but he was no match for the German heavyweight.

1933 was a fateful year for Schmeling. In his native Germany, the drums of militarism and the lash of persecution heralded the rise of Adolf Hitler and the Third Reich. This development threatened to make Schmeling persona non grata in the United States. On top of this he was knocked out by Max Baer. In this upset, some close observers detected a loss of initiative on the part of Schmeling when his best punches failed to have any effect on the iron-chinned Baer.

Schmeling's days as a top-flighter appeared to be numbered when he was decisioned by up-and-coming Steve Hamas in Philadelphia early in 1934, but he bounced back to stop arch-rival Walter Neusel in Hamburg later in the year.

In evening the score against Hamas with an 8-round knockout in Hamburg in 1935, Schmeling escaped any blame himself. But all others concerned, including Hamas' manager Charley Harvey, were excoriated in the German press for permitting the bout to continue as long as it did. Hamas, after suffering a recurrence of a football knee injury, was so terribly punished he never fought again.

By 1935 the Nazi holocaust had gained horrendous momentum and Schmeling, managed by the Jewish Joe Jacobs, found himself in the vortex of a dilemma and an eddying disapproval in the Third Reich.

Mollifying the Nazis by ditching the manager meant placing any further American appearances in grave jeopardy. Schmeling, staking everything on his great popularity with the German people, decided to stick it out with Jacobs whatever the consequences.

Jacobs also found himself in a hypersensitive situation. While recognizing its practicality, the American-Jewish community took a dim view of his involvement with the German champion, a feeling which was aggravated by the Nazi salute Jacobs found himself obliged to give when caught in the ring during the playing of the German National Anthem following Schmeling's victory over Hamas in Hamburg.

In attempting to allay protests over this gesture, Jacobs emphasized that he had held a lighted cigar in his upraised hand, thereby putting his own brand of hex on the "Heil." This revelation, readily discernible in the re-examined photo, had a counter-action overseas and Joe Jacobs never set foot in Nazi Germany again.

By 1936, Joe Louis had burst upon the boxing scene with atomic impact and a match with then champion Jim Braddock was a certainty. The idea occurred to someone—possibly Mike Jacobs himself—that a bout with the supposedly over-the-hill Schmeling would not only afford a pre-title tuneup for the sensational Louis but a sizable payday for all concerned as well.

The Jacobs forces stifled potential opposition to the German's return to America by pointing out that the prospective quick knockout of Schmeling by Louis would hold the detested racial superiority dogma of the Nazis up to world ridicule.

Discontent over the project did not completely subside and there were some mutterings of a boycott. But since both Jacobses—Joe and Mike—were playing lead roles in the negotiations this did not materialize.

As a spectator at the Louis-Paolino bout in Madison Square Garden late in 1935, Schmeling did not seem overly impressed with the one-punch demolition job that the Brown Bomber did on the hitherto punch-proof Basque. He commented tersely after the knockout, "I zee zomezing."

And indeed, he had! Spotting Louis' vulnerability to a right hand punch, the German knocked out the Brown Bomber six months later in one of the most shocking surprises of all time. Instead of the expected Louis victory and any subsequent Nazi embarrassment, Schmeling returned home to an ecstatic Germany with Der Fuehrer himself cheerleading the celebrations.

Naturally, the Nazis made capital of Schmeling's triumph as a vindication of their "superman" ideology. Discomfiture over the result in the U.S. caused a rash of propaganda to be directed at Schmeling, to the point of absurdity. Racist statements were charged to him which, in light of his record both before and after, were ridiculous.

Schmeling had fought all the Negro heavyweights available in Europe early in his career losing to one of them, Larry Gains, Canadian champion, by a knockout. The allegation that he attributed his defeat of Louis to Nordic superiority is pure nonsense. Never in his long career had Max Schmeling exhibited any traces by word or deed of Nazi racial infection.

Schmeling's return to the States to meet Louis for the championship two years later has been a matter of puzzlement to many boxing people. Since he was manipulated out of the title shot against Braddock, which he had earned on the basis of his win over Louis, many wiseacres have contended, that since Louis' title status was under a cloud, the German should have sat tight in the fatherland basking in the glory of an "uncrowned champion" and a victim of injustice.

Why Schmeling returned to try Louis again is one of the more fantastic tales of fistiana. The legend goes like this. Schmeling had married the beautiful Czech actress Anny Ondra, who, it was whispered, had found favor in the eyes of Dr. Goebbels, Nazi Minister of Propaganda. Rumors reached Schmeling that Dr. Goebbels, who was notorious for his affairs d'amour, had not allowed his interest in the beautiful lady to lag because of her marriage and the fighter is supposed to have said something about "breaking his neck."

Herr Goebbels was many things, most of them unsavoury, but he was no fool. Like many others he felt that luck had been on the side of his countryman in the Louis fight and he envisioned disaster for Schmeling if the two ever met again.

Advised of Schmeling's threat, the canny Nazi bigwig, with ready access to the ear of Hitler himself, suggested to Der Fuehrer that the prestige of Nazi Germany and its super-race obsession would be immeasurably enhanced were Schmeling to go back to America and defeat Louis again, thereby becoming the first man to ever win the championship for a second time.

One may take this story for whatever it is worth. Schmeling did return to America, to be blasted out by Louis in one round, in 1938. The clouds of war had been gathering over Europe since Hitler's accession to power and in 1939, the Wehrmacht went on the march.

Once again Max Schmeling, the Nation's boxing idol, faced a bitter choice. Succumbing to the "My country, right or wrong!" syndrome, he became a paratrooper, was hurt in the battle of Crete and saw no action thereafter.

Like virtually all fighters, Schmeling couldn't resist the compulsion to try it again 24 years after his start, at the age of 43. 14 years after their first meeting in 1938 the equally antiquated Walter Neusel evened the score with his ancient rival in a slow motion match in which Father Time was the only winner.

The saga of Max Schmeling is that of a man who was a toy of circumstance. Of ascetic habit with a yen for rustic, off the beaten path, training hideouts, Schmeling's reserved personality and character contravened the controversy that clung to him throughout his career. He was controversial without being charismatic, made so by the pressure of events beyond his control.

One of the happier aspects of his latter years has been his friendship with Louis, an obvious liking which is mutual and affords additional evidence of the unfairness of the libels directed against him in former years.

In contrast to his alleged thriftiness, he wasted little time in posting a thousand dollar reward in furtherance of the search for Gene Tunney's daughter when she was missing in Europe last year. He is expected in this country shortly to visit troubled Joe Louis in a Denver sanitarium. Soberminded and intelligent, he has done well in retirement as a business representative for various concerns, both German and American.

For all Germany's accent on the heavyweights, only one other besides Schmeling has gotten the opportunity to fight for the big title, Karl Mildenberger. Had he been called upon to face a less talented champion than Cassius Clay, Mildenberger might well have duplicated Schmeling's achievement. Off his record, he was the best German heavyweight since Max. A better than average lefthanded boxer, he did very well against a succession of invading American heavyweights during the sixties. Among those he defeated was Eddie Machen. In nine years of boxing he seldom lost and his overall record, which included winning the European heavyweight championship, was very impressive.

Walter Neusel was, for a time, the best European heavyweight, excepting Schmeling. Neusel, an aggressive blond battler, performed well in the States under the standard of the late Paul Damski and Jimmy Bronson. Walter proved good enough to win a decision over clever Tommy Loughran. But Schmeling was an obstacle to him in their homeland.

Critics abroad agree that the best all-around German fighter was the handsome Berliner Gustav "Bubi" Scholz. Like Georges Carpentier years before, Scholz fought his way up through the divisions winning the German championship as a welter, middle and light heavyweight.

A fast moving southpaw, who could both box and punch, Scholz made only one appearance in the States against tough Al Andrews in Madison Sq. Garden whom he defeated handily. This was in 1954. Although he would have been welcomed back, he never returned to the United States. Holder of the European middleweight championship, he eventually outgrew the class and after 14 years of boxing failed in an attempt to win the world light heavyweight championship from Harold Johnson.

Adolph Heuser was a hard-bitten light heavy who did well enough overseas and in the United States to earn a chance at the 175 lb. laurels then held by Maxie Rosenbloom. Nobody was beating Maxie in those days, and although Heuser gave it a good try he proved unequal to the task. . . .

Paul Maski, at one time Germany's outstanding promoter, a refugee from the Hitler terror, turned up shortly before the Second World War with Erich Seelig, also an escapee from the Nazis, and the German middleweight champion. Seelig, a busy aggressive mauler, who had twice lost to Marcel Thil in Paris, is best remembered for having brought the lustrous career of Mickey Walker to an end in New York's old St. Nicholas Arena.

Eccentric middleweight Peter Mueller, who once kayoed a referee in Germany; welterweight Gustave Eder; heavyweight Hein ten Hoff, who met Jersey Joe Walcott and was German champion; 1936 Olympic heavyweight champion, Herbert Runge, who didn't get too far as a professional before the war broke out; and junior welterweight Willi Quatuor are other names that have enlivened the German boxing scene through the years.

JEWISH FIGHTERS HAVE ACHIEVED FAME
BEYOND THEIR LIMITED NUMBERS

In law, medicine, education, finance, philosophy, psychology, sociology, literature, art, music and all forms of science, members of the Jewish faith have distinguished themselves, far out of proportion to their numbers.

While pugilism may seem far removed from these classical pursuits, the Jewish tradition in boxing is comparable. There have been mighty figures of this faith in other sports: great pitcher Sandy Koufax, and home run king Hank Greenberg in baseball; Nat Holman and Adolph Schayes in basketball; Sid Luckman, Marshall Goldberg and Benny Friedman in football; Rene Lacoste of France and Helen Jacobs in tennis; and Mark Spitz in swimming. But it is in the ring that Jewish athletic heritage is strongest and the achievement greatest.

The first person of the Jewish faith to achieve national renown in any sport in this country was a boxer, Joe Choynski. A fabled fighter out of San Francisco who, although outweighed many pounds, gained fame in legendary contests with champions Jim Corbett, Jim Jeffries and Jack Johnson, whom he knocked out in 1903.

Barney Aaron, a 19th century boxer preceded Choynski, but never gained similar recognition. More than two hundred years after his birth in 1764 the Sephardic Jew, Daniel Mendoza, retains an honored place in the annals of pugilism. A man of refinement and literacy, Mendoza was regarded as the most scientific boxer of his time. He was an especial favorite in Ireland, of all places, where he toured and lectured extensively, demonstrating the finer points of the boxing art as developed by him.

The attentive Hibernians learned their lessons well; for in the years to come such champions of Irish extraction as Gene Tunney, Tommy Loughran, Billy Conn, Jimmy Slattery, Mike Gibbons and Mike McTigue were to become paragons of the Mendoza school.

Mendoza was also admired by no less a person than George III, England's king of the American Revolutionary period, a dubious distinction from a stateside point of view, but an exciting example of the social circle in which Mendoza was accepted. Mendoza's fame endured for many years after his passing in 1836. He was extolled in Bell's "Life in London" (1855). By such passages as " . . . few pugilists can boast of such feats as this celebrated Hebrew champion." Further proof of Mendoza's versatility is found in his book on boxing published in 1789, the first ever produced by a pugilist.

All this was a long time ago. Moving into the modern era we find that these 26 boxers of Jewish extraction have been either claimants or been recognized as world champions:

Heavyweight: Max Baer (paternal).

Light heavyweight: Battling Levinsky (Barney Lebrowitz), Bob Olin, Maxie Rosenbloom.

Middleweight: Al McCoy (Rudolph), Dave Rosenberg, Ben Jeby, Solly Krieger.

Welterweight: Ted Kid Lewis (Gershon Mendeloff, England), Jackie Fields (Jacob Finkelstein), Barney Ross (Rosofsky).

Junior welterweight: Mushy Callahan (Morris Scheer), Jack Kid Berg (Judah Bergman, England).

Lightweight: Benny Leonard (Leiner), Al Singer, Barney Ross.

Junior lightweight: Jack Bernstein (Jacob Dodick).

Featherweight: Abe Attell, Louis Kid Kaplan, Benny Bass.

An Ace Fighter and Citizen

Carroll rated Jewish fighter Benny Leonard among the greatest to have ever mastered the sweet science. *The Ring* (July 1947)

Bantamweight: Abe Goldstein, Robert Cohen (Algiers), Harry Harris (Herman Sizors), Charley Phil Rosenberg (Green).

Flyweight: Corporal Izzyn Schwartz.

The greatest of all the Jewish champions was Benny Leonard. When candidates for the greatest fighter of all time, "pound-for-pound," are proposed, the name of Leonard always receives strong support. He was a boxer of such superlative skill that during his heyday it was claimed that no man could "muss his hair," slick, black, which he always kept carefully groomed. Through long years of practice he mastered a style of boxing of singular beauty and difficulty. He would rock rhythmically in and out of hitting range with a coordinated grace which was ballet-like in execution. He was highly intelligent and perfected moves which have not been duplicated since. On top of this, he was a tremendous puncher with either hand.

The list of Jewish champions might be even longer had not many of them been congested within the same period. Lew Tendler is regarded as one of the best lightweights of all time, but had the misfortune to be contemporaneous with Leonard.

The same thing applied to Willie Jackson (Oscar Tobler); Frankie Callahan (Samuel Holtzman); Charley White (Ancelowitz), all lightweights of championship potential, who found their way blocked by the invincible Benny.

The great days of the Jewish boxer lasted roughly from 1917, when Benny Leonard dethroned Freddy Welsh as lightweight champion, to 1938 when Barney Ross lost the welterweight championship to Henry Armstrong.

There were good men both before and after these dates, but it was during this 20-year span that boxing among the Jewish people reached its peak. Like all other groups their ranks comprised many who, had the fates been kinder, might have been champions of the world.

Benny Valgar, the clever New York featherweight known as the "French Flash" was one of these, as was KO Phil Kaplan, a shrewd and hard hitting welter and middleweight who rated a title opportunity, but never got one; 130-pounder Harrach Wallach of Brooklyn, one of the greatest amateur boxers of all time, had his career crippled by injury; Red Chapman (Morris Kaplan) of Boston was a clever featherweight who might have been champion with a little luck; Joe Burman, Chicago bantamweight of the Twenties, found his division crowded with an unusual number of exceptional little men; Newsboy Brown (Dave Montrose) of California was good enough to have been fly or bantamweight champion but never got the chance; Sid Terris was the best lightweight of his time but never became champion; left-hooking Ray Miller stopped Jimmy McLarnin but could never get a champion into the ring with him; middleweights of lesser calibre than Augie Ratner have worn the 160-lib. crown, but such a "break" never came Augie's way; Georgie Abrams, who came later, defeated middleweight champion Billy Soose three times, but couldn't get by Tony Zale; hard-hitting southpaw featherweight Danny Kramer of Philadelphia, clever Providence, R.I. bantamweight Young Montral, and Milwaukee featherweight Joey Sangor belong in the category of those upon whom the purple robes of ring royalty would have rested well, had fortune smiled upon them.

For some of the Jewish boys, the Star of David shone brightly at the beginning, but flickered as the opposition got tougher. New York's old East Side, "the Ghetto"—a section so prolific in fighting men that the late Damon Runyon once said its inhabitants must be descendants of a Biblical warrior tribe—suffered many such disappointments. The best remembered of these was Ruby Goldstein, later famous as a referee, once known as "the greatest prospect of all time" who proved unable to cope with the top-flighters. Lew Kersh, Sammy Dorfman, Terry Roth, Willie Siegel and Harry Felix were other "Prides of the Ghetto" of unusual potential who, for one reason or another, fell by the wayside.

As if in recollection of the royal reception tendered Mendoza in "Tara's Halls" many generations ago, Jewish boys have reciprocated by adding additional luster to the Irish names they adopted in the ring. The two Callahans, Frankie and Mushy; the brothers Young and Young; Artie O'Leary (Lieberman); Oakland Jimmy Duffy (Hymie Gold); Chapman; Eddie O'Keefe; Willie Harmon (Herman Einsman); KO Phil Delmont; Bobby Michaels (Wallach); Davey Day; Leach Cross; Johnny Clinton, Willie and Charley Beecher were all Hebrews with Hibernian nommes de Guerre.

In the years immediately preceding World War II, Brooklyn by way of Boston, came up with one of the most brilliant prospects of that period in welterweight Mike Kaplan. This good looking youngster appeared to have everything. After defeating a string of good men, among them former welter king Fritzie Zivic and the capable Cocoa Kid, Kaplan suddenly called it a career after suffering an injury in the ring.

Frustration and disappointment have plagued Jewish heavyweights. Art Lansky seemed on the way to his goal up to the time his expectations expired via a close loss to comebacking Jim Braddock in 1935; New Yorker Marty Fox was a real blaster but a victim of fickle fortune; Roy Lazer of Paterson, N.J. was impressive until tossed in with Joe Louis in 1935; Boston's Big Bill

Weinberg might have made it, but no one could ever get him to take training seriously; lanky Philly southpaw Jack Gross couldn't get by light heavy Tommy Loughran.

Brooklyn schoolboy athlete giant Abe Simon was one of the few Jewish big men to fight for the heavyweight title, but Joe Louis was the champion in his day. Big Abe, getting two chances, was no more successful than the others who challenged the Brown Bomber when he ruled the roost; King Levinsky made some good showings against Max Baer and others, but after going out in one round against Louis, the King became only a passing specimen. The Marine from Washington, D.C., Len Kanthal, looked like money in the bank after defeating Pete Rademacher and a covey of competent big fellows in the Golden Gloves, but as a professional his career never got off the ground. . . . Some have felt that Maxie Rosenbloom with his razzle-dazzle style, while only a light-heavy, might have slapped his way to the heavyweight title, had he been given the chance. The champions of his time must have felt the same way because they laughed the idea off. In recent years, Buffalo's Dick Wipperman aroused some expectations as did big Ski Goldstein out on the Coast. But Dick couldn't handle the headliners, and Ski couldn't take a punch.

The heavyweight title vacuum has been more than filled by the exploits of Jewish boxers in the lighter classes. The late Joe Woodman was one of the Old Guard who rated featherweight Abe Attell over the peerless Leonard as the best of them all, basing his opinion on the ability of Attell to handle men much bigger than himself. "Benny seldom had the worst of it on the scales," reminisces Charley Rose, "but Attell thought nothing of giving the other fellow as much as 20 pounds."

The late Barney Ross, who fought as bravely on the battlefield as he did in the ring, was the only fighter of Jewish lineage to become a double champion, as a welter and as a lightweight. In his ascent to ring glory, Ross was called upon to defeat unusually stern opposition: Tony Canzoneri, Billy Petrolle, Ceferino Garcia and Jimmy McLarnin. Ross may have been too game for his own good. In the final match of his career against Henry Armstrong in 1938 he responded angrily to suggestions by his handlers that the fight be stopped, "I'm a champion and I'm going to stay in there until I drop!" He lasted the limit, but was punished so severely that he never fought again.

One of the best boxers of his time, Jackie Fields, the former welterweight titlist was one of three American Jewish boxers to win an Olympic boxing championship—the late Sam Mosberg and Sam Berger were the others. Jackie won the Olympic featherweight title in Paris in 1924. Like Ross he had to get by formidable rivals to win the welterweight title, such as Gorilla Jones and Young Jack Thompson.

Louis "Kid" Kaplan, who put the town of Meridien, Conn. on the map, is still regarded as one of the outstanding featherweight champions. An idol in New England, the Kid's honesty was on a par with his ability. Having outgrown the class in 1927 he was propositioned by operators with a $50,000 offer to drop a decision to a contender of their own choosing along with the title. Not only was their protégé a good fighter in his own right, they advanced this come-on, "You're going to give the thing up anyway, why not get paid for it? Never mind the weight. We'll take care of the scales." Had he been present, Diogenes could have called off his search for the "honest man," for Kaplan's rejoinder was, "Look, every time I fight my friends bet a bundle on me. I wouldn't let them down for a million dollars. Now, get the hell out of here!"

Among the most remarkable performers of all time, Battling Levinsky fought 272 matches in his 20-year career, once appearing in three bouts in three different places within 24 hours! Maxie Rosenbloom was just as busy. They may have called him Slapsie Maxie but Mickey Walker, Dave Shade, John Henry Lewis, James J. Braddock, and Jimmy Slattery, who are numbered among his 185 decision victims, didn't find Maxie any joke.

Neither Solly Krieger nor Ben Jeby, middleweight champions of the Thirties, received due credit for their abilities. Krieger, a stalking dead-pan along the lines of Dick Tiger, defeated Billy Conn. Jeby had an overabundance of dura-bility and ruggedness. . . .

If a fighter deserved to become a world champion, Newark's Allie Stolz was the man. Few onlookers in the Garden the night of May 15, 1942 doubted that the flashy, sharp-punching Jerseyite had shown a clear superiority over defending champion Sammy Angott in their 15-round match. But the officials voted for Angott. Allie never recovered from this shocker.

The English Jew, Ted Kid Lewis (Gershon Mendeloff) had other claims to fame beyond his 22 meetings with clever Jack Britton. He held the welter title and most oldtimers call him the best of all the British boxers who have invaded these shores although there are some dissenters in favor of Jack Kid Berg (Judah Bergman). Berg made the most spectacular Garden debut of any foreign fighter of his time. His non-stop style earned him the soubriquet of the "Whitechapel Whirlwind," after 10 rounds of ceaseless fist throwing against Bruce Flowers, a good one, in 1929 in the Old Madison Square Garden. Berg beat the best Americans, Tony Canzoneri and Billy Petrolle among them, while winning the junior welterweight title from Mushy Callahan in 1930.

3

AFRICAN AMERICAN BOXING

At the end of 1938, two boxers dominated the fight game. They were heavy-weight king Joe Louis and triple champ Henry Armstrong, ruler of the featherweight, lightweight, and welterweight divisions, and both of them were African American. As Carroll's March 1939 article played up, "Hammering Hank" Armstrong had managed this unprecedented feat in less than ten months, while the "Brown Bomber" had defended his crown by wrecking his erstwhile conqueror, Max Schmeling, in little more than two minutes of the first round. In March 1947, *The Ring* celebrated its twenty-fifth anniversary, an occasion that Carroll used to trace the rise of "Sable Sockers" over the same period. Observing that in 1922 there were no African American champions, "just three real contenders," Carroll now counted four black title holders (heavyweight Joe Louis, welterweight Ray Robinson, and lightweights Bob Montgomery and Ike Williams) and twenty-seven leading contenders in every weight division. "A far cry," concluded Carroll, "from the hungry, haunted years of a generation ago."

By transforming the opportunities open to black fighters, boxing set the pace in banishing the worst excesses of racial segregation from other sporting activities. Reflecting in October 1960 on the US public's reaction to Floyd Patterson's triumph over Ingemar Johansson, a victory that not only saw Floyd become the first man ever to regain the heavyweight title but also brought the greatest prize in sport back to America, Carroll was struck by the complete absence of racial rancor. The contrast with the race riots that followed Jack Johnson's win over James J. Jeffries in 1910 was complete. Fifty years later, there was no clamor for "White Hopes" to avenge Johansson's defeat by a black man.

It had been very different when "Dark Hopes," the dreary prospects of African American boxers from 1910 to 1930, blighted the careers of outstanding ring men like Sam Langford, Sam McVey, Joe Jeanette, and Harry Wills. Avoided by most white boxers, the four of them were reduced to fighting each other in an endless round-robin. They endured title freezeouts, "color lines," and derisory pay. Carroll's October 1966 article, "'Dark Hopes' Showed Great Boxers with Pittance Pay," memorably calculated that for all his 252 listed fights put together, Sam Langford earned less than half the $250,000 Muhammad Ali was guaranteed for one bout alone, his first clash with Britain's Henry Cooper.

Three years later, Carroll poured evident time and energy into his biggest ever project. This was his masterpiece, *The American Black Man and Boxing*, serialized in *The Ring* between October 1969 and April 1970. The first installment focused primarily on four fighters, Bill Richmond, Tom Molyneaux, George Dixon, and Peter Jackson. Richmond and Molyneaux were former slaves whose pugilistic careers played out in early nineteenth-century England and not America, while Dixon, at various times before 1900 world bantam and featherweight champion, and heavyweight Peter Jackson were not US born. But their impact on the circumstances of the time and the future of black American boxers was sufficiently important, Carroll reasoned, to merit their inclusion in the series. Because neither John L. Sullivan nor his successor, James J. Corbett, would meet Jackson for the title, they were, according to some fight buffs, American champions only. Boxing purists insist that the first world heavyweight champion was James J. Jeffries, who had knocked Jackson out some time before defeating "Freckled" Bob Fitzsimmons in 1899.

The next decade or so witnessed both the coming of age of the black man in American boxing and his near-total exclusion from its commanding heights. Carroll's second installment again concentrated on four outstanding boxers: heavyweight king Jack Johnson; lightweight wizard Joe Gans; the original Jersey Joe Walcott, welterweight champ between 1901 and 1904; and the incomparable Sam Langford. The contemptuous ease with which Johnson, the "Galveston Giant," lifted the heavyweight crown from Tommy Burns in 1908 sparked frenzied calls, with novelist Jack London the most foam-flecked of all, for former undefeated champion Jeffries to come out of retirement and, as London expressed it, wipe the smile from Johnson's face. It was an impossible mission. Out of the ring for six years, the old "Boilermaker" eventually ran out steam and was stopped in the fifteenth round. White outrage at the result was further inflamed by Johnson's determination to be his own man, living his life regardless of what large sections of the American public deemed acceptable. Reviled because of his succession of Caucasian lovers and wives, Johnson was harried into exile, only returning to the US and a one-year prison sentence after he had controversially lost his title in Havana to Jess Willard in 1915.

Lil Artha's immediate legacy was a bigoted backlash against black boxing champions. So poisonous was the atmosphere that it was not until 1937 that another African American, Joe Louis, fought for the heavyweight crown. In the interim, a handful of black boxers won titles in lighter divisions, notably middleweight Tiger Flowers and featherweight Eligio Sardinias, "Kid Chocolate," but for twenty-two years that was it so far as boxing's richest prize was concerned. Well before Louis burst on the fistic landscape, Harry Wills, the "Brown Panther of New Orleans," an outstanding contender, failed to secure a title bout with champion Jack Dempsey. For a variety of reasons, not least of which was opposition from politicians fearful of the probable aftermath of a Dempsey-Wills fight, the match was never made. Father Time and Jack Sharkey eliminated Wills from contention in 1926. If anything, the situation worsened thereafter as the Great Depression intensified its grip. "Racial relations in the country had retrogressed to the lowest depths of Black suppression," wrote Carroll in "The Joe Louis Era," the third installment of his series. How did the "Brown Bomber" rise above this bleak situation?

For Carroll, the answer was twofold. There was Louis himself. Safely married to a black woman and carefully coached to avoid what Carroll described as the "gloating, grinning, gold-toothed Johnson-image," Joe's smashing triumphs inside the ring were accompanied by growing popularity beyond its confines. His twenty-five successful championship bouts won him respect, but his actions and statements during World War II made him into a popular hero. Donating the purses from fights with Buddy Baer and Abe Simon to the Navy and Army Relief Funds, Louis found the right words at a Madison Square Garden rally in 1942. "We'll win because we're on God's side," declared the uniformed champion to thunderous applause. With segregation in sports on the retreat after the war's end, even baseball grudgingly gave way. Signed for the Brooklyn Dodgers in 1946, all-time great Jackie Robinson was perfectly clear about the liberating influence of Louis's career. At a dinner honoring him in Chicago, he said, as related by Carroll, "There is one person I must give real and definite credit for my opportunity. His name is Joe Louis." Then there was promoter Mike Jacobs. The only color that mattered to "Uncle" Mike, whose Twentieth Century Boxing Club dominated the US fight scene from 1937 until 1948 when he suffered a stroke, was dollar green. Quick off the mark when news reached New York of a sensational puncher out of Detroit, Jacobs convinced Louis's managers that his organization could break the championship "color line" and make everyone rich along the way. Astute matchmaking, the upset of the first Schmeling fight aside, took Louis to the crown by 1937 and on to the longest reign and most defenses in heavyweight history, in the process cementing Jacobs's grip on the title.

But if box office, not bias, determined the shape of Jacobs's operations, as Carroll put it in the fourth installment of *The American Black Man and Boxing*, there were limitations too. These were set by "Uncle" Mike's sense of what matches would draw at the gate. Given that most boxing fans were white, to the end of his life he stuck to the belief that all-black bouts would not pay. Louis was kept away from useful black challengers such as Curtis "Hatchet Man" Sheppard, Lee Q. Murray, and Leroy Haynes, and outstanding African American fighters Archie Moore and Charley Burley never fought in the Garden while Jacobs ran the show.

What changed things was the advent of TV and the replacement of the ailing Jacobs by Jim Norris and his International Boxing Club. Product sponsorship greatly diminished the importance of "live" gates, and with huge numbers of home viewers watching five televised boxing shows a week in the early 1950s, the racial composition of fights mattered little. Under the auspices of the IBC, African American boxers flourished, winning and defending world championships. Without fully realizing it, Carroll thought, TV viewers came to equate the successes of black Americans in the ring with the "cherished chauvinism of American supremacy." No one fulfilled this subliminal role more completely than the fabulous Sugar Ray Robinson, whose spectacular stoppages of Gene Fullmer and Bobo Olson thrilled home audiences. When Robinson retired, his unprecedented Madison Square Garden farewell attracted a large, predominantly white crowd, recalled Carroll, which showered the Sugar Man with admiration and affection.

The three African American heavyweight champions who followed Louis— Ezzard Charles, Jersey Joe Walcott, and Floyd Patterson after Rocky Marciano retired undefeated—were, like him, Carroll argued in the fifth installment of his series, "sober-minded men, reluctant limelight-seekers, who made the champion's race immaterial." Charles, who some observers thought never again fought with the same ferocity after killing an opponent in the ring, was characterized by Carroll as the most "unobtrusive, unacclaimed and underrated champion of all time." Overshadowed by the great Joe Louis, Charles is now best remembered for two valiant losing efforts against Marciano in 1954, rather than his KO defeat three years earlier by ancient Jersey Joe Walcott, five-times challenger, father of six, and Methodist lay preacher. Floyd Patterson, the youngest man to win the heavyweight championship and the first to regain it, although cast in the same mold, was an enigmatic individual whom the public never quite understood but admired for his sportsmanship. "The Hermit of Scarsdale [New York]" was twice flattened in less than a round by a very different character, Charles "Sonny" Liston, whose fearsome scowl so intimidated opponents at the weigh-in that most of them fell quavering after his ponderous pursuit brought them within range of his clubbing punches. Despite a criminal record, "mob" connections, and the best efforts by Patterson's manager, Cus D'Amato, to deny him a title shot, Liston's pole-axing left jab and crushing left hook took him all the way to the championship. After his second victory over Patterson, he seemed invincible. "That Liston," joked one comedian, "I wish he'd fight Russia!"

Of the few dissenting voices, one was very much louder than the rest. It belonged to a brash young man, Cassius Clay. In Part VI of *The American Black Man and Boxing*, Carroll argued that Clay's rise to the championship marked the climax of the African American "takeover in heavyweight excitement." Capitalizing on his good looks, natural wit, and extraordinary ability, "The Greatest" mesmerized the American public. Spouting doggerel, he called the round in which his opponent would fall. By 1962 or so, Clay was already the most advertised athlete in the world. Like Jack Johnson in all respects but one, Cassius, proud and loud, was far removed from his quiet black predecessors. But where Johnson enjoyed a succession of white women, Clay came to hold a different position: only black women would do for him. Framing the backdrop of the about-to-become Muhammad Ali's exuberant celebration in February 1964 of his upset defeat of the "Big Old Ugly Bear," his nickname for Liston, was, as Carroll expressed it, "a coterie of dark-suited young men, of serious mien, later identified as Black Muslims." Although Ali's embrace of Islam disconcerted sections of the public, his fans mostly stayed loyal, enthralled by a series of victories against every leading heavyweight contender. In June 1967, having refused induction into the US Armed Forces on the grounds that he was a conscientious objector, Ali was convicted in Houston's Federal Court of draft evasion and sentenced to five years in prison. Released on bail pending appeal, he was immediately stripped of his crown by boxing's various governing bodies, *The Ring* alone standing firm on the principle that titles are won and lost in the ring. As divisive as the Vietnam War itself, Ali's emblematic court case was still unresolved at the beginning of 1970 when Carroll puzzled over the principles and contradictions involved.

The April 1970 issue of *The Ring* carried the seventh and concluding installment of *The American Black Man and Boxing*. Carroll's judicious summation of the series pointed to its underlying theme: because boxing was for decades the only professional sport from which African Americans were not excluded, the ring occupies a unique place in US black history. Boxing presented the sole opportunity for the African American man, in Carroll's heartfelt words, "to assert his manhood, long suppressed by slavery and the aftermath of racial bias." For many years, wrote Carroll, black boxing champions were "the most visible representatives of a repressed race the very existence of which, except in menial capacities, was largely ignored by the great mass of Americans." Taken as a whole, boxing engendered respect for black men and lifted them out of "the anonymity imposed by social injustice," elevating African Americans as champions of the world to a height that for too long was beyond their reach elsewhere.

––––––––––––

March 1939	Sepian Sockers Supreme
March 1947	Sable Sockers to the Fore
October 1960	Boxing Sets Pace in Fair Play
October 1966	"Dark Hopes" Showed Great Boxers with Pittance Pay
October 1969	I. The American Black Man and Boxing
November 1969	II. Johnson, Gans, Walcott and Langford Salient as Negro Stars Embellished Ring Annals
December 1969	III. The Joe Louis Era
January 1970	IV. Television Helped Vastly in Destroying Color Line; Robinson Reign Spectacular
February 1970	V. Charles, Patterson Too Quiet; Liston Too Involved; Then Came Brash Mr. Clay
March 1970	VI. Clay's Rise to Championship Climax of Negro Takeover in Heavyweight Excitement
April 1970	VII. Negro Achievements Galore in Boxing Have Battered Down Old Racial Barriers

SEPIAN SOCKERS SUPREME

Colored Boxers Made Great Headway in 1938—
Every Division Has Its Quota of Negro Stars

The boxing world in the year 1938 was clearly dominated by that mighty se-pia-hued pair, Joe Louis and Henry Armstrong. The thunder fisted Brown Bomber turned in what was easily the outstanding individual boxing perfor-mance of the year when he smashed his erstwhile conqueror, Max Schmeling, into complete submission in less than a round of whirlwind action. His smaller contemporary carved himself an everlasting niche in Pugilism's hall of fame when he performed the unbelievable feat of winning three world's champion-ships in less than ten months, thereby becoming the first man in the long his-tory of the prize ring to hold three world's titles at one time.

To find worthy rivals among men of their own race for Louis and Armstrong in point of boxing achievement it is necessary to drift back through the mists of time to the days of the immortal trio of Gans, Walcott and Dixon. There have been many Negro champions since these legendary figures held forth in the prize ring but none of them save perhaps Jack Johnson attained the promi-nence of Louis and Armstrong.

Back in the early days of this century and the latter days of the last one, colored pugilists stood out in an era marked by such men as Bob Fitzsimmons, Terry McGovern, Kid Lavigne, Jim Corbett, Abe Attell, Frank Erne, Kid McCoy, Joe Choynski, Tommy Ryan, Jim Jeffries and Battling Nelson. Against men such as these Gans, Dixon, Walcott, Jackson and Johnson pitted their strength and skill in contests that have come down through the years as classics of the prize ring. In those days the Negro boxer reached the peak of his power in the ring and tales of the prowess of these men reached the far corners of the earth even as does that of Armstrong and Louis today.

America also acclaimed these dusky titans of forty years ago and Dixon, for example, enjoyed a popularity in this country equalled by few pugilists of the past or present. These men were all readily granted opportunities to win world's championships, and Dixon was crowned a world champion on no less than three different occasions. Gans' ability was such that he was dubbed the "Old Master" by the sports writers of the time and boxing's old guard still insists there never has been a lightweight of his dimensions.

Following the passing of these three, the Negro race began a gradual decline from its high place in pugilism, a decline which continued on until the late twenties. Not until the sudden appearance of Louis on the scene did the sable sons of the cesti approach the high place that had been theirs decades ago.

There have been many explanations advanced for this long subjugation. The escapades and gallivantings of Jack Johnson are frequently mentioned as causing the condition. Not especially opprobrious to modern eyes, Lil Artha's carryings-on none the less antagonized and aggravated a large portion of the American public of his time. Following Johnson's winning the heavyweight title from Jeff in 1910, colored fighters found it next to impossible to engage in championship matches for many years. In fact, sixteen years elapsed before the late Tiger Flowers met the great Harry Greb for the middleweight title in 1926, in the first title match given a Negro in America since the Johnson-Jeffries affair.

From his earliest days at *The Ring,* Carroll devoted deserved attention to the achievements of black boxers. *The Ring* (March 1939)

The wave of bitterness that swept the country in the aftermath of the 1910 bout made mixed matches both unprofitable and dangerous for a long time, and this made the lot of the colored boxer a most difficult one for almost a score of years. Although the Walker boxing law became operative in New York State in 1920 and did not specifically forbid mixed bouts, the late William Muldoon, at the time chairman of the New York Commission, and Governor Alfred E. Smith, fearing a recurrence of the rioting that followed the Jeffries-Johnson bout, turned thumbs down on them. It was not until 1922 that the ban was lifted when Irish Johnny Curtin engaged Danny Edwards in what was the first mixed main event held in New York City under the Walker law. The same taboo prevailed in other American cities that permitted professional boxing from 1910 to 1920, and it was not until Johnson's reign as heavyweight king had been ended for some time that mixed bouts seeped back into the boxing schedules.

Another likely reason for the submergence of Negro fighters during this era is the mathematical one that these things often go in cycles. Every now and then one particular race or group is pre-eminent in fistiana, at various times in boxing history. Irish, Jewish, Italian or Negro boxers have almost monopolized the top positions. The rise of Louis and Armstrong may simply be the inevitable law of averages working out.

Most cities in this country were still averse to mixed bouts in the early twenties, and much of the credit for paving the way for his successors should go to the late Tiger Flowers. Not only was he the first American colored man to receive a chance at a title in many years, he was the first of the post-war Negro fighters to engage in mixed bouts in many American cities. His church-going reputation, piety, and humility made an impression on the American public that greatly benefited his race and its fighting men. The Georgia Deacon soon became a popular figure all over the country and the way had been smoothed once again for men like Louis and Armstrong.

Then came Kid Chocolate, back in 1928, and the satiny Cuban with the vivid personality dispelled the last traces of the bitter feeling of the Johnson era. The glossy-headed hero of Havana captured the American public like no little man had since the days of Dixon. He drew tremendous gates in his all too brief career, won two titles and narrowly missed another and was one of the greatest sporting idols of his day. With the advent of Chocolate, bans on mixed bouts were lifted in practically all Northern cities, and the lean and hungry days for the dusky gladiators were at an end.

Close on the heels and contemporaneous with the magnetic Chocolate were a horde of capable colored mittmen such as Young Jack Thompson, Bruce Flowers, Baby Joe Gans, Black Bill, Gorilla Jones, who found the going much easier than it had been for their less fortunate brethren in the previous decade.

These men were all better-than-fair fighters but they were hardly to be classed with the Negroes of the days of Gans and Dixon. Not until the year 1938 when Louis and Armstrong were to become ringdom's supreme rulers was the colored brother to regain the position he had held in those golden days.

Whether Louis or Armstrong is entitled to the palm as the outstanding boxer of the year is, of course, a matter of opinion, but there can be no disputing their ranking as the two foremost fighters of the day. While the devastating Detroiter enjoys a domination over his rivals unequalled by any heavyweight champion of the past, the barrel-chested little St. Louisian's record is a saga of almost incredible accomplishments.

Undefeated for the second successive year and facing the best men in three divisions, feather, light and welterweight, during that time, Armstrong is clearly one of the greatest boxers that ever lived. Of this long parade of vanquished foes only one really made the going tough enough for the double champion to be given any kind of a chance in a return bout, Lou Ambers, the ex-lightweight king. All the others were thoroughly outclassed and whipped. Henry climaxed his year's achievements in brilliant fashion by his stirring victory over big, power-punching Ceferino Garcia, one of the most dangerous men in the ring today. Few fighters in history would have been capable of conceding this terrific hitter twelve pounds as Armstrong did. This was a feat worthy of a Gans, Dixon or a Walcott.

Hustlin' Henry has clearly earned the right to be ranked along with the greatest men his race has produced. After years of trial and tribulation his career reached a crashing crescendo in 1938 and he is a cinch to go down in history as one of the most amazing men who ever followed a ring career.

At the present moment at least Joe Louis towers so far above the rest of the unlimited division, he is the one man monopoly of the class. No champion was ever as far removed from the available opposition as this somber socker. A threat to Louis' position may come out of nowhere in the coming year even as Joe did himself but there is certainly no one in view right now who figures to make the Brown Bomber work up a good sweat.

One of the pleasanter aspects of Joe's reign as heavyweight champion has been the complete acceptance of the Detroiter as heavyweight champion by the public. When Johnson held the title the feeling was general throughout the land that civilization was doomed unless the title passed from the hands of the man with the golden smile. Gone are the days of the white hope hysteria when every muscle-bound truck driver, stevedore, laborer or what-have-you was looked upon as a potential savior of an harassed humanity.

Today sporadic efforts to arouse the public with white hope tournaments and talk are met either with general apathy or ridicule by American sports writers, the most fair-minded and impartial group of men in the world. Louis' career definitely proves that so long as a champion comports himself with grace and dignity, his race or nationality is a matter of little consequence. Louis occupies a position with the present-day public somewhat similar to that held by the great Peter Jackson in California many years ago. Jackson was universally admired and respected and to this day many refuse to regard John L. Sullivan as a world's champion because he never met the Australian champion.

In a world tormented by a tidal wave of intolerance, the American attitude toward Louis stands out like a beacon of hope on a stormy night. Gone are the disturbances, bitter words, frenzied feelings and aroused instincts that characterized the reign of Jack Johnson. What small feelings there are against Louis when he boxes are the natural ones for the underdog against the superman. Dempsey in his prime also experienced the same sort of sentiment.

It is well to remember that no race or group has ever maintained a permanent supremacy in pugilism. At the time colored boxers happen to be in the ascendancy; a decade from now this may no longer be the case. Be this as it may, one thing is becoming fairly certain, and that is that the year 1938 presented two worthy successors to the mantle once worn by Gans, Dixon and Walcott in Joe Louis and Henry Armstrong.

SABLE SOCKERS TO THE FORE

Negro Race Has Forged to Front with Its Members Occupying a Strong Position in the Development of Fisticuffs during the Last Quarter Century

Outstanding development in boxing during the past 25 years has been the rise of the Negro fighter. Present day fight fans find it hard to believe that back in 1922 when this magazine appeared for the first time, there were no Negro champions, few contenders.

The fortunes of the Colored man in the prize ring ebb and flow with the tides of tolerance. At the turn of the century, the sable sockers enjoyed an eminence in the ring that approached their present high position. Gans, Walcott, Dixon and Peter Jackson led a legendary legion of mighty mittmen.

These men were not only great fighters they were public idols. Gans' name is spoken of with near reverence by those who knew and saw him. Awed Australians erected a monument to Peter Jackson. With the possible exception of Terry McGovern there never has been a little man adored by his followers as was George Dixon.

Because of the unusual esteem in which they were held, the Negro prospered comparatively in the squared circle of 50 years ago. The rise of Jack Johnson changed all this. Not a bad fellow by present day standards, the man from Galveston possessed the unhappy faculty of kindling the passions of bigotry, hate and prejudice as few men ever have.

Johnson's ability remains unchallenged. Those who censured him most in the days of his glory unhesitatingly concede his greatness today. His prowess was never the question, Johnson's braggadocio, his pettier peccadillos, might have been passed over as in the final analysis they harmed no one. But his many romances were something else again, unconventional that they were. Added to his numerous other indiscretions, they whipped up a whirlwind of resentment that reached into every recess of the republic, dropped a blanket of bitterness that covered the country for years and years.

During Johnson's reign as heavyweight king, he himself showed considerable aversion towards meeting Negro contenders. To give him just due he had demonstrated his superiority over the three most formidable men of the time, Langford, Jeannette and McVey, but none of them ever got in there with Lil' Artha for the title. The country developed an adverse complex as far as mixed bouts were concerned. Boxing itself fell into general disrepute during the time.

It was outlawed in most places as the Johnson era saw the Negro boxer and the ring game hit an all-time low. Public temper was such that 16 years were to elapse before a Negro man was to get a chance to fight for a world's championship in America following Johnson's victory over Jeffries in 1910.

The mood against mixed bouts played right into the hands of most of the champions not overly anxious to meet dangerous challengers anyways. The great Harry Greb finally gave the late praying Deacon Tiger Flowers a chance at his middleweight crown back in 1926. Flowers was actually the first man to break the spell that hung heavy over the land following Johnson's reign. Presented before and accepted by the public as everything that Johnson was not, Flowers, who was actually a man of devout humility, broke down the bars in many cities throughout the nation back in 1924, 1925 and 1926.

Doomed to go down in history as the prize victim of the intolerant trend of the times was Harry Wills. The old Brown Panther was caught right in the middle, and although the most potent challenger of Dempsey, never gained the opportunity to fight for the heavyweight crown. In Wills' case it was particularly unfortunate, for if ever a man led a stainless life, it was the menace of Dempsey's day. A model family man, and one of the greatest proponents of clean living, Wills is today a wealthy man in his mid-fifties who looks years younger and is one of Harlem's most solid, substantial, and respected citizens. But his fistic fortunes were caught in an ebb tide and he never got his chance.

In all fairness to Dempsey himself, Jack never actually drew the color line. Unlike John L. Sullivan, who bluntly declared he would not fight a Negro man and that was that, the Mauler never went on record as saying he would not meet Wills because of his race. Because of the temper of the times, he could have done this (as his successor Tunney did) and gotten away with it.

In his early days Jack fought several Colored men. According to his own statement he first realized his own prospects as a pugilist when he flattened George Christian, a pretty good man, in one round. Weighing 170 pounds he got in there with big John Lester Johnson, no setup by far, and gave a good account of himself when just a kid. Left to his own resources there is good reason to believe that Dempsey would have met Wills. The feelings of Manager Kearns and Rickard on the matter, is something else again. This pair realized that they had a bonanza and naturally risking it, as a bout with Wills would have, did not exactly appeal to them. So, with the cloud of the Johnson era still hanging like a pall over the land, and with memories of the disturbances and disruptions that followed the Johnson-Jeffries fight, they capitalized on the public distrust of mixed bouts, and a Dempsey-Wills bout remained in the land of dreams.

Wills' contemporaries, some of them dangerous men, suffered a like fate as far as title matches went. Kid Norfolk, Leo Flynn's thunderbolt; Panama Joe Gans, a welter who fought heavyweights, were two outstanding men of the time who were never even considered when title bouts were talked about. . . .

Following the winning of the 160-pound title by Flowers, things loosened up considerably for the Negro clouter. The bars still remained as rigid as ever as far as the heavyweight crown went, as the Old Dark Shadow of Leiperville, Pa., George Godfrey, was to find out. In the lighter classes though, a weak link in the chain of oppression had been disclosed and the promised land began to appear dimly in the distance.

Spindly Panama Al Brown demonstrated his superiority over the world's bantamweights in such decisive fashion that he became bantamweight king. Young Jack Thompson, a fine combination boxer-hitter, won the world's welterweight championship. Gorilla Jones, whom Clevelanders still consider the greatest middleweight of all time, won a claim to the world's 160-pound crown. John Henry Lewis brought the world's light-heavyweight title back to Phoenix, Ariz.

Other capable Negroes of the late twenties and early thirties, who performed creditably, although minus titles, were Black Bill, Bruce Flowers, Baby Joe Gans, Al Gainor, Larry Gaines, Tiger Payne, Jack McVey, Allentown Joe Gans, Oscar Rankins, Larry Johnson, Chick Suggs, Tiger Roy Williams, and Danny Edwards.

By all odds the most spectacular and magnetic Negro fighter of that period was flashy Kid Chocolate. The appearance of the Cuban lad on the scene excited fight fans as they hadn't been in years. Under the spell of his sunny disposition and vivid personality, additional barriers were lifted and the way was further cleared for the resumption of the Negro boxers' former high place in the sport. Chocolate won the featherweight championship, drew great crowds in every appearance, flashing across the boxing sky like a brilliant meteor in an all too brief career.

Much progress has been made since that July day in 1910 when Jack Johnson shattered the hulking Jeffries, but in the division the Texas dock walloper once ruled the bars remained down.

Just about the time that Chocolate's career was fading out, a stolid, tan-skinned youngster was plodding along in the amateur ranks out of Detroit. He had already been singled out as something out of the ordinary as a boxing prospect, but few realized the impact he was to make not only upon pugilism but upon contemporary history. The Joe Louis era was dawning.

With his career still unfinished, still supreme in the field, it is too early to rate the effect of Joe Louis upon contemporary thought in America. That it has been monumental is evident. It far transcends the business of boxing alone, reaching into every corner of our national life.

Even as Jack Johnson, a single individual, set back the march to better understand a generation, so has Joe Louis affected American civilization in the reverse fashion. In a recent magazine article, the country's outstanding sports columnist, Dan Parker, sports editor of the *Daily Mirror*, made the astounding assertion "Joe Louis has influenced interracial relations for the better more than any member of his race that ever lived and that includes Booker T. Washington and Dr. George Carver." At first thought this statement about a pugilist seems irrational but upon further consideration it becomes indisputable.

A Detroit police official recently disclosed that of the playmates and companions of his boyhood Joe Louis was the only one who never got into any kind of trouble. This is indicative of Louis' career. The most minute examination of his record fails to uncover any facts or actions detrimental to his character. It is reasonable to assume that there is possibly no other worldwide celebrity of the era who can claim this distinction. No one is perfect but upon the basis of conduct and deportment, Joe will have to do it until somebody better comes along. A man of his unusual gifts might be excused for becoming impressed with his own importance, slipping up once in a while as is expected of every human. Louis has set an example of modesty that is unparalleled.

How has all this affected the progress of Negroes in not only boxing but in many varying fields? The whole stereotyped conception of the Negro as one unable to stand success or prosperity as demonstrated by Johnson has been laughed away as ridiculous by many who formerly held to this distorted opinion. Results have been that new avenues of opportunity have been opened to him. The old arguments have been so thoroughly refuted by the standards set by Louis that today we find organized baseball and pro football turning a helping hand towards the Negro athlete. Aristocratic Yale University rejoices in the exploits of the great football player Levi Jackson, the first Negro member of a Blue eleven. When the records are all in and the chips counted it will be obvious that Joe Louis more than any other individual is responsible for this wonderful trend of the times.

Louis' record as a champion is too familiar to warrant much repeating in this article. There never has been a champion in any sport like him. A man who towers above the field as overwhelmingly, and one who answered every challenger whoever it may be.

When you mention Louis, you account for the present high position of the Negro boxer. Today the publicly drawn color line has vanished. The public will no longer stand for it. During the Louis regime the boxing game has enjoyed more of a certain respectability than it ever has before. It must be admitted that the stability of Promoter Mike Jacobs as the game's outstanding promoter has had considerable to do with this.

Luckily Louis received more than an assist in lifting the Negro fighter to his present pinnacle from Henry Armstrong. Armstrong too was a far cry from the old false conception. A polished highly intelligent fellow, a poet of all things, well-spoken and educated, Henry formed with Louis a double play combination that sent many bigots back to the dugout from which they may never emerge.

The Human Hurricane from St. Louis set a record that will probably never be equalled when he held the featherweight, lightweight and welterweight titles simultaneously.

Twenty-five years ago there were no Negro champions, just three real contenders. Contrast this with the situation today. Besides the great Bomber, Bob Montgomery and Ike Williams share the lightweight laurels, Ray Robinson at long last is 147-pound kingpin. The field of contenders is clearly dominated by Negro sluggers. Elmer Ray and Jersey Joe Walcott, Curtis Sheppard, Jimmy Bivins, Lee Q. Murray, heavyweights; Billy Fox, a man who has knocked out every opponent he has faced, and Ezzard Charles, the Cincinnati sensation, Archie Moore, St. Louis smoothie, Billy Smith, Booker Beckwith, veteran Lloyd Marshall, and Jack Chase, light-heavyweights; Charley Burley, Holman Williams, Sam Baroudi, Bert Lytell, middleweights; Tommy Bell, Cecil Hudson, California Jackie Wilson, Chuck Hunter, Beau Jack, O'Neill Bell, welterweights; Willie Joyce, Bob Bratton, Wesley Mouzon, lightweights; Jimmy McAllister, Cabey Lewis, feathers, and Harold Dade, the bantam king.

It's a far cry from the hungry, haunted years of a generation ago. Remarking about the present change in conditions, Mr. Dan Morgan, sage of sockology, stated: "Yes sir, years ago fellows like Jeanette, Langford, McVey and Johnson himself, called themselves the luckiest guys alive, when they got away with a thousand dollars. Today a couple of guys like Ray and Walcott need a truck to carry the thousand dollar bills home."

Respected and popular Billy McCarney, old Professor of Fistiana, offers an interesting observation anent the high place of Negro pugs today. "They have a better rating than they ever had before," opines Uncle Will. "The Negro fighter today may not be any better than the real old timers, but he is generally better educated, more polished on the average and a perfect gentleman at all times. Of course this is due to most of them imitating Louis so no matter how you look at it you always come around to Joe."

That the public approves of the present state of affairs is evident by booming boxing gates throughout the country. The old nonsense about two Negro boxers not being an attraction is disproven every night. Walcott and Ray sold out the huge Garden recently. The same thing is happening everywhere.

The regime of Joe Louis as heavyweight king will go down in history as an era when tolerance, decency and fairness flourished as never before. Long may he reign.

BOXING SETS PACE IN FAIR PLAY

Ingemar Johansson lay prone on the canvas. The world heavyweight championship was back in the United States and the crowd in New York's Polo Grounds was joyously heralding its recapture with prolonged semi-hysterical cheers for the victorious Floyd Patterson, who made history by regaining the title.

Nationalistic emotions have been rare in stateside crowds. One of the reasons is due to America's near monopoly of fistic championships in all divisions except in the flyweight and bantamweight classes. Because of this durable domination of boxing, American audiences have long since become jaded to any "flag waving" demonstrations occasioned by a boxing bout.

Still another reason is the polyglot makeup of the American population, taking in, as it does, many citizens only a generation or so removed from ancestral Europe. Such as these find considerable satisfaction in an overseas invader's success, minimizing any intense nationalistic fervor. But there seemed to be a resurgence of nationalism on all sides when Patterson's hand was raised in triumph, and waves of applause and jubilation cascaded over the old Polo Grounds.

Of course, there was a time back in the nineteenth century when such an attitude was the prevailing sentiment. Boxing historians in detailing the career of John L. Sullivan never neglect to mention old John L.'s unforgettable declamation following his defeat by James J. Corbett—"Gentlemen, Thank God I was beaten by an American!"

Old Stars and Stripes Custom Abandoned

For many years U.S. born champions belted their middles with a gaudy sash of stars and stripes. This custom was still popular when Dempsey won the title and there are pictures of the old Manassa Mauler so attired. Use of the national colors in such fashion was long ago ruled out by staid boxing commissioners as being beyond the pale of propriety, but it is significant that the straight-laced New York arbiters who ban the use of all tights and bathrobe embellishments, make a notable exception in the case of former Olympic boxers who, as professionals, are exempt from this regulation. They are permitted to wear their Olympic bathrobes with the huge letters USA emblazoned on the back.

In analyzing the reaction to Patterson's triumph, one of the most popular over here in some time, students of mass psychology have fingered a number of interesting points. The U.S. public had come to resent Johansson's lackadaisical contempt for both proper conditioning and Patterson whom he regarded as an inferior fighter. It was a reflection on American methods and American ability in general. Secondly, with the nation's traditional leadership being challenged in so many areas in recent years, the public was ripe for an affirmation of American superiority no matter where, and took Patterson's smashing victory as a "shot-in-the-arm" reassurance that in the long run, Uncle Sam always winds up at the head of the parade.

So, Patterson, practically written off in pre-fight predictions, suddenly found himself a national hero. The press throughout the country made Floyd the subject of editorial tributes. The "New York Daily News" comment was typical. Its tremendous readership, largest in the country, found itself nodding assent to a "Well done, Floyd!" caption topping the paper's lead editorial the day after the fight.

The City of New York's civic acclamation was one of a continuing string of fetes and receptions which have honored the only man ever to regain the world heavyweight championship.

Of even greater import than the "flag waving" flavor which permeated Patterson's victory was the sharp realization of the great social advances made in the country in the past half-century. Fifty years ago in Reno, Nevada, Jack Johnson, of the same race as Patterson, won the heavyweight championship of the world by beating James J. Jeffries.

Disturbances of Past No Longer Face Public

Many otherwise sane and stable people took the Negro's winning as though the end of the world had come, unleashing a cataclysm of concentrated bitterness across the country.

Disturbances in which many were injured, broke out in such cities as Washington, Pittsburgh, Atlanta, Omaha and Chicago. Tension gripped New York when a riotous welcome to Johnson at Grand Central Station verged on boiling over into a racial conflict.

In the wake of the fight came press diatribes of such an incendiary nature that even the barest quotes from them are out of order today. Out of the whole messy business came the expression "White Hope" which has since entered the language as a colloquialism meaning an aspirant after something with little chance of gaining it.

Some extremists went so far as to view the development as a national ca-
lamity, a racial regression boding ill for the future of the Caucasian race. Sports
artist-writer Robert Edgren, who admired Joe Gans but hated Johnson and
worshipped Jeffries, sought to case the catastrophe by claiming that Jeffries
had been doped, an allegation which curiously has been currently echoed by
Johansson apologists. Edgren's assertion was taken seriously by many grasping
at any kind of straw to rebuild their shattered morale.

Strangely enough, boxing and its people formed an oasis of reason and
fairness in the midst of the desert of distorted thinking which blanketed the
rest of the country. Johnson never lacked individual supporters in boxing
outside his own race. His main sparring partner and corner man at Reno was
big Al Kaufman. His chief second was Billy Delaney. His strongest press sup-
porter was famed sports columnist and cartoonist, T.A. (Tad) Dorgan, and Nat
Fleischer, now The Ring editor and prominent among his financial backers was
New Yorker George Considine.

Race No Issue in Support by Experts

Boxing people in taking a position for either Johnson or Jeffries did not allow
the issue of race to enter into it. A conspicuous example of this was to be found
in the opinions of great middleweight, Stanley Ketchel, and heavyweight contender Sam Langford. Ketchel, who had been barred from visiting the Jeffries
camp, was all for Johnson, and Langford, who disliked Johnson, was equally
strong for Jeffries.

Another incredible facet of the fight, completely out of tune with the tempo
of the times, was the part played by Billy Delaney, a famous trainer of those
days. Delaney, after a bitter dispute with Jeffries, whom he had conditioned
for years, went over to Johnson and was given much credit for the Negro's easy
victory. Delaney's knowledge of Jeffries' style, which he imparted to Johnson,
and his masterful coaching from Johnson's corner, aided the Galveston giant to
batter Jeffries into submission. Also lending aid and encouragement to Johnson
were Harry Foley and "Prof" Burns. One cannot resist wondering in just what
field and from what university the good professor gained his degree.

On the other side of the picture, Negro heavyweight Bob Armstrong was a
hard and conscientious worker in Jeffries' cause.

Nor did the crowd at the fight evince any extreme bias. Tad has described
the ringside as being evenly divided in sentiment. He reported " . . . as many

of them had their money bet on Johnson as on Jeffries." Jeffries' defeat, which became obvious in the early rounds, was received by the 16,000 present with complete equanimity.

All the evidence is that a half-century ago, boxing and its people were far ahead of the general public in evaluating a man for what he was, and what he could do, rather than on any ethnic grounds.

The area of racial relations is one in which the much-maligned sport of boxing has always been far in advance of the general public and all other sports.

Dark Clouds of Passion Are Rapidly Disappearing

Even the principals in the famous battle, Johnson and Jeffries themselves, were unaffected by the public virus over their meeting. Recourse to the records fails to reveal any feeling or action by Jeffries which might be construed as fanning the flames of prejudice.

To his last days, Johnson always spoke very highly of the man he had defeated. He often said, "Jeffries was a fine man and the cleanest fighter who ever stepped into a ring. I don't doubt he could have gotten away with any kind of foul or dirty work in our fight if he cared to, but he fought the cleanest fight of any opponent I ever faced."

The fifty years which have passed since Johnson met Jeffries in 1910 make this year the golden anniversary of a boxing match which had a grave social impact on the country. The dark clouds of passion which hovered over the fight and the times were a long time disappearing, but today their disintegration is about complete if the public reaction to Patterson's triumph is any criterion.

Of course, a complete victory over the forces of bias is still to be won and there is still some distance to travel to reach that Utopia where it is non-existent. But one thing is certain: the sport of boxing will continue to be in the van in the march to better understanding between all peoples and races.

"DARK HOPES" SHOWED GREAT BOXERS
WITH PITTANCE PAY

The Jack Johnson Era, with all its controversy, remains one of the most intriguing periods of boxing history. This was again brought out by the unusual interest aroused by a recent piece on the "White Hopes" spawned by the racial passions of that period, in the July issue of this magazine.

Although the impetus which gave rise to it was unsavory, the silly, especially by today's standards, search for a Caucasian to dethrone the ebony champion did have its stimulating effects.

Although it stressed quantity rather than quality the great search for a man to beat the unpopular Johnson resulted in an activity among the heavyweights that exceeded anything before or since. From the horde of aspirants who sprung up in every corner of the land a Nordic nemesis to Johnson finally arrived in big Jess Willard.

Johnson hardly had been picked off the steaming Havana campus while shading his eyes from the sun in 1915 than the fickle public, with shouts of "Fake," began a campaign of ridicule against the White Hopes. It has continued to this day.

The sun shone far more brightly for the "White Hopes" during Johnson's reign than it did for the Negro big men who had the ill fortune to be his contemporaries. Hopes were never darker for colored mittmen than during Johnson's time and for many years thereafter.

Jack's gold tooth grin cast no rays of happiness upon his Negro challengers, notably Sam Langford, Sam McVey and Joe Jeanette. In the smaller classes the effects of the Johnson era were so drastic Negro fighters were virtually barred from title consideration in the United States.

Johnson won the title in 1910 and it was not until 1926, when Deacon Tiger Flowers got a shot at the middleweight title, that this barrier was breached.

Of all the Negroes active during this parlous period Langford suffered the most. The public liked Sam but its appetite for Negro champions had been destroyed by Johnson. Poor old Sam, one of the greatest fighters of all time, never got the chance to wear a boxing crown.

In 22 years in the ring, Sam showed a clear superiority in every class from lightweight to heavyweight, facing such immortals as lightweight champion Joe Gans; welterweight marvel Joe Walcott; fabled middleweight Stanley Ketchel; and Jack Johnson himself. But along the way Langford could never get any champion into the ring with him with a title at stake.

Let it be understood that the term "Dark Hopes" refers not to pigmentation but to the dreary prospects which were the lot of Negro fighters from 1910 to 1930. Things were no brighter for Jeanette, a fine heavyweight from New Jersey, than they were for Langford during this time.

Jeanette met Johnson no fewer than nine times before Lil' Arthur became champion. Following his victory over Jeffries at Reno in 1910, Johnson had no time for Jeanette. Jack admitted that the difference between them in ability was too slight to risk any further encounters. Had this slim advantage been in Jeanette's favor rather than in Johnson's in this series, and had Jeanette been tabbed by fate to occupy the heavyweight throne, not only the history of boxing but of the nation—at least in racial matters—might have been vastly different.

For Jeanette was everything that Johnson was not. His interracial marriage had none of the abrasive effects of Johnson's upon the public. He was reticent where Johnson was garrulous; retiring where Johnson was arrogant; a reserved family man with none of the flamboyancies which afflicted Johnson's private life. How would the public have accepted a man like Jeanette as the first Negro heavyweight champion? Probably in the spirit with which it accepted Joe Louis years later.

Sam McVey completed the triangle with Jeanette and Langford during Johnson's time. McVey made a career of battling these two. In twenty years of battling, he met Langford 15 times in a series spread over the U.S., Europe, Australia and South America. In the endless round-robin of matches among Langford, McVey and Jeanette, the most fantastic occurred in Paris on April 17th 1909. Jeanette was knocked down 21 times in this one, but was finally declared victor in the 49th round when McVey called a halt, announcing that he could not see.

Harry Wills made the trio a foursome in 1914. In the next decade, besides meeting McVey and Jeanette, he fought Langford 22 times. With the bars being up against them Wills and Langford advertised their meetings as being for the "Colored Heavyweight Championship" which gives some idea of the desperate straits to which these outstanding men had been driven.

Like the radioactive fallout of an atomic explosion, Johnson's reign far outlasted his years as champion, in its dire effects upon the Dark Hopes. It thwarted Wills' chances of ever getting a crack at Dempsey despite the exemplary record of the old New Orleans Brown Panther as a boxer, a man and a citizen.

Pickings were so lean for colored boxers in those times that purses of less than one hundred dollars were common. "The biggest purse I ever got for a fight was $10,000 for fighting Iron Hague in London. The top money I ever got in this country was $3,000 for fighting Gunboat Smith. Very often I got no more than $150 or $200 for my fights," the great Langford revealed. Wills did somewhat better. Big Harry used to say he welcomed a week's work on the docks for $15, so scant were his ring earnings in the days just before and after World War I.

With such meagre returns, and White Hope competition confined to Caucasians, Negro fighters of lesser renown had little to which to look forward. Some of them, like Big Bill Tate, kept alive by acting as sparring partners. Dempsey was a favored employer. Some actually trained White Hopes. Jeanette and Bob Armstrong were quite active in this respect. John Lester Johnson could be depended upon to give a good account of himself, when he got the opportunity, as young Jack Dempsey found out when he faced John Lester in a New York club back in 1916.

Battling Jim Johnson—a mammoth of a man—proved a stubborn antagonist for the "Big Four" of Langford and Co. on several occasions and fought Jack Johnson in Paris to a fuzzy finish in 1914, the only Negro boxer to meet Johnson as champion.

Then there was a hodge-podge of local standbys scattered from Coast to Coast whose missions in life were mainly as "customers" for Langford, Wills etc. Some of them like Young Peter Jackson, George Cole, George Gunther, Larry Temple, Dave Holly and Klondike, were good fighters in their own right, but the great majority, such as Jack Thompson, Battling Gahee, Silas Green, Kid Cotton, Cleve Hawkins, Roughhouse Ware, Black Bill, and Morris Harris, had little to recommend them save a willingness to risk the Langford thunder for a dubious payday. For business reasons, Sam's efforts against them were often merciful. Good enough to make Langford and Wills extend themselves, Jeff Clark, a protégé of the late Jimmy Bronson's known as the "Joplin Ghost", was a fine boxer who might have gained title status as a light heavyweight in more favorable times. Jeff outpointed both Langford and Wills.

On such rare occasions when a well-known White Hope crossed the line to meet any of the above, some "pre-arrangement" often was suspected. A one-sided split of the purse was a fact of life for Negro boxers of the drab decades between 1910 and 1930. It is hard to imagine a drearier outlook than that which faced the dark hopes of that period with its pittance pay, "color lines," and title freezeouts. Because of the championship chill, smaller Negro boxers virtually vanished from the ring not to reappear again in any numbers until the late Thirties.

If it were possible to aggregate the total earnings of every active Negro boxer between the years 1910 and 1930 it would fall short of the total earnings of former heavyweight champion Floyd Patterson alone. Langford said that he averaged less than $500 a fight, which means that Sam, with 252 listed fights, averaged less than half the quarter million Cassius Clay was guaranteed for the Henry Cooper affair alone.

Before shedding too many tears over this depressing review of the dark days of the dark hopes let us not forget that boxing was then the only professional sport in which Negroes were allowed to participate.

The Louis era was the great catalyst in transforming the rejections of old into the receptivity of the present. Joe's reign as king was as beneficent as Johnson's was malignant. Langford, Jeanette and Wills, fine men who lived to ripe ages, by their stoic acceptance of a harsh fate plus their stature as fighting men, made their own contributions to the freedom which now illumines all professional sports.

I. THE AMERICAN BLACK MAN AND BOXING

A re-examination of the role of the Negro in American history has become a major factor in the readjustment of racial relations in the United States. New disclosures of the part played by the Black Man in the making of America are constantly forthcoming and as the movement continues to gain momentum, added revelations are doubtless in store. Most of this information comes as a surprise to the general public, until recently completely unaware of the facts presented.

For better or worse, down through the years, the Black history most publicized and familiar to the mass American public involved the Negro's exploits in the ring. The seismic tremors of Jack Johnson's career continue to reverberate and Joe Louis remains the great Colored folk hero of the American people.

The reason for this is quite obvious. For many decades boxing afforded the only avenue of escape by the Black Man from the suffocating anonymity of repression imposed upon him by social conditions.

The world of entertainment offered some release, but even here the Negro's talents were circumscribed until fairly recently. In almost any other field, including all other professional sports, Black exclusion was part of the country's social pattern.

While their participation in boxing was not without its inequities, particularly during the period following Johnson's becoming champion in 1908, Negroes were able to rise to the top in this profession by becoming world champions and gaining world-wide fame in the process. Along with this repute came financial gain far exceeding that available to them anywhere else.

The comparative welcome extended to Negroes in boxing is a puzzling anomaly, considering the punishing aspects of the sport. One would imagine that due to its bodily contact, boxing would have been the last instead of the first sport to lower the bars to inter-racial competition, but the reverse has been true. Boxing under the Marquis of Queensbury rules appears to engender respect rather than hatred between opponents and the effect of the sport in this country, save for the Johnson era, has been towards racial amity rather than friction.

Bonds of friendship between ring rivals of different races have been strong and sincere. Former opponents of Louis never have anything but kind words for Joe.

Another paradox of pugilism has been the eagerness of Caucasians to direct or sponsor Black aspirants in the ring, dating back to the 18th century, when

Bill Richmond, the first Black fighter of record, appeared in the British prize ring under the patronage of the Duke of Northumberland.

Richmond was truly fortune's favorite. When British General Percy, later the Duke, arrived in his native Yorkshire, England, upon his return from the American Revolution in 1777, he numbered among his spoils of war the young son of a Negro slave woman appropriated from the chattels of a New York minister, of all people. The Duke took such a liking to the lad that he gave him the upbringing of a member of the nobility.

The boy adapted readily to this genteel life; learning his lessons well in the exclusive school to which the Duke's prestige had gained him admittance. The Duke further indulged the lad by dressing him in the finest clothes, which he wore with elegance. Everything went fine in the community where, Negroes being oddities, young Richmond became a local favorite. This happy situation developed some flaws as the young man entered the romantic years and began to engage in flirtations with town belles who responded favorably to his attentions.

This development was ill-received by British soldiers stationed in the town and finally one of them, one Docky Moore, after tongue-lashing the Duke's young ward, set upon him physically, sending him home weeping to the Duke. Enraged by the attack, and provoked by his youthful ward's docility in the face of it, the Duke peremptorily ordered the lad to challenge the soldier upon pain of lashing if he refused to do so. Faced with this choice young Richmond did as the Duke requested and gave the soldier such a thorough thrashing, that the town bully, a brawling blacksmith, resentful of the Negro's gay attire and popularity with the ladies, took it upon himself to avenge the battered redcoat. His challenge was for a public 'prize fight' with side bets at a spot in the town known as The Groves. The huge blacksmith proved no match for Richmond, and was thoroughly battered. The Duke after 'yelling himself hoarse' at the bout and collecting his winning bets enthusiastically decided to train his young bondsman for the ring.

This was how it all began and the Duke of Northumberland, with an assist from sex, a British soldier and a blacksmith, forged the chain of circumstances which linked the destiny of the Black Man to boxing. Despite his small size, Richmond, fighting under the aegis of the Duke, disposed of lesser opposition so handily he eventually faced England's legendary Tom Cribb, the most famous bareknuckle fighter of his time and champion of England. Richmond proved unsuccessful against Cribb, who outweighed him some 30 pounds. According to the journal "Boxiana," he fought until the age of 50. Along with his boxing reputation, Richmond's manners and urbanity were so decorous and he was held in such high esteem that he spent his final years as the proprietor of a London sporting inn frequented by the well born and the aristocratic patrons of various sports. He passed on, respected and admired by all, on December 28, 1829, at the age of 66.

England remained the seat of boxing in the early 19th century. The Black fighter who followed Richmond, Tom Molyneaux, is sometimes referred to as the first American champion. He was a former Virginia slave who on the strength of his fighting ability against other slaves in plantation scuffles had in some manner earned his freedom and, equally mysteriously, made his way to England, where he appeared in 1809. Tom landed penniless, friendless and unknown, but his imposing physique so impressed one Bob Gregson, a sporting man and coffee house owner, that he contacted Richmond who took him in hand as a possible challenger to the invincible Cribb.

In what would become a defining seven-part series, *The American Black Man and Boxing* saw its first installment published in October 1969. *The Ring* (October 1969)

The two men were as opposite as the poles and strong arguments for the theory that environment is the decisive determinant in the course of life. On the other hand, Molyneaux had come out of American slavery, untutored and undisciplined, and these were the chains of his bondage which he was never able to break.

Unlike his mentor he was a big man, a legitimate heavyweight, and in preliminary contests soon proved himself a worthy rival for the British champion. Richmond's prestige was so great that Molyneaux had no difficulty gaining the necessary backing for a match with Cribb and when the men met on December 18, 1810, wagering was heavy on both sides. The match was fought under the archaic London Prize Ring Rules which had little resemblance to the Queensbury code followed today.

The fiercely contested struggle ended in the 33rd round in a welter of pandemonium not unlike a present-day soccer riot, with Cribb being declared the winner.

On the basis of this confused conclusion to the first meeting, Molyneaux asked for and received another chance at Cribb. Not even the persuasive Richmond was able to convince the unmanageable Molyneaux of the necessity of proper condition. He showed his disdain for both Cribb and conditioning by consuming "a whole chicken and a huge apple pie washed down by large quantities of porter" 10 minutes before the fight. He proved no problem for the Englishman the second time around, succumbing in the 11th round. He offered little resistance, several times falling to the canvas through sheer exhaustion.

Molyneaux's decline was hastened by a general physical disintegration brought about by dissipation. He ended his days in Ireland in pathetic fashion; his once powerful frame emaciated and his constitution shattered by his excesses, Molyneaux died on August 4, 1818.

The Black beginnings in the ring had their inception in England. What boxing among Negroes there was in the ante bellum period was confined to plantation entertainment 'bouts' between husky slaves. Negro boxers appeared in the North following the Civil War but there was little public reaction to them until the appearance in Boston of George Dixon in the early Nineties.

Dixon, a native Nova Scotian, was the first genuine Colored sports hero in the United States. He was the first recognized Negro boxing champion, winning the bantam and featherweight championships. Surprisingly, he suffered little from the prejudices of the period. He was patronized by a wealthy and influential group of Boston sports figures who engaged Tom O'Rourke to handle him.

O'Rourke, a bulldoggish, adamant character saw to it that Dixon rarely got the worst of it during his long and lustrous career lasting from 1886 to 1906. O'Rourke was such a powerful personality, that with the footprints of Sherman's Civil War invasion still fresh on Southern soil, Dixon fought a mixed bout against the amateur champion Jack Skelly in New Orleans in 1892 without any significant incident.

Dixon's popularity with the public grew as his fame increased, aided by his habit of promenading through the poorer sections of towns and distributing coins and bills to the ragged inhabitants. This largesse, while humane, was to haunt his final years with poverty. But drink was his real undoing and the way was downward following his defeat by, and his loss of the featherweight championship to Terry McGovern in 1900. He appeared in England and fought for several years after that but his glory years were long gone.

Dixon never overcame his failing for liquor, dooming himself to an untimely end in 1909 at the age of 39. Some idea of the hold George Dixon had on the American public comes in the public response to his passing. His body lay in state in a New York funeral parlor for three days during which thousands of those who had idolized him for his ring greatness and his generosity bade farewell to the first great Negro 'super-star,' a modern term which well describes him.

Contemporaneous with Dixon in writing a 19th century chapter to this history, Peter Jackson, West Indian-born champion of Australia, arrived in this country in 1888 with the announced purpose of gaining an opportunity to become the champion of the world.

His reception was incredible. Wealthy members of the prestigious California Athletic Club gave him a royal welcome and a delegation of sporting men led by the most noted sports writer of the time, W.W. Naughton, was at dockside to enlist themselves in the cause of the Black Australian.

Although Jackson proved to be a cultured gentleman of refinement, and was hailed as such throughout his many years in the United States, he never gained his objective. Despite Jackson's gift for saying the right thing at the right time and a genius for allaying any bias with his formal dignity and manners, John L. Sullivan was able to take refuge behind the 'color line' in denying the Negro aspirant his chance.

While this did not sit well with a goodly proportion of the public and clouded Sullivan's claims to world championship status, there was no way to force John L. to abandon his position. Dethroning boxing bodies were unknown in those days and had such a move been attempted, John L.'s adulation by the public was so deep-seated it would never have been tolerated.

Jackson took his denial with the resigned decorum which added to his stature as a man. Sympathy for his cause gained him such popularity that, as was the custom in those days, he toured the country meeting 'all comers' in exhibitions and was well received upon the stage, playing the leading role in 'Uncle Tom's Cabin.' His most notable contest in this country was the classic 61-round draw with Jim Corbett in San Francisco in 1891.

Jackson's fame and prestige were further enhanced following his victory over Frank O. Slavin, the British Empire champion, in London in 1892. Sullivan was no longer champion, having been beaten by Corbett. But upon his return to America, Jackson found Corbett now unwilling to oppose him a second time.

Stunned by the futility of his quest, Jackson, a lover of the good life to begin with, now surrendered himself to the indulgences of dalliance. Liquor and women drained him of his vitality and skill and he was a pitiable knockout victim of James J. Jeffries in his final fight in 1898. His body wracked by tuberculosis, his mind and spirit tormented by frustration, Peter Jackson expired in his adopted homeland of Australia in 1901 at the age of 40.

Boxing purists insist that the Jeffries-Jackson fight was the first one for the world heavyweight title. They deny anything more than the American championship to John L. Sullivan because he would not fight Jackson. Because of John L.'s disputed title, Corbett and Bob Fitzsimmons also have flawed championships.

Although like Dixon he was born elsewhere, Peter Jackson's impact on the circumstances and the future of the Negro boxer in America was monumental. A victim of injustice, he contributed much towards molding a favorable image of all fighters generally and is a towering figure in the history of Black boxers in the American ring.

Here in abridgment is a recounting of the highlighted Negro fighters of the 19th century. There were other great ones, notably Joe Gans and the Original Joe Walcott, but these two fought well into the 1900s.

Several important points are pre-eminent in this essay. The first shows that even the pioneer Negroes in the ring had little difficulty gaining white support and sponsorship. Secondly, that in three of the four individuals dealt with here, the blandishments and temptations of success had sorry consequences, and third and most important three of the four were held in such high popular regard by the public of their era they served the dual role of being goodwill ambassadors in an ethnic sense as well as being famous fighters.

II. JOHNSON, GANS, WALCOTT AND LANGFORD SALIENT AS NEGRO STARS EMBELLISHED RING ANNALS

The larger than life likeness in bronze of Joe Gans which enhanced the inner lobby of the old Madison Square Garden in New York for many years, served as an unprecedented sculptured tribute to a boxer whose career had highly salutary social results.

As far as is known no pugilist has ever been so honored by so distinguished an artist as Mahonri Young, the statue's creator. Recollections of Gans' career in the ring prove it was well deserved. Fifty years after his death in 1910 memorial respects were paid by a Baltimore delegation to this one time lightweight champion in graveside ceremonies. That the celebrants honoring the memory of this Negro fighter a half century later were predominantly white is testimony to the lingering hold that Gans has had in the affection of the public.

In No. 1 of this series we have dwelt upon the popularity enjoyed by, and the favors extended in the last century to pioneers Bill Richmond and Tom Molyneaux overseas, and to Peter Jackson and George Dixon in this country. Gans exceeded all of these in his reception by the people, enjoying a peculiar immunity from racism.

Coming from a Southern city, Baltimore, he was held in such high esteem he shared honors as the city's outstanding sports figure with Babe Ruth, the greatest of all baseball players, for many years.

Gans' uncanny appeal was rooted in a personality which strongly projected the 'nice guy' image. He was taffy colored with features often referred to as 'semitic.' He was no grinning teeth-flasher, rarely smiled and was pleasant mannered and self effacing. He had a weakness for gambling and was no stranger to after dark dalliance. This was diluted with discretion.

As a boxer he was a wizard, coldly deliberate and calculating. In this day his style would be called 'computerized.' He was known as the Old Master, for a couple of reasons, the first was the precise expertness of his boxing; the second, for his mastery at 'going along' with an opponent whom he outclassed with a minimum of hurt to his foe, with viewers none the wiser.

Gans perfected this art of 'carrying' an opponent up to a point at which it almost proved to be his undoing. There was a period in Gans' career of twenty years when his efforts were corrupted by unsavory influences which controlled and intimidated him. This led to his being party to the Gans-Terry McGovern travesty in Chicago in 1900 which fomented such a scandal that boxing was outlawed in that city for many years. But not even his admission of fakery proved potent enough to dispel the Gans mystique with the adoring public, which took the attitude that the champion had been an unwilling but helpless victim of pressures exerted upon him by unscrupulous manipulators.

Gans became lightweight champion two years after the McGovern disaster, by beating Frank Erne. He was invincible at his weight for several years thereafter, finally losing the championship to Battling Nelson in 1908. By that time tuberculosis, which was to take his life two years later, had ravaged his vitality.

That Gans, at a time when intolerance and racial bias were at flood level in this country, should have been a genuine hero of the ring is incredible.

Wherever he appeared in his travels throughout the country, Gans would conduct boxing clinics in gymnasiums where he demonstrated and instructed youthful aspirants in the finer points of the art. This created a chain reaction of good will for the Negro fighter. The most promising youngsters would attach themselves to Gans' entourage for a time. A couple of Italian prospects, the Lenny brothers, Eddie and Harry, were among those who became good boxers as Gans proteges.

Following his untimely death at the age of 36 in Baltimore, Gans was eulogized throughout the nation as not only one of the greatest of ring champions but as a vital contributor to racial amity.

" . . . Probably the greatest fighter who ever lived was Joe Walcott, the Barbados Demon . . . " wrote the late T.A. 'Tad' Dorgan in the New York Journal in 1925 " . . . the more one thinks about Walcott's deeds in the ring the more wonderful he appears to be. You must remember that he stood but five feet one inch tall and at his best weighed 137 lbs." The original Joe Walcott, active in the ring from 1890 to 1905, may have been all that Tad said he was but he did not exert the social impact upon his time that Gans and Dixon did, although he was a contemporary of both and managed by the same man who handled Dixon, Tom O'Rourke.

During the next 15 years, never weighing more than 142 pounds, he was a ring wonder, often defeating men weighing 40 pounds more than himself. Notable among his victims was the fine lightheavyweight Joe Choynski. Walcott was truly a ring phenomenon but strangely enough he had more trouble with men smaller than himself, such as Gans and the aggressive lightweight champion Kid Lavigne. He became world's welterweight champion by knocking out Rube Ferns in 5 rounds in 1901, the second black fighter in ring history to gain that distinction.

In today's ratings Walcott would have been a 'superstar' as he continued to terrorize the larger classes.

As might be expected from one who has run off to sea as a child, Walcott was of a roving disposition and not without his idiosyncrasies. An injury caused by a revolver which went off while he was toying with it almost cost him his hand in 1905, hampering his effectiveness in the ring thereafter.

His loss of his championship to Dixie Kid in 1904 was occasioned by a general mixup at the bout's finish in which O'Rourke precipitated a riot. Walcott regained the title but relinquished it for good to Honey Mellody in 1906.

Undistinguished by Dixon's largesse and magnetism and Gans' mystique, Walcott never became the idol they were. But his fantastic exploits accelerated the burgeoning prestige of black boxers during the late 19th and early 20th centuries.

This prestige seemed clearly on the rise as this century progressed into its opening decade. But, rightly or wrongly, the public demanded one concession in return for the plaudits it bestowed upon the black champions. In the uncomfortable racial climate which clouded those times, modesty in victory and discretion in conduct was deemed mandatory on the part of Negro boxers. Jackson, Gans and Dixon had conformed, more or less, to these qualifications, thereby gaining the popular reward. As a consequence, people conditioned to a certain behavioral pattern were totally unprepared for what Jack Johnson had in store for them. They would not have been had they explored the reasons for Johnson's nickname of 'Lil Artha.'

For as long as anybody could remember back in his native Galveston, Tex., John Arthur Johnson had been a non-conformist. As a precocious teen-age strong man on the Galveston docks, 'Lil Artha' lifted such heavy bales and whipped so many adult dock wallopers that the question "Did you hear what Lil Artha done?" became so repetitious that the nickname 'Lil Artha' stuck to him to the end of his days.

As a sparring partner in the training camps of better knowns he was equally fractious, taunting. He baffled his employers with a variety of boxing tricks which came naturally to him. As the first black heavyweight champion of the world, Johnson remained in character. No man's career or personality has ever had such a contradictory analysis to the contemporary public shaken up by his sharp departure from the Jackson-Gans image. Johnson was a gloating braggart; a philandering romancer; a stirrer of racial passions; a discredit to his people; an ingrate; a fabricator; a fugitive from justice; and, above all, a ridiculer of the then cherished dogma of race superiority.

Today the wheel has come full circle, directly opposing the appraisal of sixty years ago. Johnson is now looked upon by segments of a more tolerant society as a proud warrior asserting his 'black identity'; a Casanova with an unmatched appeal to women; a turn of the century militant in manly opposition to oppression; the noblest and most fearless of all the black champions; a rebel against exploitation; a gifted user of words and statements; a victim of Caucasian injustice and the first Negro to expose the 'superiority' thesis as a lot of nonsense.

Both these interpretations are extreme with the truth lying somewhere in the middle of this opinionated spectrum.

Johnson entered the ring in 1897 and in a few years established himself as the most dangerous threat to champion Jim Jeffries. Jeff did not publicly draw the 'color line' as John L. Sullivan had drawn it, but he announced his retirement and attempted to pass on his crown to a self appointed designee, Marvin Hart. Smallish Tommy Burns defeated Hart in 1906 and was widely regarded as world's champion.

Johnson, like his predecessors, was able to mount considerable white support both moral and financial. This enabled him to harass Burns clear around the world. He finally cornered him in far off Sydney, Australia. Not satisfied with demonstrating his complete mastery over the Canadian, his bald pate glistening and gold teeth gleaming, he taunted his foe and the ringsiders before the match was finally halted in the 14th round.

Among those most upset by Johnson's jibes and exhibitionism was the novelist Jack London, covering the fight for American newspapers. His dispatches hysterically beseeched Jeffries to come out of retirement to 'redeem' the Caucasian race. Jeffries, who had ballooned up to 300 lbs., at first ignored these entreaties but a $100,000 offer from promoter Tex Rickard convinced him of the nobility of the crusade.

On July 4, 1910, Johnson defeated Jeffries as convincingly as he had whipped Burns. In a tumultuous aftermath, mobs set upon rejoicing Negroes in cities throughout the country, with lives lost and many injured in serious disturbances. These eruptions exacerbated an already tense situation, giving birth to the 'White Hope' era.

Johnson's private life had also taken a turn which added to the gravity of the circumstances. His first wife had been a fair skinned Negro woman whom he accused of deserting him for a jockey. Losing this kind of decision to a flyweight impelled Johnson, he explained, to cross racial lines in his future relations. After a succession of pallid paramours he married his first white wife, socially prominent Etta Duryea, in 1909. Johnson undeniably had a way with some women as well as much personal charm, and all might have been well had Miss Duryea not committed suicide in 1912.

Even the great Negro educator, Booker T. Washington, joined in the outcry which blasted Johnson from all sides. With use of legal chicanery, the Mann Act was invoked against the Negro titleholder and he fled to Europe by way of Canada, disguised as a member of a Negro baseball team. Johnson, joined by his third wife Lucille Cameron, also Caucasian, remained in Europe until the outbreak of World War I made his Paris residency uncomfortable.

His defeat by Jess Willard in 1915 in Havana will probably rate as the most controversial fight of all time. Still considered a fugitive from justice, he returned to his native land where he was sentenced to serve a year in Leavenworth prison. He was probably the most pampered prisoner in the annals of incarceration. He hobnobbed and played cards with the warden, entertained friends and visiting dignitaries, gave boxing exhibitions on weekends and in all respects received royal treatment. Following his release, the rest of his life was without outstanding incident. Irene Pineau, a woman of refinement and beauty, also white, remained with him after they were wed in 1925 until 1946, the year of his death.

During Johnson's reign his great contemporary Sam Langford clearly ranked as his most formidable challenger. But Johnson, who defeated Langford in a handicap match in 1906 turned a deaf ear to Langford's challenges. Although Sam was never a champion, a coterie of supporters, of whom octogenarian Charley Rose is one of the few survivors, has called the Boston man the greatest fighter of all time.

It is interesting to conjecture what the public response, and the course of race relations would have been, had Langford and not Johnson been fingered by Fate as the first black heavyweight champion of the world. There were vast personality divergences between the two men. Johnson was a firm believer in the modish advertising pitch, "If you got it, flaunt it!" Langford was in the Gans mould, reticent and retiring. The squat native of Nova Scotia had a fondness for liquor but as far as is known showed little or no interest in the type of interracial amours which were at the seat of Johnson's misfortunes.

Johnson's career had such historical impact because of the racial passions it conjured up. Viewed in retrospect his life seems innocuous save for the tragedy for which he was not directly responsible, and which led to his persecution. There is no record of his ever having done any particular harm to anyone. The women who married him did so of their own volition and during the last years of his life he became noted for his jaunty beret, amiability and general good humor.

But the favorable current evaluation of the first Negro heavyweight champion was not the public's judgment of Johnson sixty years ago. His career's effects were accurately summed up in this comment in the Negro periodical, the Pittsburgh Courier of Sept. 17, 1960, "From July 4, 1910 bells tolled for every Negro athlete for 27 years! Contraction of opportunity for Negro athletes to vie on an interracial basis began immediately . . . in an ever tightening tensing anti-Negro quarter of a century."

III. THE JOE LOUIS ERA

Political scientists, psychologists and sociologists have been inching along of late towards a belated recognition that the part played by sports in weaving the fabric of the social pattern may be far greater than has been realized. This delayed discovery of the double-domes has long been dwelt upon in the pages of this magazine. The review of the career of Jack Johnson in the preceding article of this series offered ample affirmation of this premise.

Johnson's life, particularly its romantic episodes, brought every brand of bigot out of the woodwork. These mischief-makers seized upon the chocolate-hued heavyweight champion's vanilla-flavored love life as convincing evidence that the sole goal of the liberated black was intermarriage and this race mixing, according to their reasoning, could mean the doom of the proud Caucasian. The tragedy of the times was that the public went along with this ethnocentric conclusion and every black citizen of the United States suffered to some degree from the backlash of the Johnson era.

An immediate result of this bias was a clamping down on the acceptance of Negro fighters as world champions, despite the hero roles played by Gans and Dixon prior to Johnson's rise. This development was greeted with much relief by contemporary champions, happy with the fact that the public attitude permitted them to bypass dangerous Negro contenders without resorting to drawing the 'color line.'

The unwritten ban on Negro world champions in this country lasted 16 years, until finally breached by the late Tiger Flowers, who won the middleweight championship from the great Harry Greb in 1926. Flowers, a docile, ante-bellum type Southern Negro, had earned this opportunity largely through a cleverly conceived campaign built around his piety—conducted by his manager Walk Miller, a shrewd Southerner from Flowers' native state of Georgia.

Along with this, Flowers' manners, ability, sportsmanship and humility brought him sincere respect and admiration. When he died suddenly in 1927 the state of Georgia declared a day of public mourning and he was the subject of a moving eulogy by then heavyweight champion Gene Tunney, which was widely circulated.

The Negro fighter who suffered most, and whose career almost capsized in the cross currents of the Johnson carry-over, was the late Harry Wills. This was ironic, for no two human beings were more unlike. Wills, standing 6 feet 3 inches tall and weighing 210 lbs., was one of the most magnificently built men ever to appear in the ring. Wide shouldered, slim-waisted and prodigiously strong, he was known as the Brown Panther of New Orleans. No fighter was ever more aptly nicknamed. He was as unassuming as Johnson had been flamboyant. He remained married to the same woman for more than 40 years and his private life was as serene as Johnson's had been storm tossed. Small enough to be a jockey in his youth, his tremendous physique was the result of a fetish for physical conditioning and the clean life.

By 1916, Wills, having survived an extended series of matches against Langford, Sam McVey, and Joe Jeanette, loomed menacingly on the heavyweight horizon. The same day that Dempsey won the world heavyweight championship from Jess Willard, July 4, 1919, Wills beat Sam Langford in St. Louis for something called the 'colored' heavyweight championship.

Scant public notice was paid to this but from that time until 1926, Wills was far and away the most formidable contender for Dempsey's crown. They never met, for a variety of reasons. First, the effluvia fomented by the Johnson critics still clung like a contagion to the racial climate. Secondly, promoter Tex Rickard, his gambling house background notwithstanding, was hardly inclined to risk such a money maker as Jack Dempsey against a foe of Wills' formidability. Needless to say, Dempsey's manager, Jack Kearns, who had managed Wills, concurred. Third, and most important, despite the glaring contrast between Wills and Johnson as personalities, political figures voiced dismay over the probable aftermath of a Dempsey-Wills fight, recalling the Johnson-Jeffries disturbances. Hence the locale of such a match posed a great problem. Governor Al Smith of New York was adamant in his disapproval of such a bout in this state.

Wills continued to challenge Dempsey, but to no avail, even going into the courts without success. Wills did not lack support. He was widely hailed as the 'Man Jack Dempsey feared' and some sportswriters, notably T.A. 'Tad' Dorgan, of the N.Y. Journal directed a drumfire of derogation against Dempsey for his failure to answer Wills' challenge. Wills' manager, Paddy Mullins, a politically well-connected, one-time saloon keeper with associate Lew Raymond, kept Wills' cause in the public eye.

After years of controversy the Dempsey-Wills business finally came to a head in 1926 when James A. Farley, then chairman of the New York State Boxing Commission, denied Gene Tunney a license to fight Dempsey by declaring Wills the rightful contender. This ploy pushed both Dempsey-Tunney fights out of New York and at the same time spotlighted Farley with a national prominence which eventually moulded him into a towering political figure.

Wills' defeat by Jack Sharkey, following Dempsey's loss to Tunney in 1926, wrote finis to one of the most controversial chapters in boxing history, the Dempsey-Wills affair. The long-drawn-out wrangle had not been without some profit to Wills. In 1925, free-lance fight promoter Floyd Fitzsimmons, backed up by automobile manufacturing money, paid Wills a $50,000 retainer for his signature for a prospective Dempsey-Wills match. Nothing ever came of it, and the fifty grand provided the foundation for the affluence Harry Wills enjoyed as a real estate owner until he passed on at the age of 73.

Wills was not the only capable Negro boxer to be side-tracked by the backlash brewed by the bigotry of the Johnson Era. Kid Norfolk, a fine man personally and a top contending light heavyweight, who died early this year, never got the title opportunity he deserved. Panama Joe Gans, a West Indian welterweight protégé of famed fight manager Leo P. Flynn, suffered a similar fate.

When Joe Louis first appeared on the national scene in 1935, racial relations in the country had retrogressed to the lowest depths of Black suppression, this

The American Black Man and Boxing series would see Carroll's artistic talents turn to depictions of America's black boxing icons. *The Ring* (March 1947)

was the time of the Great Depression, worsening an already despairing situation. In many respects conditions were even bleaker than they had been at the turn of the century for the Negro.

Since Flowers in 1926 there had been four Negro champions—Al Brown, bantamweight; Young Jack Thompson, welterweight; Kid Chocolate, featherweight, and Gorilla Jones, middleweight. Of these a satiny skinned, sleek, 'Patent Leather Kid,' Chocolate, had made by far the most dazzling impact on the public. Beautiful in action, his iridescent style and personal charm had made the ebony Cuban the most popular Negro boxer since Dixon.

Despite this breakthrough in the lighter classes, one conspicuous barrier remained in the most important category, the heavyweights. Since Willard's victory over Johnson in 1915 no Negro had fought for the heavyweight title. Following Dempsey, Tunney, Schmeling, Sharkey and Carnera had gone along with this tacit exclusion. For the record, Max Baer was the first champion to publicly announce that he would disregard this practice.

Compared to the outlook in other sports for Negroes, the situation in boxing was utopian. The most stringent color line in American life was to be found in professional baseball. Professional football and basketball followed similar lines. In amateur golf, and tennis, Black participation was unthinkable in the Thirties, and Negro athletes were so few and far between on college gridirons, courts, and diamonds that they were oddities. Sports in those times were a reflection of the racial mores of the country.

This was the racial atmosphere in which Louis first arose. His prospects appeared as bleak and barren as a lunar waste but Joe Louis was one of the most fortunate of men. "A man is master of his fate but fortune is its mistress . . . " And Joe Louis had better luck with Dame Fortune than ladies-man Jack Johnson or homebody Harry Wills ever had.

Louis had been propelled into the heavyweight picture at a most propitious time. In 1935 the long-time domination of boxing in New York by Madison Square Garden was being contested. A Hearst newspaper sports writing combine, Damon Runyon, Bill Farnsworth and Ed Frayne, 'angeled' by money-man Mike Jacobs, was in rebellion against the Garden monopoly.

For a number of years, the writers had co-operated comfortably with the Garden in the promotion of big-time boxing in support of the Hearst Milk Fund. Complications had come about between the Fund sponsors and the newly installed head of the Garden boxing department, the cocky and contentious James J. Johnston, due primarily to personality clashes.

Bulwarked by the vast publicity potential of the Hearst newspaper empire, the Garden opposition appeared formidable. Meanwhile, Louis had hit the national headlines by way of a sensational streak of successes in the Midwest. The Garden's reaction to this Negro phenomenon was stymied by a stubborn hangover of Johnson-phobia in its directorship.

While an inner-council debate dragged on about just what to do about Louis, Mike Jacobs, showing signs of being far different from the mere figurehead many anticipated, took the initiative. He scurried out to Louis' home town of Detroit, convinced Louis' handlers, suave, sophisticated bankroll men, John Roxborough, a Michigan University graduate, and Julian Black, that his organization with its press connections was capable of breaking the heavyweight championship 'color line.'

Louis' debut in New York was a smash hit. He knocked out former champion Primo Carnera in thrilling fashion, then followed up by disposing of another ex-champ, Max Baer, in equally spectacular style, in the fall of 1935. Mike Jacobs soon demonstrated that he was a promoter of unusual efficiency and effectiveness. Grumpy and inarticulate, plagued throughout his life by ill-fitting dentures, he had the mechanistic mind of a computer. This, added to his rare talents of manipulation, eventually made Louis champion of the world after it appeared that Louis' defeat by Schmeling in 1936 had ruined everything for Joe.

Schmeling's victory automatically made him the No. 1 contender for the heavyweight title, then held by 'Cinderella Man' James J. Braddock, who had defeated Baer as a 100–1 shot. With the Nazis in power in Germany, the prospect of a Hitler-acclaimed champion was abhorrent to many. Among these was Joe Gould, Braddock's manager, the son of a rabbi. But Gould was no man to allow sentiment, however strong, to dull his bargaining powers. In return for side-tracking the German, he drove a hard bargain. Besides demanding an excessive split of the 'gate', he exacted an agreement from Jacobs calling for a percentage of Louis' earnings to be paid to himself and Braddock for the next 10 years. The promoter gagged on this, but had no choice only to acquiesce. Over the years he made Gould's collections as difficult as possible and the manager died claiming monies still due him.

Seeing a faint chance of regaining control of the heavyweight champion, Madison Square Garden swiftly signed Schmeling to meet Braddock, with the champion already training to meet Louis in Chicago. The Garden people went through all the motions and the expense of staging a mythical Braddock-Schmeling fight, complete with advertising, preliminaries, and a formal weigh-in of Schmeling on the announced date—hoping against hope that the

New York commission might declare the German the heavyweight champion by default. This turned out to be the original impossible dream.

Louis became the second Negro to win the world heavyweight championship, by knocking out Braddock in Chicago in 1937, causing cataclysmic celebrations in Black communities everywhere. Not all this exuberance was good clean fun, much of it was tainted with hooliganism, but Louis' winning the championship did have a therapeutic effect upon the spirits of the colored population sickened by the Depression and generations of gross deprivation and racial oppression.

The general public's reaction to Louis was a far cry from the reflex hostility which Johnson encountered. One of the reasons for this was that mass intelligence had progressed far enough to fend off the kind of racial propaganda which had turned the streets of cities into racial battlegrounds in 1910. The other reason was Louis himself.

Instead of the gloating, grinning gold-toothed Johnson-image which the public had found so exasperating, Louis, his towel-wrapped head lowered, after humbly mumbling into a ringside microphone, left the ring in a manner more like a man going to the gallows than one making a triumphal exit. This was a vivid demonstration that—racial agitators to the contrary—not all Negroes were alike.

Adding to the popular acceptance of Louis there was also the reassurance that the interracial romantic interludes characteristic of Johnson which had caused a national psychosis were not to be expected from Louis, who had crossed no racial lines in taking Negro Marva Trotter to wife two years before. This departure from what bigots claimed was the norm for Negro successes proved a powerful plus for Louis, particularly in the South.

With Louis now champion, Old Mike Jacobs, who had first made his presence felt as the shadowy secret backer of Tex Rickard years before, moved methodically and effectively to consolidate his position. He turned out to be a dubious 'angel,' as his newspaper partners faded one by one from the picture. Roxborough and Black remained the nominal managers of Louis with razor scarred, master boxing teacher Jack Blackburn as trainer, but Mike gradually took on the actual direction of Joe Louis himself.

Under his exclusive promotion, Mike managed Louis masterfully, making few mistakes in directing and protecting the affairs of the champion. With Louis as his trump card added to his own Machiavellian technique, Mike Jacobs reigned as the virtual dictator of boxing from 1937 until he was incapacitated by illness in 1948.

Joe Louis held the heavyweight championship longer than anyone else, 11 years, and defended it successfully more times than anyone else, 25. Of these defenses, the most dramatic was his return match one-round knockout of the man who had defeated him, Max Schmeling, in 1938.

The unfairness of the campaign to impute Nazi contamination to Schmeling has become obvious in the intervening years. There have been few more sincere friendships and genuine liking between one time ring foes than that between Louis and Schmeling.

Prior to World War II, respect rather than adulation had been the public attitude towards Louis. His actions and statements during the great war changed this feeling to one of idolatry. He made himself a living legend when at a Madison Sq. Garden rally in 1942, in uniform, he pronounced the words which became a rallying cry of World War II. "We'll win because we're on God's Side." In a subsequent reply to those critical of the nation's treatment of the Negro, Joe came up with the crushing, "There's nothing wrong with this country that Hitler would fix." From that point on, Louis became an American folk hero who could do no wrong.

The war over, Joe was hailed on all sides by an adoring public who felt that he would have willingly accepted front line action had it been called for. Following the victorious conclusion of the war in which thousands of Black servicemen had participated, a movement accelerated against the exclusion of Negroes in sports and in other areas of American life.

The most obdurate and traditional of these barriers, the 'Color Line' in baseball, had been breached early in 1946 with the signing of Jackie Robinson, by the General Manager of the Brooklyn Dodgers, Branch Rickey. Powerful opposition to Rickey's move among players, owners and press seethed ominously below the surface of a pseudo-compliance. A major factor in keeping this antagonism sub-rosa was the great popularity of Joe Louis with the American people. Rickey admitted he had taken this into consideration in signing Robinson. Jackie himself was well aware of the liberating influence of Louis' career. At a dinner honoring him in Chicago in 1948 he said " . . . There is one person I must give real and definite credit for my opportunity. His name is Joe Louis."

Louis himself had undergone personality changes since his early days. Inclined towards sullen withdrawal as a youth, he came back from service with a new joviality which, while always reserved, gained him a reputation as the funnyman of the heavyweight champions. His dry wit has enhanced his already favorable public image.

He had his share of virtues but thrift and money management are not among them. Consequently, he has been beset by tax troubles running into hundreds of thousands of dollars, but this had resulted in no impairment of his popularity. The public deduction is that his dereliction here is largely due to his own naivete in money matters and the irresponsibility of his advisers.

Intransigence—which had considerable to do with his first defeat by Schmeling—is also prominent among Joe's human failings. Rejecting all advice to stay retired and undefeated (Gene Tunney was among those who implored him to do so), Joe returned to the ring even though he received an unprecedented sum of $150,000 plus a yearly stipend of $15,000 from James D. Norris when he first called it quits in 1949.

Even after being soundly beaten by Ezzard Charles, he stubbornly resisted the entreaties of well-wishers not to go on, but persisted in fighting until he was literally blasted out of the ring by the late Rocky Marciano, who seemed genuinely saddened that he had been forced to do so.

Any suspicion that Louis's hold on the people might be waning vanished following his recent hospitalization in New York. During his short confinement the hospital was inundated with calls and wires from all over the world. In still another divergence from the Johnson experience, Louis is today more popular among white than among black Americans. Many young blacks to whom the harsh, oppressive, period in which Louis had to make his way is as remote as the Iron Age, see the old Brown Bomber as an anachronistic relic of the past, irrelevant to the mood and militancy of the present. Not having been around in Joe's day, they are unable to make comparisons between Negro opportunities then and now. These are many times greater and the example and career of Joe Louis played a notable part in this advancement.

For all his greatness and social impact, Louis must give way to a little man when the greatest boxing accomplishment of the Louis era is singled out. This honor belongs to Henry Armstrong, who during the Thirties was the featherweight, lightweight and welterweight champion, simultaneously.

Armstrong, a public hero in the Gans and Dixon tradition, was a remarkable performer. His style of boxing was unceasingly aggressive, a sharp departure from the stand-up classic moves of the majority of Negro boxers. Well-spoken and educated, a high school graduate, his career complemented Louis' influence on public thinking very well and he is still widely admired and respected. Famed for the power and precision of his punching in the ring, the blows of Joe Louis were equally damaging to the bias and bigotry that infected the social conditions of the time.

Carroll's work often made maximum use of space, as
seen in this overview of Henry Armstrong's storied career.
The Ring (August 1938)

IV. TELEVISION HELPED VASTLY IN DESTROYING COLOR LINE; ROBINSON REIGN SPECTACULAR

In the opening article of this series the point was made that for many decades boxing was the only professional sport from which Negroes were not excluded. In every other avenue of American life, black repression created almost insurmountable obstacles. While this limitation of opportunity has been a sorry reflection on our society it has been, like it or not, a harsh fact of life.

Even in the ring, racial parity left much to be desired and while Mike Jacobs deserved great credit for maneuvering Joe Louis into the heavyweight championship of the world, by and large, Negro fighters did not fare too well in Mike's regime. Although Louis was the busiest of champions, Uncle Mike, as the actual manager of the Brown Bomber, followed the familiar pattern of steering the champion clear of such 'Black Menaces' as Leroy Haynes, Lorenzo Pack, Jack Trammell, Curtis "Hatcher-man" Sheppard, Tiger Jack Fox and Lee Q. Murray. These were not great fighters and none of them figured to beat Louis but they were all dangerous punchers. Like his longtime partner, Tex Rickard, Jacobs could see no sense in jeopardizing his "Golden Genii," Joe Louis, when richer returns and softer opposition were available elsewhere. Quarantined into a quarrelling quorum of their own, these Negro heavies proceeded to batter each other into oblivion.

While Jacobs ran the Garden such outstanding Negro fighters as Archie Moore, Charley Burley, Ezzard Charles and Lloyd Marshall never fought in the big arena, the mecca for all boxers. In all fairness to him, Mike couldn't have cared less about racial complexion since he was color-blind to every shade save dollar bill green. What did concern him was the racial balance of the championship roster. The box office, not bias, determined his modus operandi. Looking at the 10–1 white-black ratio in the population, Mike reasoned that the gate receipts had to suffer if title bouts took on too dark a hue. Future developments were to prove him wrong. But he never completely relented on this position.

The entry of the electronic age, which gave professional boxing another dimension, television, forced a re-evaluation of Mike's position. The appearance of the TV sponsor diminished the importance of the "live" audience. When a stroke removed Jacobs from the picture in 1948, the late James D. Norris speedily filled the vacuum. Jim installed retired champion Louis as part of his newly organized International Boxing Club, with a $150,000 stipend, adding direction of Madison Square Garden to his control of the Detroit Olympia and the Chicago Stadium; placing Negro lawyer Truman Gibson in charge of his Chicago operations; making Harry Markson director of boxing in the Garden; and solidifying television's ties to boxing promotion.

Under the new system, crowd attendance was no longer vital. A sponsor picked up the tab for a guaranteed number of shows with the main bout fighters guaranteed a stipulated amount for each show. This figure, beginning at $3,500, eventually rose to $7,000 in the late fifties, with exceptions for championship fights.

With the take no longer wholly determined by the box office, an immediate result of the new arrangement was the erasure of what remained of any color lines in boxing. The public, now freeloading by way of home TV, cared little about the racial composition of the fights. The public responded so avidly to boxing on home TV in the early fifties at one time there were five weekly televised boxing shows. The reason for this was obvious. Before the advent of TV boxing, only a small minority of the people could be classified as "in person" boxing fans, due largely to the often overlooked fact that professional boxing has always been the most expensive of spectator sports. Even in this TV era, ringside seats for the first Liston-Clay match at Miami were priced at $250. Good seat attendance at fights has always been far beyond the pocketbooks of most of the population.

The TV industry seems to regard its early dependence on boxing as an embarrassment and rarely mentions it, but details of the Jersey Joe Walcott-Ezzard Charles heavyweight title match in Pittsburgh are illuminating. When the promoters announced that the match was not to be televised, in 1951, a nationwide clamor of anguish by purchasers of TV sets reverberated from coast to coast. With millions of TV sets stockpiled and awaiting a rush of customers, a state of panic hit the big manufacturers. They hurriedly banded together and handed over a $100,000 kitty to the promoters, who allowed the fight on the air lanes, with the local area blacked out.

That both contestants were black made no difference—as had been feared for so long—to the public. They wanted to see the fight, and that was that. This public receptivity led to the adoption of a recast racial policy on the part of the Norris organization. During most of the 10-year existence of this outfit the majority of the world champions were Negroes. Any lingering fears over public resistance to this "Open-Door" development were dispelled in 1951 when the middleweight championship match between America's Sugar Ray Robinson and the brown-skinned Briton, Randy Turpin, attracted the largest amount of money ever taken in for a title match below the heavyweight division.

At the time of the inception of the IBC in 1949, television, then in its infancy, showed little signs of any departure from the traditionally negative approach towards Negro opportunity. As it had done for generations, boxing filled the breach by providing what little exposure there was on the magic eye for colored people. So much so, that comedian Dick Gregory was to observe that the only Negroes he saw on TV were on the Friday night fights.

In the past few years rapid moves have been taken to rectify this condition. But for a long while if Negroes were seen at all on television, it was usually on the IBC boxing programs. In retrospect, despite its forced dissolution by government edict due to monopolistic accusations and its allegedly sinister attachments, the Norris operation proved to be not only a boon to blacks but a bargain to the general public.

Once again, in conjunction with boxing the Black man had made contacts with a large segment of the population from which he had been isolated. Under IBC auspices, Negro fighters flourished. In living rooms, comfortable, gratis and for nothing, one could see Floyd Patterson win the heavyweight title by knocking out Archie Moore; Moore win the light heavyweight title from Joey Maxim; lightweight champion Joe Brown defend his championship against a succession of challengers, with noteworthy performances; Ezzard Charles won Louis' vacated title by beating Jersey Joe Walcott; and lightweight champion Jimmy Carter, featherweight champion Sandy Saddler and welterweight champions Kid Gavilan, Virgil Akins, Johnny Saxton and Johnny Bratton. Armchair audiences saw Archie Moore survive some rough going in a title match against Yvon Durelle and the great Sugar Ray Robinson score classic one punch knockouts over tough Gene Fullmer and Bobo Olson.

The country's racial climate notwithstanding, the American public, without fully realizing it, has come to equate the success and achievements of Black Americans in the ring with the cherished chauvinism of American supremacy. For better or worse, the obsession of American superiority is deeply ingrained in the national psyche. As indigenous to, and products of, the nation, America's Black champions have served as subliminal symbols of U.S. supremacy. No one ever fulfilled this concept of the American Negro boxing champion more completely than Sugar Ray Robinson.

In his long years in the ring Robinson's career often took on the complexion of a love-hate romance with the American public, with spells of estrangement and unpopularity interspersed with the general adulation accorded him as the greatest boxer of his time. But all's well that ends well, and like re-united lovers at the end of a play, Sugar Ray and the public wound up in each other's arms when Madison Square Garden staged an unprecedented farewell to him four years ago.

The tribute, brainchild of the Garden publicist, John Condon, turned out to be an emotional occasion with a large crowd, predominantly white, pouring out its admiration and affection for the retiring champion. In the long history of the ring nothing quite like it had occurred.

As a non-conformist along the lines of Jack Johnson, to whom he has personality resemblances, Sugar Ray showed signs of rebelliousness as far as back as his Golden Glove days when he was always among the leaders in making demands for more meal money, etc. As a professional he did not endear himself to boxing people with such cracks as, "An actor makes faces and his agent gets ten percent. A fighter bleeds and his manager gets 33⅓ percent. Who thought this up, anyway?" Suiting his action to the word upon the death of his original manager, a New York brewer, he replaced him by merely changing George Gainford's title of trainer to manager.

Of far greater gravity, unfortunately, were his World War II difficulties which, at one time, threatened his continuance in boxing. But in recent years the authorities as well as the public, not unmindful of the humiliations and inequities experienced in the segregated Army of World War II by Black servicemen, has allowed tolerance to temper its judgement of Robinson's wartime actions.

Public aggravation was also exercised by Sugar Ray's air of hauteur and occasional arrogance, embellished by such affectations as rainbow-colored Cadillacs and a trailing chain of retainers of obscure employment. There were also departures from good taste, such as his presence on the golf course in Cleveland the day following his match with Jimmy Doyle in Cleveland in 1947. Doyle lay critically ill in the hospital. Many considered this callous and his remarks at the inquest after Doyle's death did not reflect kindly upon him. But, in a subsequent bout on the coast shortly after, he donated his purse to the mother of the deceased fighter.

Some of his actions kindled criticism by the press to which he sometimes responded unpleasantly and this did not help matters. He made insomniacs out of promoters and fight people by an addiction to postponements, often for the vaguest of causes.

Television money was one of his prime concerns. No one was more adamant in getting his full share of the ancillary rights than Sugar Ray. Claiming that fighters generally are natural targets of exploitation and that he himself had been the victim of many a hard bargain in the beginning, Robinson, once in the driver's seat, drove the hardest of bargains for himself.

Ingratitude was another charge frequently levelled at Robinson. His answer to that was that too many people try to live off fighters. But for all their abrasiveness, his antics, however irritating, were rarely harmful and the credit side of his character was impressive. First and foremost, as an example of clean living and its benefits, he could not be surpassed. No one had ever seen him take a drink of liquor or use tobacco in any form. Few men paid more attention to conditioning and proper care of the body than Robinson, thereby setting a worthwhile example to the young people of the day.

No one fought more cleanly in the ring. Save for an incident in Germany where his unfamiliarity with European rules caused a commotion, it is hard to recall his ever being warned by a referee or criticized for any infraction of the rules of sportsmanship laid down by the Marquis of Queensberry. He has never been known to complain publicly over a decision although he had good reason to do so. Particularly in his first match with Paul Pender in Boston, which cost him the championship, and in his drawn match against Gene Fullmer in 1960, which prevented him from winning the middleweight championship for the sixth time.

As a sportsman in the ring Ray was a paragon. He was never known to take any unfair advantage while in action and there is no record of his ever having criticized, ridiculed, accused or spoken harshly of any opponent in his quarter century of boxing.

Individual opinions of his ambivalent personality have ranged from the recent encomium by Richard Watts, drama critic of the New York Post, calling him "The most delightful of men," to highly caustic comments written by Negro reporter Sam Lacey for a Baltimore paper some years ago.

Whatever the contradictions in his chameleon-like personality there is complete unanimity on his super-ranking as a boxer. Among the oceans of words lauding his extraordinary gifts as a fighter those of Harry Markson, director of boxing in Madison Square Garden serve as the most explicit. Wrote Markson, " . . . during the height of his career, Sugar Ray Robinson didn't lack a single attribute which the great fighters need. He had a left hook, a right cross, defensive skill, the will to win, ring generalship, speed of hand and foot, courage, a sense of pacing, a variety of punches, the ability to size up an opponent after a round or two, split second reflexes, magnificent legs, and the ability to reach superior heights when the situation required it. Some keener students of boxing than I may have discovered a flaw, but I didn't see it and if Robinson had any, where and when did they show?"

It must be added that Robinson did all these things in the ring with the unmatched grace, rhythm, and finesse of a virtuoso. Handsome features and a streamlined sepia toned physique gave his boxing an artistic quality.

Five times middleweight champion and once welterweight champion, his return to the ring after a two-year retirement, during which he delved deeply into the delights of Paris where he was a public hero, was, at first, deplored by friends and well wishers. Many had tried but no fighter had returned to the wars after such a luxurious layoff at the age of 34 with success.

After absorbing a trouncing from rough Tiger Jones at the outset of his return to the ring, he seemed doomed to a like fate but, displaying an iron willed determination, he fought his way back to the championship. This was an achievement ranking with Henry Armstrong's holding three world championships at one time

As an active ringman Robinson remained in the spotlight longer than anyone else. Among the unforgettable performances that made him an international idol for so long were his atomic one-punch knockout of Gene Fullmer; his picture book boxing which turned back the welterweight challenge of Kid Gavilan; his super-skillful display against light heavyweight champion Joey Maxim before the 105 degree temperature caused his collapse; his uphill struggle against Tommy Bell, his most stubborn foe, to win the welterweight championship; his defeat of Randy Turpin, blood streaming from a bad cut, to regain his middleweight championship and his playing the matador to the bull-like rushes of "El Toro" Jake LaMotta in winning the middleweight title for the first time.

It was never a secret that, like Gans long ago, Sugar Ray did not always have a knockout in mind when he stepped into the ring. The late Dan Parker once commented, " . . . no mother ever carried a baby more tenderly than Sugar Ray could carry an opponent when in the mood."

One of the strongest critics of Joe Louis for fighting too long, Ray Robinson refused to heed his own advice and the sight of the once peerless boxer—his efforts manacled by middle age—struggling against youths in the final stages of his career was not a pleasant one. But not all his deftness deserted him. At the age of 45, he was still giving a fairly good account of himself. It is a further tribute to his ring stature that in 25 years of ring warfare he was never actually knocked out.

Plagued by law suits, liens, attachments, and mismanagement during the latter years, he came upon a treasure trove when the U.S. government returned a quarter of a million dollars to him which had been held for tax emergencies since the Turpin fight 18 years ago. Today he actually appears better groomed and handsomer than in his prime. He lives well, is active in show business and has no apparent worries. The coat holders are long gone and he chauffeurs his own car.

His past imperfections and improprieties forgotten, Sugar Ray is still swarmed about when he appears in public. As long as the American preoccupation with preeminence exists he will no doubt remain idolized as a national symbol of the kind of excellence which the country worships.

V. CHARLES, PATTERSON TOO QUIET; LISTON TOO INVOLVED; THEN CAME BRASH MR. CLAY

Theoretically the heavyweight champion of the world is able to defeat any man alive in physical combat under the civilized code laid down by the Marquis of Queensberry.

This implies a superiority which, when demonstrated by a black man, caused considerable discomfort to that portion of the population plagued by the psychosis of "White Supremacy" 60 years ago. The noisiest disclaimer of this type of thinking was novelist Jack London, who, speaking for those of similar views, screeched for a Caucasian crusader "To wipe that golden smile forever off the black man's (Johnson's) face."

While some found the occupancy of the heavyweight throne by a member of a race less than 50 years out of bondage unnerving, this racist notion was more neurotic than national. The current idea that Jack Johnson was confronted by a white monolith of opposition is nonsense. Had this been the case he would never have become the world champion in the first place.

A conspicuous defector to the Negro's cause was Jim Jeffries' erstwhile trainer, Bill Delaney, who after a bitter dispute with the Boilermaker, denounced him, took over the training of Johnson; acted as his chief second; and was largely instrumental in the Negro's easy victory over Jeffries in Reno, Nevada, in 1910.

Johnson's long pursuit of Tommy Burns prior to his winning the championship from the Canadian in 1908 took money. This enterprise was financed by a syndicate of New York gamblers who couldn't have cared less about Nordic superiority and cleaned up in bets on the Black man's victory over Jeffries. Even the white hope safari of Johnson's time was primarily a propaganda product of scheming fight people, rather than any hysterical concern by the general public over white "redemption" in the ring. More often than not, the white hopes were objects of ridicule and derision by cartoonists and writers of the period such as Tad Dorgan, Bud Fisher, W.O. McGeehan, Hype Igoe, Bugs Baer, Damon Runyon, and Ring Lardner.

Joe Louis' long and benign reign as heavyweight champion, during which a generation existed approvingly, conditioned the people to a behavioural pattern which was consistently followed by the three Negro world champions who succeeded him, Ezzard Charles, Jersey Joe Walcott and Floyd Patterson. These were, like Louis, sober minded men, reluctant limelight seekers, who made the champion's race immaterial.

Under this bland dynasty, interrupted by the late Rocky Marciano from 1952 to 1956, and by Ingemar Johansson for a short period, the public grew to regard the heavyweight championship as raceless.

Charles, who followed Louis as champion by beating Walcott in 1949 and then defeating the "unretired" Louis a year later, went to an extreme of self-effacement. This Georgia-born Cincinnatian was the most subdued, reticent, unobtrusive, unacclaimed and underrated champion of all time. Well spoken, but rarely talkative; not bad looking; a high school graduate; well groomed; with a placid private life and a commendable record in World War II, Charles' abilities were largely nullified by his negative personality.

It is interesting to speculate what the public reaction would have been 60 years ago had a man of Charles' tepid temperament been the first black heavyweight champion. Since Charles lived an ultra-quiet life, the public of his time never really got a chance to know him. But, despite this, the general response to him was friendly, and his reserved dignity made a favorable impression. Along with that he was a fine fighter. Small for a heavyweight, some of the fire he had generated as a slashing middleweight seemed to go out of him following the death of Sam Baroudi, a middleweight who expired after a bout with Charles, a shocking mismatch, in 1948. For the remainder of his career his efforts seemed haunted by this tragedy, a development which often brought him criticism as overly cautious.

Wide popularity never came to Charles. His defeat of Louis, despite an obvious let-down on his part in the latter rounds of the one-sided battle, did not make the public happy. Negroes were particularly disconsolate over the downfall of the legendary champion. The result of this was to make him even more withdrawn and aloof. It was not until his first losing effort, against Rocky Marciano, when, past his prime, he made a valiant try, did public adulation come his way.

Charles' last years in the ring were highly consistent with his expressed feelings when at his best. He asserted a dislike for boxing, rarely attended fights, but had to be driven from the ring by personal edict of various boxing commissions when he persisted in continuing to fight while risking grave consequences to his health.

For one who earned $800,000 and lived conservatively throughout his career his later financial insecurity has proved baffling. Hospitalized for many months in Chicago, he was the object of a benefit last winter at which a considerable amount of money was raised, with Marciano a prime participant.

Charles, whose unusual first name was derived from the surname of the white doctor who delivered him at birth in his native state of Georgia, belongs among those whose ranking as a boxer is being elevated by retrospection and nostalgia. He narrowly missed becoming champion for a second time, in his fourth bout with Walcott in Philadelphia, in 1952. His sensitivity over not replacing Louis as an idol could have accounted for his somber personality.

The transference of Jersey Joe Walcott from the top of a trash heap on a city dump truck in Camden, N.J. to the heights of world-wide fame accentuates the role of the ring in affording the black man a ladder of ascent from the most dismal depths. Nowhere else is such an escape possible, and Jersey Joe is a prime example. Talked off his job on a garbage truck by a glib local boxing figure, Vic Marsillo, in 1944, after retiring from the ring three years before, Walcott went on to become the heavyweight champion of the world. For no greater investment than coal in the bin and food and clothing for Walcott's wife and five children, Marsillo and partner Felix Bocchiccio garnered more than a million dollars for themselves and the boxer.

Past 30 at the time, Walcott had shown good prospects as a heavyweight in his youth. But he had been a casualty of the Jacobs modus operandi during the great days of Louis, when Negro heavyweights were maneuvered into belaboring each other into obscurity in small town fights for smaller purses.

For want of something better to do, Marsillo convinced first himself, then Walcott and Bocchiccio, that Walcott, despite his age, still had the potential. A match with Joe Baksi, then a ranking heavyweight contender, proved Marsillo right as Walcott, picked as an overage pushover, won the decision over the rugged Baksi. Rejuvenated, Walcott went on to his first match with Joe Louis, a controversial contest in Madison Square Garden which many thought he won on the basis of the two knockdowns he scored over the waning Brown Bomber. The decision went to Louis.

If a boxer receives one chance to win the heavyweight championship of the world, he is favored by fortune. If he gets two shots, Lady Luck truly is his paramour. Walcott received five chances to become the heavyweight champion! After failing a second time against Joe Louis, he was twice unsuccessful against Charles. In a fifth attempt, he became champion by knocking out Charles in Pittsburgh in 1951.

The fight's conclusion left him trembling with emotion in the center of the ring, his hand upraised in an evangelical gesture, as bedlam raged behind him. He uttered these words of thanks, "The good Lord has answered my prayers as I knew he would. I am telling you young folks never to give up in despair. No one thought I could do it but me and the good Lord and if you think you can do something I am telling you young people you can do it!"

Walcott's privations, perseverance, fatherly appearance and large family won him a ready rapport with the public, particularly women, intrigued with the idea of a father of six besting younger men and becoming a world champion. Although no Johnson for garishness and gloating, Walcott was more articulate than Louis and far more gregarious and outgoing than Charles. Adjusting well to his new role as celebrity, he specialized in personal appearances up until the time Rocky Marciano's thunderous right ended his term as champion and brought a temporary halt to the dark domination of the heavyweight division, in 1952.

Louis, Walcott and Charles were not the kind of men to kindle racial passions. The late Rocky Marciano's success against them was viewed in the light of pure competition, and nothing else. Marciano himself, personality wise, was cast in the same mold as the Negro champions who preceded him, a man given more to modesty than braggadocio. The acceptance of Louis, Charles and Walcott as men and champions solely, minus any ethnic connotation, had been so complete that the term "white hope" had fallen into disfavor. It was never applied to Marciano.

Marciano's retirement, undefeated, in 1956, cleared the way for young Floyd Patterson to become the fourth American Negro to be declared the heavyweight champion. For many years sponsorship of black fighters had been largely concentrated among Americans of Irish extraction, O'Rourke, McMahon, Flynn, McCarney and McKetterick. Italians were becoming more and more prominent in this role. Felix Bocchiccio had by some magical means maneuvered Walcott into five opportunities to become champion and Cus D'Amato was to revolutionize the management of Negro fighters. Not even the Norris regime, although it made great progress in this direction, had eliminated all the inequalities which confronted Negro fighters. At the time D'Amato and Patterson came on the scene, it was still routine for a black fighter to make whatever concessions had to be made in arranging a match, as to weight, purse distribution and experience.

D'Amato soon made it clear that he was going to have none of that. If anybody was going to make any concessions it was going to be the other guy and not his Floyd Patterson. An adamant bachelor, Cus' egocentricity took such a stubborn course that throughout his early career Patterson had all the better of it every time he stepped into the ring. D'Amato forced the Norris IBC to revise its television fee for his fighter, a difference of some $40,000 in Patterson's first meeting with Hurricane Jackson. Cus' approach as Patterson's manager was so far out of line with what had been the time-honored custom that it was regarded as effrontery by many. The unyielding mentor was called eccentric, among other things.

Patterson was managed better than any Negro boxer before or since. He became richest of them all. He was actually only a light heavyweight whom D'Amato fattened up into a heavyweight. Some of his most lucrative purses were gained against opponents of dubious credentials as challengers hand-picked by the crafty D'Amato. When Marciano called it quits, the heavyweight crown was up for grabs with Patterson, Hurricane Jackson and light heavy-weight champion Archie Moore the leading aspirants. Patterson defeated both of these without too much trouble and made several highly remunerative de-fenses against inept opposition before losing in 1959 to Ingemar Johansson, from whom he gained the championship the following year.

Patterson's peculiar personality and unnatural shyness which were more amenable to psychoanalysis than socializing, prevented his ever becoming a public favorite. Rescued from a troubled childhood by institutional care, he had a mania for seclusion and weird disguises, all designed apparently to mystify the public. In this he succeeded, at the same time obscuring any issue of race so completely that Cassius Clay was to brand him in later days "A colored 'white hope.'"

But for all his clandestine ways—and these included an interracial mar-riage, which the present-day public, in sharp contrast to earlier times, ignored completely, Floyd Patterson's credentials as a fighter are noteworthy. He was the youngest man ever to win the heavyweight championship and the only man to win it back after losing it. Although his ring assets, which featured light-ning-fast punching combinations, were flawed by the fragility of the natural 175-pounder which he was, his overall record is impressive. Late in his ca-reer, important contests with both Jerry Quarry and Jimmy Ellis were decided against him. They could just as easily have been in his favor. As an American Olympic boxer in 1952 his exploits stand unequalled.

The public admired Floyd Patterson for his calm and quiet ways and his sportsmanship. He refused to criticize any adverse verdict. But the public never quite understood him. In this the fans were as one with the fighter, who often gave the impression that he was trying to escape from himself. But for all that he earned more money in the ring than any other boxer on record, almost eight million dollars! His share from all sources, including theatre television, for his first match with Sonny Liston in Chicago in 1962 is listed at two million dol-lars! Since he was stopped in two minutes and six seconds this breaks down to a rate of almost $16,000 per second! This figure makes Patterson, a Negro, on a time basis, the highest paid human being in history. This is something for social scientists and economists to ponder.

The emergence of Liston brought to the fore a world champion with an "anti-social" background. There are sociologists who might dispute this by saying that Sonny, one of 22 children of a poverty-blighted family, was set up as a target for society's best blows by his early environment in the Arkansas back woods.

Liston ascended the heavyweight throne with a record of 20 arrests, most of them minor, but including a five year stretch in the Missouri State Penitentiary for a felony.

Not everyone agreed that a man with such a past should be eligible to fight for the championship, but Patterson himself turned out to be the deciding factor. The rift between Floyd and manager D'Amato has had elements of mystery and has never been fully explained by either party. But there was no question about the cautious manager's disapproval of Liston as a Patterson opponent. Although the suspicion persists that the break between Floyd and the manager was due to something deeper, this was the reason given. In turning thumbs down on Liston, D'Amato was acting in character. Cus long had displayed a disinclination to risk his prized protégé against colored challengers and it was inferred that this had become disturbing to Patterson.

On his merits, Liston had clearly earned the opportunity. Slow footed and lumbering, he was a powerful, numbing puncher. Barely able to read and write, Sonny understood the meaning of psychology even if he never would have been able to spell it. Of menacing physical proportions, his fearsome glowering at his foes was designed to and did strike terror into most of them. This war of nerves, which usually reduced his rivals to quavering flight, plus a pole-axing left jab and a crushing left hook, enabled him to amass a knockout-studded record with only one defeat in 10 years of boxing, since his release from prison. . . .

Following his release, Liston was not able to avoid brushes with the law, usually for automobile violations, charging this to police harassment. He was also caught up in the net of the Kefauver investigations of 1965 with the interrogators showing a keen interest in the names of some of his supposed sponsors, Vitale, Carbo, and Palumbo. These were people who, the authorities charged, were not unknown to the Mafia. Although evidence to the contrary was not lacking, Sonny disclaimed any connection with these parties with this bit of droll philosophy, "Before you can convict anybody for murder you have to come up with a body. Before you can convict me, you got to come up with one of those guys as my manager. You can't do it."

Such observations were not unusual with Liston, as witness this one on the inequities of occupation. "A lawyer can get you sent away to jail for 20 years, but he still gets paid. A doctor can kill you but he still gets paid. Them guys can't lose. If I had to do it all over again, I would never be a fighter."

Rocky Marciano was powerfully built but short, as was Jersey Joe Walcott. Charles and Patterson were slightly built as heavyweight champions go, but Liston looked the part, both in the ring and out, of a man able to best any living human in any kind of fight. His one-round demolition job on Patterson in their second meeting added to this illusion, and comedian Joe E. Lewis spoke for the world when he cracked, "That Liston, I wish he'd fight Russia!" No other heavyweight champion, not even Louis, Marciano or Dempsey exuded such an aura of invincibility as Liston following his defeats of Patterson. But there was one dissenter; faintly at first but growing ever louder, sounded the clarion call of brash young Cassius Clay, "I am the Greatest."

VI. CLAY'S RISE TO CHAMPIONSHIP CLIMAX OF NEGRO TAKEOVER IN HEAVYWEIGHT EXCITEMENT

Public acceptance of a Negro world heavyweight champion, uncomfortable and unwilling in 1910, particularly in the South, had become so favorable 50 years later that the sponsorship of Clay, a young Negro fighter, by a combine of affluent business men was taken as a matter of course.

In the general confusion, controversy, chaos, and contention which have surged about Clay, too little note has been taken of the unprecedented initiation of his career. No heavyweight champion-to-be had ever set sail for the title convoyed so auspiciously. Upon his return to his native Louisville, Ky., as the Olympic light heavyweight champion in 1960, wheels were speedily set in motion organizing a syndicate of 11 Louisville businessmen, eight of them millionaires, to take over the management and direction of Clay. This combination, all white and of southern background, offered the following proposition: The fighter was to be paid a $10,000 signing bonus, and guaranteed a yearly income of $4,000 for the first two years. He was to receive 50% of his purses, with the syndicate paying all expenses. He was to receive $500 a month for "walking around money"; 15% of his share was to be put into an annuity (now said to be worth $100,000) which would begin payment at the age of 35.

The prime mover in this setup had been William Faversham, Jr., son of a famous actor of years ago, and a business success in his own right. Well aware of their own virginity in the vineyard of professional boxing, the businessmen made a wise choice in engaging the Dundee brothers, Angelo and Chris, to handle the competitive side of the Clay enterprise.

While the Clay cartel was not permeated by pure altruism, its members were far from welfare candidates. The initial investment of $2,500 each was insignificant for men of their financial standing. Prior to the dissolution of the arrangement in 1966, the return from this small outlay had been sizable, but hardly staggering, considering the wealth of the men involved. But motives and pecuniary results aside, the formation of the Louisville syndicate had a deeper social significance. This southern action had once again demonstrated the peculiar power of boxing in eradicating racial bias. The restrained and raceless reigns of Negro heavyweight champions, Ezzard Charles, Jersey Joe Walcott and Floyd Patterson, following Louis, had lulled the public into a seeming unawareness of the ethnic extraction of the heavyweight crown wearer.

The interruption of boxing's sepia syndrome by Rocky Marciano and Ingemar Johansson had occasioned no mass rejoicing over the return of the world championship to Caucasian auspices; a far cry from the "whooping and hollering" which had resounded nation-wide when Jess Willard defeated Jack Johnson in 1915. Champions Charles, Walcott and Patterson made the big title colorless in more ways than one. Their personalities, which were inclined towards drabness, had removed much of the iridescence which traditionally enhances the championship. Not even the great Louis, for all his magnetism, really qualified as a colorful figure. Rocky Marciano was one of the most formidable of all champions but was easily lost in the faceless crowd.

Up to the arrival of Clay, only Johansson showed glints of glamor. His reign was brief. The public had come to equate the heavyweight champion of the world with an equanimity which bordered upon boredom. No sooner had he turned professional than Clay showed that he was something else again. Necessary changes in racial mores had been accomplished by Louis as world heavyweight champion, most famous Negro of his time, by keeping his mouth shut. This mission accomplished, Clay reasoned, the time had come to reverse course and sound off.

Helped no little by the publicity attendant on his unprecedented sponsorship, Clay moved quickly to capitalize on his good looks, natural wit, and extraordinary ability by attracting attention to himself in a variety of unorthodox ways. He antedated the current "Black is Beautiful" motif by exaggerating his handsomeness. He exuded an irrepressible effervescence energized by a pseudo-praise. It took no more than a few early victories over mediocrities to make Clay's battle cry "I am the Greatest!" become familiar to the nation. As his opposition became more newsworthy and his performances more impressive, he amplified this slogan with his own variety of poetry, a ding-dong doggerel which became a public divertissement. " . . . When you come to the fight, don't block the gates or bar the door . . . for Archie Moore will fall in four." He rhymed, to the amusement of the multitudes, by now completely entranced with the most effusive fighter since Max Baer. Beneath the peripheral persiflage there was a submerged stratum of seriousness evident in Cassius' application to the art of boxing and to body conditioning.

By 1962, Clay had become the most advertised athlete in the world. Women's magazines, unusual outlets for sports publicizing; radio and television programs which rarely took note of boxers; sports page coverage which blanketed not only the country but the world, made the name Clay a household word. It might have all been for naught had Clay not possessed extraordinary ability. He whetted public interest with a spectacular gimmick of naming the round in which his foe "would fall," and made it stick. As an extrovert and an exhibitionist, he became an international topic of discussion.

Sonny Liston, then champion, could not be called a public idol but no heavyweight champion had ever been held in such awesome respect, and not without reason. In his wake he had left a pile of terror-stricken knockout victims, including former champion Floyd Patterson; his forbidding background; glowering façade; huge size and muscular development, magnified the illusion of might and menace which was Sonny Liston in 1962.

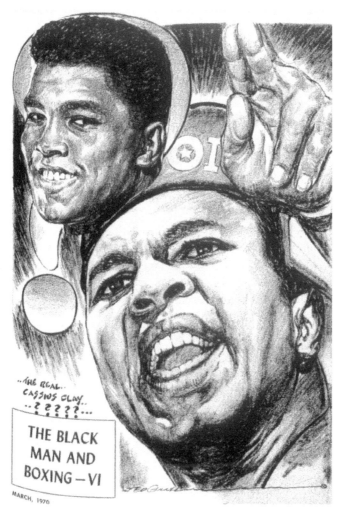

..THE REAL..
CASSIUS CLAY
..? ? ? ? ?..

THE BLACK MAN AND BOXING – VI

MARCH, 1970

Although he often questioned Ali's political pronouncements, Carroll nonetheless respected his demonstrable ability in the ring. *The Ring* (March 1970)

Facing this fearsome confrontation, Clay responded with barbs of badinage and ridicule directed against the burly titleholder, whom he dubbed "The big old ugly bear." The public, by now conditioned to Clay's carryings-on, was taken aback by this show of disrespect to Liston who was installed a prohibitive favorite to beat the brash young challenger when they climbed into the ring in Miami Beach, Fla., early in 1964.

For those who would denigrate the part played by boxing in the Saga of the Black Man in America, the financial details of the first Liston-Clay fight should be enlightening. Spectators paid as high as $250 for a ringside seat, a phenomenon in itself. The bulk of total receipts of $5,686,000, came from theatre television. Of this vast amount, Liston is listed as having received $720,000. If his luxurious way of life in Las Vegas is any indication, Sonny wound up with a good part of it. Clay's share came to $360,000.

Considering what it paid out, the public received an unsatisfactory ending with Liston sombrely surrendering the world's championship by refusing to come out for the 7th round. The spectators came to the conclusion that Clay's speed was too much for Sonny to overcome. Clay had fled through most of the match, which had been evenly fought up to the unexpected finish. Upon being proclaimed champion he went into a delirium of exultation, screaming and gesticulating. Forming a backdrop to the celebrating was a coterie of dark suited young men of serious mien, later identified as Black Muslims.

On the way to winning the championship, Clay had brought the boxing game back into the limelight it had occupied in the days of Louis and Dempsey. He was an international conversation piece. The word charisma was invented for him. A galaxy of starry qualities, looks, wit, gregariousness and talent were all fused into a traffic-stopping personality. Viewed from the perspective of personal magnetism, Clay truly was the "Greatest!"

But, like the cloud on the horizon no bigger than a man's hand, there were whispers and rumors gradually growing into inquiries, pursuant to Clay's relationship with Malcolm X, later expelled, but at the time the most dynamic disciple of Elijah Muhammad, Messiah of the Black Muslims, a separatist Islamic offshoot with overtones of Black supremacy. The passing of time with its revelations of the Muslims as a non-drinking, non-smoking sect with puritanical ideas about such things as women's dress; plus the emergence of much more aggressive activist elements of the Black community, has tempered public trepidation over the followers of Muhammad. But at the time, 1964, membership in the Black Muslims was categorized with card carrying in the Communist Party.

Prior to the first fight with Liston, Clay had been evasive about his Muslim connections and the extent of his involvement. This ended the moment his hand was raised in triumph over the dreaded Big Bear. The public reeled over the new champion's ready admission that he was not only a Muslim but a thoroughly indoctrinated one. Outside of a hasty downgrading of his potential value as a commodity in such ancillary ventures as TV, the movies and endorsements, there was no hint of interference with his future activities in the ring. Briefly, the ideology of the Black Muslims as elucidated by Elijah Muhammad is directed against the past slavery, which they consider the ultimate crime and the first cause of the social ills which afflict the country. This affliction, according to Muhammad, precludes an integrated society. They espouse a form of apartheidism with complete separatism as far as is feasible from the majority white group.

Of all the Negro champions, Clay, off his background seemed the unlikeliest to embrace this ethnocentric evangelism. Unlike practically every outstanding Black fighter of the past, Clay, in his early years, had been comfortable, unmarred by the desperate deprivation of the sharecropper's shack or the ghetto slum. The name, Cassius Clay, had been that of one of the most famous abolitionists of the 19th century. Along with that, his career had been launched under a white sponsorship unmatched by any other Negro fighter.

Negro athletes generally, and Negro fighters particularly, having had such rough going in their early years and carried away by the blessings of monetary good fortune, have veered away from the religious and political radicalism now prevalent in the country. It is interesting to speculate how Clay would have reacted to the preachments of Malcolm X had his boyhood been plagued by hunger and hardship. Perhaps the results would have been the same. Then again, who can tell?

However uneasy the public may have been over Clay's religious attachments, it had little effect upon the support given his fighting. The receipts from all sources for his first title defense, against Liston in Lewiston, Maine, in 1965, exceeded $1,600,000, with Clay taking down $480,000. For the second time the public finished second best. Sonny faded away after less than two minutes of the first round, as Clay stood above him yelling for the one-time terror to "get up and fight."

As world champion, Cassius Clay, meeting and outclassing all challengers both here and abroad from 1964 to 1967, established himself as one of the greatest boxers of all time, an accolade readily conceded him by all, his out-of-the-ring turbulence disregarded. Only one of his matches has been close: his meeting with Doug Jones in 1963. In all the others, his great speed; keen ring brain—the result of a 114-fight apprenticeship in the amateur ranks; excellent condition, and sharp hitting have made his opponents appear futile.

Clay's Black Muslim attachments seemingly made little difference to the fight conscious public. He earned more than five million dollars in five years. But, as his involvement with the movement grew greater so, too, did the concern over his draft status by the Selective Service system. Previously turned down for obscure reasons, he was ordered to report for induction in Houston, Tex. Clay now calling himself Muhammed [*sic*] Ali, as a Black Muslim "minister," refused induction on the grounds of conscientious objection. On June 20, 1967 he was convicted in Federal Court in Houston for draft refusal, sentenced to five years in prison, and fined $10,000.

Clay's absorption into the Black Muslims had automatically sealed the doom of the Caucasian cartel which had sponsored him, a development which was co-incident with the review of his original draft status. Various boxing bodies, including the New York State Commission and the WBA, fell over themselves in the rush to dethrone the draft-defaulting champion. This attitude was not unanimous, however. The Ring Magazine refused to withdraw recognition, asserting that Clay's appeal to higher courts, staying his incarceration, voided the right of any authority to take away his title.

The case of Cassius Clay has proved as divisive among the people as the Vietnam war itself. Although he is not allowed to leave the country, Clay moves freely about in a supporting base of alienated youth, protestors against the war, and a sizable part of the Black population. His status among the so called "silent majority" of Americans is less secure and many organizations including veterans are determined to keep him inactive until a final disposition of his case. Besides his ministerial pretensions, in his appeal to the Supreme Court, Clay racialized his case by charging "lily whitism" to the Selective Service system, stressing the absence of Negroes on the local boards.

Clay is a fighter first and last, and fight people, always practical, are at a loss to understand his thinking. "The guy says he doesn't want to kill anybody. O.K. but he must know that there is more chance of his being sent to the moon than being sent to the front lines. He admits he is fighting for money and by now his time would have been over. He'd be back bigger than ever with a million bucks waiting for him to start fighting again." There is something to this line of reasoning. But Clay insists that his objections are conscientious and money is secondary to his principles.

With Clay, contradiction has been a way of life. In the years since his war difficulties brought his luminous career to a jarring halt, some of his pronouncements have come uncomfortably close to the "hate-Whitey" excretions of the extremists, but no Black fighter ever gained fame under management as milky as Muhammad Ali.

Some of his statements have antagonized super-patriots but no professional flag-waver has stated the case for the country any stronger than Clay in the 1960 Olympics, when he replied to a probing Russian reporter, "The U.S.A. is the best country in the world, including yours. I ain't fighting alligators and living in a mud hut."

The kaleidoscope character of Clay projects itself in wordy waves. He is at one and the same time, childish and mature; obliging and stand-offish. Any compilation of his comments emphasizes his complexities. "I believe it's human nature to be with your own kind. I don't want people who don't want me. I don't believe in outside trouble. I'm no fool, there's no referee in the street." Here is a statement to gladden the heart of the deepest down-in-Dixie diehard. In the same vein, "Integration is death. I want my baby to come out looking like me. . . . " It is a supreme irony that on the social issue of miscegenation which all but destroyed Jack Johnson, Cassius Clay, the most controversial champion since Johnson, is in agreement with the critical public of Johnson's time.

"It's downgrading to see a Black man making love to a white woman. That's what happens when they get a movie role. They're a disgrace. I refuse to downgrade Black women by appearing with white women. I'm a separatist. Elijah Muhammad taught me to stay with my own people and respect the Black woman. Black men, as soon as they make money in television and movies, right away go with white women. That's a disgrace." As Jack Johnson spins in his grave the handsome Clay has thus far shown no signs of insincerity on this score. His first wife, a Negro show girl whom he divorced because she strayed from the rigidities of Muslim dress and habit, has been succeeded by a statuesque beige beauty of grace and charm, Belinda Boyd, also a Muslim.

Clay says he refused to play Jack Johnson in a European movie because of the former champion's interracial love affairs. Bigots of his time who insisted that Johnson's attitude on intermarriage was normal for successful Negroes must also be gyrating beneath the sod in unison with the man they vilified. Clay is at his logical weakest on the question of race relations. In attempting to clarify his separatism, he responds "I don't hate tigers, nor am I anti-tiger. But if a tiger broke into this room now I would break out, because my knowledge of his nature and mine lets me know we can't get along together."

Clay's attitude resulted in the staging of a successful tournament by the WBA involving eight of the outstanding heavyweights, five of whom were Colored—Thad Spencer, Leotis Martin, Ernie Terrell, former champion Floyd Patterson and the eventual winner Jimmy Ellis. It also brought to the fore a rough, tough, highly formidable, claimant of the championship recognized in New York and six other states, Joe Frazier. Recent efforts to bring about a meeting between Clay and Frazier have been abortive.

Clay's suspension last year from the Black Muslims plus a denial of the use of the name Muhammed [*sic*] Ali by Elijah Muhammad has not lessened his allegiance to the cult leader. He declares to point out that the son of Elijah, Herbert Muhammed who succeeded the syndicate as his manager, also suffered suspension some time ago.

Everyone agrees, that as good a boxer as he was, Cassius Clay had still to reach his full potential and that his money-making possibilities were limitless had his career kept to a conventional course.

VII. NEGRO ACHIEVEMENTS GALORE IN BOXING HAVE BATTERED DOWN OLD RACIAL BARRIERS

Throughout this series the point has been stressed that for many years boxing was the only professional sport from which Black Americans were not excluded.

As a consequence, there is a communion between the Negro and the ring which makes the sport unique in the history of the Black man in the United States. The present proliferation of Negroes in all professional sports provides an incredible contrast to days gone by and a happy prognosis for an eventual curing of the ills of prejudice.

Crowded stadiums and vast television audiences attest to the public acceptance of this racial amalgam on gridiron, court and diamond. The popularity of this space age 'New Order' in sports should come as no surprise when the careers and achievements of the Black champions of boxing are reviewed.

The Negro fighter was the Great Pioneer of sports. When all other doors were closed to members of his race, he was a champion of the world, the acknowledged best. It is a paradox that the public, notwithstanding its racial malaise, reacted to the Negro boxer as a champion not with antagonism or resentment, but with acclaim and homage.

There is no form of hero worship conceivable which has not been accorded the Negro champions. They have been received and lauded by presidents, governors, mayors and every kind of public dignitary; honored with parades, banquets, testimonials and civic receptions without end; subjects of books, plays, movies, radio and TV offerings which have been invariably favorable; pursued by women of every ethnic extraction; hailed as conquering heroes both here and abroad; besieged by autograph seekers and idolizers and forgiven transgressions for which ordinary citizens would have sorely paid. With few exceptions for the Negro world champion, kudos has been the name of the game.

It would be unrealistic and inaccurate to assume that there has not been a price to pay. As a rugged contact sport, boxing has its hazards and while its fatalities are not enveloped in the flaming death of auto racing nor do they approach those of football numerically, for a time, ring tragedies were striking Negro boxers in disproportionate numbers. Only two such accidents involving world champions have occurred. Both victims, Davey Moore and Benny Paret, are among the champions listed herein.

The greatest and most obvious danger in boxing comes from fighting too long. Virtually every Negro fighter of prominence put his well-being in jeopardy by wearing out his welcome in the ring. The recent findings in a survey of the Royal College of Physicians in London concluded that while severe brain injury is uncommon among boxers, a danger of brain damage exists if exposure is prolonged. This is a danger which can be clearly circumvented or even eliminated by retirement at the proper time.

In the past, outstanding boxers have been most reluctant to do this, shifting from place to place to avoid the resolutions of the various boxing bodies to prevent them from continuing. In former years, limitation of employment elsewhere had made Negro boxers particularly vulnerable to the hazards of extending their careers beyond health-wise boundaries. There seems to be less disposition to do this today as commission bans become more co-operative and opportunities elsewhere for Blacks increase. Eye injuries, usually retinal, are a menace to boxers and those so afflicted should be quickly barred.

Human weakness of the too-much-too-soon syndrome has been the bane of all boxers; leading all too often to the dissipation of thousands of dollars. Negro boxers have been no exception, to say the least. As the mainstay of Madison Square Garden boxing during the World War II period, former lightweight champion Beau Jack was responsible for receipts of more than $1,000,000, but his last stop was a Miami hotel shoeshine stand which, incidentally, clears him more than fifty dollars a day. The introduction of the lawyer and the accountant into the fiscal lives of fighters is designed, and appears destined, to make this type of fate improbable for modern boxers. Joe Frazier's corporate setup is indicative of this new trend, which allots a certain amount of his money to the boxer while retaining control of the major part of it.

There are scant traces of any inequalities in the ring game today. But for many years, particularly during the Prohibition Era, when betting on boxing was at its peak, the Black fighter often found that a lucrative match was polluted with a "proposition." The late Bill Farnsworth, then sports editor of the New York Journal-American, thought this was the case when he covered the Young Jack Thompson-Jimmy McLarnin match in Madison Square Garden back in 1930. Wrote Farnsworth, " . . . It is the opinion of this writer that the fans who witnessed the Jimmy McLarnin-Young Jack Thompson fight at the Garden last night were sitting in on one of the cleverest barneys of all time in the history of boxing. The official decision of the Evening Journal is that of Hype Igoe, our most able boxing expert, and old Hypus thinks that McLarnin won and that he won strictly on the up and up. Bill Corum figured Thompson the winner. A draw was the worst the Negro should have received, as he scored the points. But regardless of who won, it is the writer's belief that Thompson was under a pull. He could have won the decision from here to his native California and back had he wanted to . . . just as sure as I am writing this piece Thompson never tried to win this fight. Whenever the Negro came out from under wraps, he gave McLarnin a boxing lesson, making the baby-faced Irishman look like an amateur . . . "

Color blindness in awarding a close decision has come to be taken for granted nowadays, with no reason to believe otherwise. But for many years this was not the case, and the Negro boxer's edge had to be very substantial in a mixed championship bout. One of the victims of this persistent practice years ago was Kid Chocolate, who in these equitable times probably would have been a triple champion. The decisions which went against him would probably have been in his favor when he fought Tony Canzoneri for the lightweight championship and Jackie Kid Berg for the junior welterweight crown back in the Thirties, were he boxing today.

The characters of the Caucasian managers of the Negro champions were, over the years, as variable as human nature itself, running the gamut from outright roguery to genuine affection for their charges. In all fairness to them, the management of Negro fighters, frightfully frustrating at best, was not without some personal risk. Tom O'Rourke, once attacked by irate ringsiders at a Dixon [sic] fight in Providence, R.I., narrowly escaped with his life. Such incidents were not uncommon in the old days. A consensus of the cognoscenti, besides those mentioned in previous articles, names such people as Gil Clancy, Papa Bob Levy, Bobby Melnick, Eddie Walker, Luis Guitterez, Charley Johnston, Suey Welch, Jersey Jones and Jake Mintz as having done well by the Negro boxers they managed.

Boxing, like life itself, exists in sunshine and shadow, its darker recesses illuminated by fame's spotlight, money, and the adulation of the crowd. For many years the Negro boxing champion was the most visible representative of a repressed race, the very existence of which, except in menial capacities, was largely ignored by the great mass of Americans. Therefore, the fighter found himself in the isolated role of a kind of ambassador to a majority group from a minority with which it commonly had little contact.

How well Gans played this part has been explored in a prior piece, and Joe Louis, as heavyweight champion, was the most famous Negro of his time. Of all the great Negro boxers of the past, Archie Moore best symbolizes the public favorite. Archie, who came upon his great days late in athletic life, was a virtuoso at playing upon the strings of public affection. An opportunist who turned this talent to a worthwhile purpose, he showed that retirement has not diminished his instinct for the proper gesture by reading a poem written by him and dedicated to the memory of the late Rocky Marciano at a boxing show on the Coast some months ago.

Taken as a group, the Negro champions—with rare exceptions—give the lie to baseball manager Leo Durocher's oft-quoted "Nice guys finish last." By and large they fit comfortably into the 'good guy' category. Products mainly of rugged early environments and barren circumstances, some of them surmounted juvenile indiscretion to become distinguished for good natured likeability and commendable conduct.

The presence of foreigners on the accompanying list accounts for the designation of "colored." There is considerable confusion among Americans both black and white, as to the acceptable nomenclature for those of African or part African descent. To keep everyone happy throughout these articles, a variety of terms has been used. In their native countries none of those listed probably would be referred to as 'Negroes.' But all of them are sufficiently dark-skinned to have been confronted with the problems—receding but not extinct—familiar to Americans of color in the United States.

All of these overseas champions, national heroes in their homelands, performed in the United States, leaving lasting impressions on the sporting public. One of the first, as well as one of the most pathetic and ill-used of these visitors, was the Black African from Senegal, Battling Siki. The tragic trek of Siki from his ancestral Africa to death in a Hell's Kitchen gutter in New York encompassed heroism in World War I; winning the light heavyweight championship from the faded French idol, Georges Carpentier; losing it to the Irishman Mike McTigue, in Dublin on St. Patrick's Day, and a turbulent stay in this country which culminated in his murder. This was a crime in which the authorities, after apprehending a suspect who allegedly confessed, proved so derelict in enforcing justice that the New York Daily News caustically commented " . . . The white man's law failed to avenge the boy from Africa's jungles." And indeed, it had not. Two bullets in the back had been civilization's gift to the man they called the "Jungle Boy." Freedom for his killers was our society's farewell.

Many years were to pass before another Black African, Dick Tiger, was to prove by contrast the fallacy of categorising men of similar ethnic strain. The ailings which were Siki's—eccentric behavior and overindulgence in liquor—were, and are, as alien to Tiger as could possibly be. The Nigerian was the other extreme in the personality spectrum. The last word in formal dignity and decorum, this affable African family man in his long years of campaigning in the United States, exceeded all foreign fighters for popularity.

On the whole, U.S. boxing aficionados have taken so kindly to dark-skinned Latin American boxers that their popularity here has equalled that in their own countries. As mentioned previously, the charismatic Kid Chocolate was a major factor in regaining the ground lost by Negro boxers following the Johnson era, and Kid Gavilan, now a U.S. resident, ranked near the top of the fighting favorites of his time.

Another key to the cause for the high favor in which colored champions have been held is the American obsession with meritorious achievement. The feats of such legendary fighters as Louis, Armstrong and Robinson are supplemented by Sandy Saddler's retiring as a fine featherweight champion; Joe Brown's record of defending the lightweight championship successfully more times than anyone else and Emile Griffith as a welterweight twice winning the heavier middleweight championship.

The great majority of the champions served an apprenticeship as amateurs and as such the Black boxer has enjoyed equal eminence. The procession of Golden Glove, national, international and Armed Service champions has been unending, reaching a roaring crest in 1952 at the Helsinki Olympic Games when the United States won five Olympic championships; the winners, led by Floyd Patterson, all being Negroes.

American affluence and medical advances are rapidly making small statesiders a vanishing species, and this lack is keenly felt both in the amateur and professional boxing ranks. Today America's boxing strength has become concentrated in the larger classes with Clay, Frazier, Ellis and light heavyweight champion Bob Foster being Uncle Sam's standard bearers.

All-time selection is a game anyone can play revolving as it does around personal opinion. The fact that he is a contemporary undoubtedly helps his case, but any present-day consensus singles out Ray Robinson as the greatest Negro fighter of all time. What disagreement there is, comes from those to whom the past is present. Their dissent cannot be ignored however for they do have the advantage of long experience. Conspicuous among these are Nat Fleischer, Editor of this magazine, still loyal to Jack Johnson, as first choice and hardy veteran Charley Rose, who places Sam Langford at the top. Veteran confrere Jersey Jones joins Archie Moore in rating non-champion Charley Burley as the all-round best. Space limitations preclude any extended exposition of the reasons for the appended selections but complete records of all those so named are accessible in the Ring Record Book and disputants are welcome to their own choices and rankings.

For many years chances to become champions did not come easy for Negro fighters with the result that many colored boxers of title qualifications remained merely contenders throughout their boxing careers. Among these were Lloyd Marshall, Chick Suggs, Baby Joe Gans, Allentown Joe Gans, Flyweight Black Bill, Jack McVey, big George Godfrey, Jim Bivins, Charley Burley, Tommy Bell, California Jackie Wilson, Gene Burton, Tiger Jones, Cuban Kid Tunero, Pedro Montanez, Percy Bassett, Holley Mims, Henry Brimm, Bert Lytell, Holman Williams, Cocoa Kid, Al Gainer, and Australian aborigine Ron Richards. Some of these received title chances but most of them, for one reason or another, did not.

The Black man's achievements in boxing take on added lustre through such observations as that of the Belgian essayist Maurice Maeterlinck, "Boxing is the discipline of violence. It is violence civilized by conventions that are almost courteous. It is not degrading. It is a sport in which skill is required. Combative instincts are an integral part of our nature and those people who lack these instincts, lack mental energy."

Boxing's benefits to the Black man have been manifest in creating a respect for him engendered by his courage, physical prowess and discipline in the ring, by lifting him out of the anonymity imposed by social injustice; by providing a means of contact other than one of subservience between the races, and elevating the Negro as a champion of the world to a height which was, for many years, beyond his reach elsewhere.

Whatever one's feelings about pugilism, the position of boxing in any recounting of the Black man in America cannot be minimized. Throughout these articles an attempt has been made to drive home the realization that for many years this sport presented the sole opportunity for the Negro to assert his manhood, long suppressed by slavery and the aftermath of racial bias. The Black man's response to this challenge is historical. Success in boxing necessitates physical courage, strength and muscular coordination; fortitude under the stress of pain; body condition and emotional control. Whatever the milieu in which they predominate, these are qualities which warrant the highest respect as the so-called masculine virtues.

4

BRAINS VS. BRAWN

Although inclined by temperament to favor brains over brawn, Carroll knew that punchers were always in with a chance. His article by that name in the June 1939 issue of *The Ring*, written on the eve of "Two Ton" Tony Galento's match with Joe Louis for the heavyweight crown, was a prescient and eloquent warning to the "Brown Bomber" to watch out for his opponent's murderous left hook. From Jack Dempsey vs. Luis Firpo, when the crude "Wild Bull of the Pampas" came within a hair's breadth of separating the "Manassa Mauler" from his senses and the title; through light heavyweight Paul Berlenbach finally catching slick boxing Jimmy Slattery; to middleweight great Stanley Ketchel, outpointed nearly all the way by "Philadelphia" Jack O'Brien, ending the fight in the tenth and last round with a single sensational blow; and many more examples too numerous to relate, victory could always be snatched from the jaws of defeat by one mighty punch.

But what were the secrets of hitting hard? An article in *The Ring* for April 1941 recalled Carroll's encounters over the course of a single day with Jack Johnson, in *Ring* editor Nat Fleischer's unwavering opinion, the greatest of all heavyweight champions; boxing experts "Dumb" Dan Morgan and "Professor" Billy McCarney; old-time "White Hope" Gunboat Smith; peerless former lightweight king Benny Leonard, himself a devastating puncher; and Jack Kearns, Dempsey's onetime manager. Each one of them had a different explanation. Johnson was adamant that stance and balance was the key. Others attributed punching power variously to nervous tension or concentration or body drive, or as Leonard insisted, it all came down to confidence. Fleischer himself thought wide shoulders held the secret. Belying his spindly legs, onetime blacksmith and former heavyweight title holder Bob Fitzsimmons's extraordinary upper body strength meant he could punch with the best of them. Or maybe there was no secret after all. Declared McCarney, "When all is said and done, the best hitters all came by their punching powers naturally."

If anything could offset punching power, thought Carroll in April 1940, it was stamina. He had particularly in mind Henry Armstrong whose never-ceasing attack wore down one opponent after another. Because twenty-, forty-, and fifty-round fights were things of the past, stamina now tended to be over-looked as a vital ring asset, but those boxers who possessed it took some beating. Harry Greb famously set a terrific pace from start to finish, as did light heavyweight "Slapsie Maxie" Rosenbloom and, in the lighter weight divisions, Jackie "Kid" Berg and Pancho Villa. The "Nebraska Wildcat," Ace Hudkins, was another fighter who never seemed to tire, beating good men in four divisions, from lightweight to lightheavy. Stamina and endurance were often enough to overcome heavier poundage, superior skill, or greater hitting power.

Some twenty years apart, in the June 1942 and June 1964 issues of *The Ring*, Carroll mulled over the question of boxing styles. The classic upright stance of past heavyweight champion James J. Corbett, relying on defensive use of the straight left, had largely been replaced by the savage slugging style of Jack Dempsey. A few exceptions aside, notably 1920s light heavyweight champion Tommy Loughran, the old-school style of defensive boxing was largely obsolete a decade later. By present-day standards, Billy Conn was a clever boxer, acknowledged Carroll in 1942, but the fiery Pittsburgher, he concluded, was much too prone to trading punches ever to qualify as a defensive master of bygone days. What old-timers would have made of Cassius Clay/Muhammad Ali's style can only be guessed at. "The Greatest's" fast-stepping, quick-thinking dismantling of plodding Sonny Liston in February 1964, a fighter deemed unbeatable on the basis of his two crushing victories over Floyd Patterson, prompted Carroll's musings a few months later about fistic greats and their style nemesis. Joe Louis always had difficulty with opponents who got down low against him, most memorably in his first fight against the Chilean Arturo Godoy, who, by crouching almost to the ground, received the vote of one of the judges. Even all-time great Sugar Ray Robinson had trouble with fighters who, on his own admission, he had "to look for," boxers who kept moving, bobbing, and weaving.

Why, Carroll wondered in *The Ring*'s March 1955 issue, were some fighters able to keep going for much longer than others? The careers of Jersey Joe Walcott, Archie Moore, and Sugar Ray Robinson each stretched over three de-cades. It couldn't be size alone. There were too many exceptions to the notion that smaller men matured faster than heavyweights. World flyweight champ Pascual Perez of Argentina was still going strong at age thirty-five, while former heavyweight contender Tami Mauriello was washed up at twenty-four, an age when champion Rocky Marciano was still in the amateur ranks. Close to hand was the example of recently retired welterweight contender Tony Janiro, whose career had peaked when he was barely out of his teens and was effectively over by the time he was twenty-one. Carroll concluded that one thing was for sure. Fast living at twenty-one was unlikely to produce fast movement at thirty-one.

Sugar Ray's remarkable ring longevity may have been helped by the fact that last to go is a fighter's punch. But the fact that in Robinson's case power was exceptionally combined with peerless boxing skill caused Carroll to return time and again to the perennial question of boxer vs. puncher. In October 1963 middleweight contenders Joey Archer and Rubin "Hurricane" Carter met in Madison Square Garden, with the smart boxing Archer winning a close ten-round split decision over the thunderous punching Carter. With the referee and one judge voting 5–4–1 and 6–4 for New Yorker Archer and the other judge seeing it as 5–4–1 for New Jerseyite Carter, a ringside poll immediately after the fight found the press 9 to 5 in favor of Carter. The biggest problem, as Carroll understood it, was the weight accorded for misses. Some experts thought that the ability to make an opponent miss was boxing at its best and should be counted the same as punches landed. Others believed that unless there was a countering blow as a result of the miss, the scoring should not be affected. These differing interpretations caused Archer's supporters to cheer whenever he made Carter miss, but because Joey rarely attempted a countering punch, he was condemned by the "Hurricane's" fans.

There Carroll left the question until nearly seven years later when Scotland's brilliant Ken Buchanan outpointed Panama's Ismael Laguna, himself no mean boxer, for the lightweight title. The dazzling skills displayed by both fighters on that occasion prompted Carroll to reflect on what he termed boxing's central contradiction. At one and the same time, the sweet science glorified the KO, nullifying everything that had happened before it, while it also celebrated under Marquis of Queensbury rules the art of self-defense. Did the ability to avoid punishment rank alongside the power to inflict it? Those who insisted that boxing was a game of skill needed to look no further than the lightweight division itself. Joe Gans, Freddy Welsh, Benny Leonard, Sammy Mandell, Tony Canzoneri (one of Carroll's all-time favorite fighters), and in recent times Joe "Old Bones" Brown were all exceptionally talented boxers, Gans and Leonard particularly so. Buchanan, who self-consciously modeled his moves along the ropes on Sugar Ray Robinson, was believed by Carroll in December 1971 to be one of the cleverest boxers to have sat on the lightweight throne. Always gratifying to see skill prevail in the ring, declared Carroll, since it gave the lie to the idea that brute force was boxing's dominant characteristic. Alas, Carroll would live long enough to see Buchanan's title pass to Roberto "Fists of Stone" Durán. He would have relished Durán's befuddled loss—"no más"—to boxing master Sugar Ray Leonard.

June 1939   Puncher Always Has a Chance
April 1940   Stamina Is a Great Ring Asset
April 1941   Secrets of Hitting
March 1955   Age vs. Experience
June 1964   Every Fistic Great Has Style Nemesis
December 1971   KOs Thrill but the Name of the Game Is Boxing and
                   Buchanan Proves It

PUNCHER ALWAYS HAS A CHANCE

Some years ago in a signed article, Gene Tunney, retired undefeated heavyweight champion of the world, made a surprising statement in the course of his treatise on the ring game and its ramifications. A punch, proclaimed the learned Gene, is the best defense! This statement is not too amazing by itself, but coming from a master of the finer points of the pugilistic art, it was a real eyebrow lifter. What Mr. Tunney obviously meant, was that the possessor of a wallop inspired a respect in his opponent that caused said opponent to withhold his attack, through fear of being nailed by a finishing blow.

Tunney's declaration is brought back to mind by the recent announcement of the signing of Louis and Galento for a title match this coming June. While there is a general disposition throughout the world to laugh off the animated beer barrel from Orange, New Jersey as a dangerous threat to the Brown Bomber, it cannot be denied that the colorful Italian can punch. Much has been said and written of Tony's lack of any kind of defense, but it might do the critics some good to ponder over the wise words of Tunney regarding a punch as a defence mechanism in boxing.

Few boxers in the ring today have less claim to mastery of the intricacies of defensive boxing than Galento, but still and all, here is the Jersey Jumbo matched to meet the champion of the world. What Leroy Haynes and Lorenzo Pack have forgotten about the fine points of boxing Galento will never know, but they paid off on Tony both times as Leroy and Lorenzo wound up on the canvas. Some of Galento's recent bouts have been regarded with mixed emotions by many, but last summer before he was floored by Kid Pneumonia, the moon-faced mauler really possessed a punch—and how!

If by the time June rolls around, Galento has regained that robust riotousness that was his prior to his illness, and all the steam of last summer is back in that left hook, he must be given some kind of a chance against even so great a fighter as Joe Louis. Why? Because it has been proven many times in the past that a man with a punch has a chance.

Galento is crude, but no cruder than Firpo. Louis is great, but no greater than Dempsey, and if ever a man missed a world's title by an eyelash, the old Wild Bull of the Pampas was the man. Some still stoutly declare that the shaggy maned South American didn't miss it at all but actually won the world's crown that September night in 1923. Ever since that memorable evening, there have been speculations as to what would have happened had a manager and handler like wily old Leo P. Flynn, shouting Joe Jacobs, or cagy Jack Kearns been behind the Argentinian rather than the non-English speaking nonentities that the frugal Firpo retained to represent him. The bout might have possibly ended ten seconds after Dempsey was catapulted out of the ring by the lumbering Luis, with the Argentinian champion of the world.

On form, Firpo could be conceded no more chance against the swift striking Dempsey than Two Ton Tony is given against the equally lightning-like Louis, but the old Wild Bull had a punch, and that was almost enough. It might have been more than enough had penny-pinching Luis Angel seen his way clear to hire a competent American advisor. This is probably the most eloquent example in recent ring history of the danger that pure and simple punching power alone presents in the prize ring to even the greatest of fighters. Dempsey was as close to defeat as it is possible for a man to be, when Firpo knocked him out of the ring after being floored himself a couple of times in their primitive struggle. Dempsey came back to flatten the Argentinian in the second round, aided by a liberal interpretation of the rules, but Jack had one narrow escape that night.

Benny Leonard had a somewhat similar experience against hard smashing Charley White. White was almost purely a puncher. The Chicagoan possessed one of the hardest left hooks in ring annals and made trouble for every good fighter he ever met. He was a good fighter in other respects, but not to be classed with the masterful Leonard as an all-round performer. Still in their East Chicago fight back in 1920, White landed his left hook and "a la Firpo" knocked Benny Leonard out of the ring. How long Benny stayed out is still a matter of argument, but great fighter that he was, he caught up with Charley and knocked him out. In connection with this one Leonard talks interestingly, and also discloses his keen ring generalship and quickness to capitalize on a rival's slightest error.

"I noticed," says Benny, "after I got the fog out of my noodle after tumbling out of the ring, that White never threw his left hook without slightly raising his left foot first. I went along with Charley for a couple of rounds after being knocked down until the ninth round.

"A slow thinker, White must have thought I was tiring for in the ninth I saw his left foot raise off the canvas just a bit, and as he made this movement I threw as hard a right as I ever did in my life, beat him to the punch, and down he went. The referee seemed to be taking his time counting and White got up before the count was over.

"He was in bad shape, and I wrapped him up another pill and he went down again. I took no chances on the referee's arithmetic this time and counted along with him and raised my own hand at the count of ten. White was slow but could he punch!"

Joe Louis and his very capable board of strategy should be the last to make little of Galento or any other hitter's chance in the light of past developments. Schmeling was, if possible, a shorter ender than Galento will be, in his first meeting with Joe in 1936. But again the German could still punch and the rest is history. The public, Mike Jacobs, and Louis and his mentors all forgot that the Black Uhlan was a hitter and discounted his chances, thereby setting the stage for one of the greatest ring upsets.

No prize fighter went further with a punch and punch alone, than Paul Berlenbach, former light-heavyweight champion of the world. Although a powerful man physically, the Astoria Assassin was not punch-proof himself, and his boxing skill was that of a muscle-bound wrestler, as he began his athletic career as a grappler. The plodding German could really lay them in though, his left hook to the body was a numbing blow that seemed to paralyze his opponents and render them helpless. Berlenbach couldn't box himself, but he knew the formula for the clever fellows. When he met Young Stribling in 1926 in New York, the skilful Southerner was highly favored to relieve him of his light-heavyweight laurels. The New Yorker solved the problem of the tricky feinting Stribling simply and effectively by pounding the Georgia boy's arms until he could hardly raise them, with his deafening left-handed blows, and winning the decision handily.

Stribling wasn't the only above the average boxer who found the Astorian's punch too much for him. Another victim of Berlenbach's crude punching prowess was young Jimmy Slattery. One of the most beautiful boxers of that or any other day, the stylish Buffalonian made plodding Paul look like the re-formed wrestler he was for nine rounds of their fight on September 11, 1925, in New York City. Drifting about the ring like a moonbeam on the surface of a lake, arms dangling at his side, his every move a symphony of muscular action, Slattery's boxing was like a dream come true. All Berlenbach had to offer against the slim Irish lad's dazzling repertoire of ring tricks and finesse was a punch, but that was all he needed as the willowy boy from Buffalo's old First Ward wilted under his numbing blows and succumbed to an eleventh round knockout. . . .

Not only does a puncher always have a chance; he has a chance up to the last minute! Whereby a boxer must have time to work his tricks and amass the points that give him a victory total, the man with the punch can be hopelessly behind but still snatch victory from the jaws of defeat in the waning minutes of a contest, with one single blow.

A famous instance of this occurred in the bout that was to have tragic consequences between Max Baer and Ernie Schaaf in Chicago on August 31, 1932. Far ahead on points, the ex-sailor, at the time the No. 1 heavyweight hope of the country, was knocked cold eight seconds before the final bell by one of Baer's wild rights that came whistling out of the smoky atmosphere.

The finish of the bout between the great Stanley Ketchel and the talented Philadelphia Jack O'Brien was perhaps the most celebrated example of the ever-present danger that lurks in a power-packed mitt. The superlatively clever O'Brien had a comfortable lead on points going into the last round of his ten-round contest with Ketchel back in 1909. Three seconds before the fight ended, Ketchel landed one of the wallops that have made his name famous to this day, and the gong ended the fight with O'Brien dead to the world with his head in the resin box and the referee counting over him. This was one of the most sensational finishes to a bout between outstanding men and old-timers who were lucky enough to be in the old National Sporting Club in New York City on March 26, 1909, never fail to bring this one up when great battles of the past are mentioned.

Dempsey, according to his own testimony, had another narrow escape from disaster at the hands of a lightly regarded opponent who however could punch a bit. Rickard, ignoring the fact that Carpentier, despite his small size, was a dangerous hitter, is supposed to have requested Dempsey to coast along with the 170-pound Frenchman for a couple of rounds and not disappoint the tremendous crowd, first of the million-dollar gates, with a too easy knockout. Dempsey is said to have acquiesced, with the result that the Orchid Man nailed him with his vaunted right in the second. Dempsey declares he has never been hit any harder, and went right after Carpentier from then on.

Every now and then a punch is the medium through which an otherwise mediocre boxer ascends the championship throne. Al McCoy of Brooklyn, who has come down through the years as the "cheese champ" of the middleweights, was such a one. Whatever his other abilities, McCoy could hit and one April night in Brooklyn, N.Y., in 1914, this Jewish boy closed his eyes, swung from the floor, and landed on the chin of the then middleweight champion, George

Chip, the capable Pittsburgher, and found himself the world title-holder less than a round after the opening gong. Few gave the Brooklynite a chance, but his punch took care of that.

In view of his recent performances and inasmuch as he seems to be a young man who learns his lessons well, Joe Louis does not figure to be caught napping as he was in the first Schmeling affair. He will no doubt enter the ring well prepared to offset the terrors of the Galento left hook, and being much the faster man, will probably beat the Jersey Gargantuan to the punch—but if he doesn't—and Tony should land first, it may well be the shot heard around the world, for a man with a punch is man with a chance.

STAMINA IS A GREAT RING ASSET

In ranking great boxers of the past and present, most followers of the fistic game usually rate skilful boxers and hard hitters among the top-notch fighters of all time. These critics and fans are prone to overlook one of the most valuable ring assets any fighter can possess, stamina or endurance. The ability to set and hold a pace so terrific in its intensity that the most scientific of boxers and the hardest of punchers eventually wilt under the pressure and succumb to exhaustion, has carried many famed fighters to the top of their profession.

In the old days of twenty-, forty- and fifty-round bouts, the quality of endurance was a vital one to any aspiring pugilist. In recent years the ring game has become refined to the extent that long distance contests are no longer the style, and as a result, the importance of stamina to a boxer has been generally overlooked.

That the ability to maintain a fast clip in a ring battle still is as important as of yore, is brought strongly to light in the amazing career of Henry Armstrong. While Henry possesses other necessary attributes of the great fighter, namely a puzzling bobbing and weaving defense, a cast-iron chin, and a stinging overhand right, the real secret of his success is the durability of his never ceasing attack and his ability to wear down almost any opponent.

This was strikingly evident in his recent embroglio with Pedro Montanez, one of the most slashing slugfests ever seen in the Madison Square Garden ring. In almost everything but stamina the Puerto Rican was Armstrong's equal, but in this vital asset he fell short of matching his demoniac opponent and that was his undoing. In fighting heart, ability to assimilate punishment, hitting power, boxing skill, gameness and weight, Montanez was the equal of the champion. But the outrageous Islander, whose thrilling demonstration of courage will never be forgotten, couldn't hold the fantastic pace the untiring Armstrong maintained for eight rounds. In examining Armstrong's record, it is significant that the only men to give him any real opposition were those whose endurance matched his—Lou Ambers and Baby Arizmendi.

While on the subject of stamina, Ambers has frequently shown lasting qualities about the equal of Armstrong's. The Herkimer Hurricane, in both his melees with Henry, came roaring down the homestretch neck and neck with the route-going Armstrong. Indeed, in their first battle, Lou survived a terrible going over in the early stanzas to finish up in better shape than the hustling Henry, who was considerably the worse for wear at the final gong. In their second meeting, the upstate New Yorker stepped right along with Homicide Hank and was as fresh as the little tan tornado at the finish. Whenever the question of endurance is brought up, Lou Ambers has to be rated right up there. . . .

Armstrong's blistering trail to three titles was strewn with the figures of many accomplished boxers and knockout artists—Ross, Sarron, Belloise, Beauhuld, Venturi, among others. All were masters of the art of self-defense. Garcia, Bass and Montanez all packed plenty of power in their mitts. All these were badly beaten. Only the boys who could stay with Henry's pace were able to give him any trouble.

Down through the years, the name of one man has become synonymous with stamina in the ring. Battling Nelson was the man whose endurance has become almost legendary. Old-timers tell us that the Durable Dane was neither a great boxer nor a great hitter, but his staying powers were superhuman. Some of them even say that under present day conditions and ten-round bouts, the Battler might have been just another fighter, but it was the Dane's good fortune to be around in the days of the marathon fights and that was certainly to his liking. Nelson became famous for his twenty-round brawls with such as Aurelio Herrerra, the thunder-fisted Mexican, whom he outlasted and outgamed back in 1904; and the late Jimmy Britt, to whom he lost a twenty-round verdict the same year in a fight billed as for the lightweight championship of the world.

However, the two fights which are always recalled whenever great lightweight battles are discussed, are Nelson's forty-two-round go with the great Joe Gans, which the Durable Dane lost on a foul, and his savage primitive tangle with Ad Wolgast, another route-going gladiator. That lasted forty rounds. Almost impervious to punishment in his prime, Nelson followed the tactics of Armstrong in the present day. His style was simple. He wore his more talented rivals down by the overpowering relentlessness of his unending attack until they succumbed from exhaustion.

Against the masterly Gans, whom he met three times, he dogged the peerless champion doggedly each time. Finally, in their third and last contest, July 4, 1908, with the world's lightweight championship at stake, the Old Master, weakened by weight-making and disease, finally fell before his relentless rival at San Francisco in seventeen rounds.

A year previous Nelson had caught up with the classy Californian, Jimmy Britt, with an eighteen-round knockout over the then lightweight title claimant in

Colma, Cal., and his victory over Gans at last rewarded him with a clear and undisputed claim to the world's lightweight championship.

Oddly enough, the man who conquered Nelson was of the same rugged enduring mold. Ad Wolgast, the Cadillac Bearcat, was the man who ended the Durable One's reign over the world's lightweights with a bit of help from Father Time, at Port Richmond, Canada, February 22, 1910.

Ironically, Nelson, the man who wore down the greatest, was himself run to a state of collapse and exhaustion in this losing effort that cost him his crown. This forty-five-round contest is one of the memorable classics of the prize ring. Nelson, the unflinching, the human machine who never ran down, the man whose inhuman endurance had been too much for some of the ring's great masters to overcome, himself succumbed to the same tactics. Stamina coupled with youth proved the undoing of the one-time untiring marvel of the ring, and in the forty-fifth round he slumped wearily to the floor, victim of a younger man whose endurance was greater than his.

Thus, the lightweight crown passed from the head of one tireless warrior to that of another when Wolgast defeated Nelson. Wolgast, like Nelson, was not impressively equipped with any of the ring talents. He was a good puncher, not a great one, but his stamina was enough to crown him king of his class.

The years rolled by and no boxer appeared on the fistic horizon with endurance qualities comparable to those of Wolgast and Nelson until the appearance of Ace Hudkins on the scene about fifteen years later. The one-time Nebraska Wildcat was born fifty years too late. He was a throwback to the stone age of pugilism, the days when men battled until one fell exhausted to the turf. This yellow haired toughie used to shadow box ten rounds at a fast clip in his dressing room before his fights, and then complain that he couldn't get started at the end of a ten-round go.

Hudkins was anything but clever. He was a fair puncher only, but every man who ever boxed him was mighty glad when the final gong rang. The Ace laid his head on his opponent's shoulder in the Armstrong manner and flailed away endlessly. He never seemed to tire. . . . Hudkins' stamina and little else, carried him to a fortune, and with better breaks, would have gained him a title, for even Mickey Walker himself agrees that the Nebraskan received none the better of the decision that retained Mike's middleweight title for him that rainswept night in Chicago in 1928 after ten of the bloodiest, brawlingest rounds ever seen in a Windy City ring. "When you got in there with that egg," says Mickey, "you sure knew you were in a fight. He never let up and was a real good tough fighter."

Among the big fellows there have been many more talented fighters than gold-toothed Paulino Uzcudun, but it is doubtful if any heavyweight ever possessed better staying powers. Paulino, like Hudkins, was born in the wrong era. The Basque might have been champion had he come along in the twenty-round days. As it was, he did handy with the outstanding men of his time on stamina mainly, along with an oaken ribbed body and a steel chin.

Paulino's twenty-rounder with Max Baer under an equatorial Nevada sun in Reno, Nevada, in 1931, was a test of endurance unsurpassed in recent ring history. The steaming atmosphere boiled fighters, handlers and spectators alike, and although Baer, in those days, a powerful, hard-hitting youngster, had greater physical assets, the Spaniard's iron constitution stood him in good stead that broiling day and he gained the decision. Paulino displayed the same lasting abilities in all his ring battles. Often beaten, he always acquitted himself well and was never knocked down or stopped until Louis turned the trick when his best days were long behind him.

Contemporary with Uzcudun and strongly similar to him in the possession of unusual stamina was the Cleveland Rubber Man, Johnny Risko. The blubbery Ohioan never seemed to get tired although he was built very much on the pudgy side. Like Paulino, his endurance saw him through a long and honorable career in the ring despite his lack of other outstanding talents. Johnny could throw 'em and keep throwing 'em without a let-up for any distance, and he still plays the tank town circuit every now and then when he desires a little ready cash.

In race track parlance, a horse with endurance is known as either a "router" or a "stayer," and no thoroughbred has ever attained real greatness minus this ability. This shows the importance of stamina to finely bred horses and the same thing goes for fighting men.

Bat Battalino, Billy Petrolle, Harry Greb, Mike O'Dowd, Maxie Rosenbloom, a tireless fellow if ever there was one, Tiger Flowers, were some of the great ones who possessed plenty of staying qualities. Ditto Jack Kid Berg, Louis Kid Kaplan, Pancho Villa. But some of these also had plenty on the ball besides the ability to set a terrific pace, but in many cases their stamina alone made them outstanding. Jim Jeffries, along with other abilities, probably possessed more stamina than any big man who ever lived.

Against Montanez, Armstrong, who had shown signs of decay in some of his recent outings, was more persistently aggressive than ever. Some place, somewhere, the Perpetual Motion Man has apparently replenished the supply of whatever he uses for fuel to keep his amazing fistic machinery moving. Armstrong's career is a good example of what stamina and persistency can accomplish not only in the ring, but in almost any other calling. Henry, like the other battlers mentioned, has proven that stamina and endurance are often enough to turn back all other obstacles and talents, such as weight, superior skill or greater hitting powers.

SECRETS OF HITTING

Jack Johnson, Former World Heavyweight King, and Other Experts Tell What Makes a Fighter Stand Out

The burly figure of Jack Johnson, former king of the heavyweights, passed through the door of the outer office of THE RING into the sanctum of the Editor, Nat Fleischer. With his usual broad smile, he greeted all hands, then sat himself into the huge arm chair opposite the Editor's desk.

The models of the right hand of Jack Johnson, Jack Dempsey, Joe Louis and Henry Armstrong, made by Dr. Walter Jacobs, New York dentist, were on Nat's desk. Several newspapermen were listening to a little talk Fleischer was giving on how famous fighters acquired their punching power, when genial Jack Johnson, a doleful expression flitting across his expansive features, seemed to sink a little deeper into the chair as Nat, pointing to the deformity in the knuckles of Armstrong's hand, explained why Henry hit from the side as compared to the straight shots of other great fighters.

"Too bad, too bad," chirped in Johnson. "You've hit the nail right on the head in your explanation, but there is something more about Armstrong that needs explaining." The former world heavyweight champion, with his picturesque beret covering his bald head, rose from his chair, picked up the model of Armstrong's hand, examined it closely, then picked up his own, and while looking it over carefully, repeated: "Too bad about lil' Armstrong. A great fighter who could have lasted much longer and hit much harder if he hadn't wasted so much energy. You know, Nat," he continued, while those in the room listened, "nobody ever wasted energy like that boy. He reminded me of the Niagara Falls, the way he used up all that power—much of it uselessly. There was no way in the world he could have lasted any longer than he did, fighting that way."

"What would you say was the big difference between the old-timers and modern fighters like Armstrong, Jack," interposed Nat. "Stance, stance," almost shouted the ex-champion, his popping eyes emphasizing his reply. "The old fellows like Gans, Bobby Dobbs, Corbett, and Peter Jackson, were never off balance. They had it. Why can't the fighters of today get perfect balance?"

With an alacrity and springiness that belied his 60 odd years, the limber Mr. Johnson was on his feet demonstrating, with sliding rhythmic movements, the poses and action of the great fighters of long ago. "Notice my right foot," explained Lil' Arthur, "it always points away from my body at a right angle, now look at the pictures of the old boxing masters you have hung around this office and you'll see the same thing.

"What does that mean? Just this, Peter Jackson, Corbett, Choynski, McCoy, Fitz and myself, by simply taking a quick step with that right foot, were able to move, shift and pivot ourselves in such a way that we were always in perfect position to counter, with the full force of our bodies behind the blow. . . .

"Stance is not only the secret of real scientific boxing, it is the key to real hard punching too," went on the man who is regarded as one of the great masters of defensive boxing. "Louis is a good hitter, because he is a tremendously powerful man, with the smooth muscles of a great puncher, and a great fist, but if this stance were better, he would hit even harder." "He wouldn't be allowed in the ring if he hit any harder," laughed Nat Fleischer.

"But, Jack," I cut in, diplomatically, "I thought you were known more for your boxing than for your hitting." "Aha," Jack came back, "I was waiting for that, take a look at the record book, young fella, and you'll find out that Jack Johnson and not your Dempsey or Louis scored the most knockouts of all the heavyweight champions. And," he added, "against better men."

"Well, Jack, would you say that balance made Dempsey a great hitter," asked Fleischer. "You know he had anything but the stance of you old timers." "Dempsey had a style of punching all his own," explained the man from Galveston. "He punched out of a weave. He swayed from side to side then threw his whole body forward and often upward in sending a punch at his opponent. The blow would land with the weight of his whole body behind it and he threw it plenty fast, like a bullet. That's where he got his tremendous hitting power."

"It's a strange thing," pondered Fleischer, "how some fighters can punch and others cannot." "Nothing strange about it. How do you expect a fellow like Conn, for instance, who is never properly balanced, to be a hard hitter, with all the jumping around he does. He's never set. Now, Benny Leonard moved around, too, but he was always balanced and that's why he could punch," was Johnson's rejoinder. "Of course, some people can just punch and that's that. I remember old Fitz. Fitz was pretty old when he boxed me, but that old bald headed freckle face . . . how he could hit. He threw a punch at me that would have been the end of Jack Johnson if it had landed. It hummed like a swarm of bees, when it went by my head.

"Langford and Walcott were another pair of hard punchers, lemme tell you. That Walcott, he was a killer. Langford, too, with those arms almost down to his ankles, and those wide shoulders was one tough puncher." "Shoulders, that's where it comes from," chirped in Fleischer. "Take a look at Lew Jenkins, he looks like a tag of bones till you examine his shoulders and back. Fitz was the same way, all his power was in his shoulders. . . ."

"But poor Henry," broke in Johnson, "if he could only have saved a little of that energy for a rainy day, what a difference it would have made! How I wish a fellow like Bobby Dobbs had only been around to show Hank how to get the most out of the endurance the good Lord gave him," finished Johnson as he exited sadly from the office.

Johnson had barely closed the door behind him, when the sage of fistiana, the irrepressible Dumb Dan Morgan, came bustling in, trailed by big Gunboat Smith, one time star heavyweight. "I just saw Johnson downstairs, the old boy looks good," began the voluble Daniel.

"Yes, we were just discussing hitters and why they can hit," said Fleischer.

"Why they can hit? Easy—nervous tension, that's the answer." "Show me a jittery, nervous fighter, and I'll show you a guy who'll knock your block off. Dempsey couldn't stand still in the dressing room or in his corner before a fight, that meant that when he got out there he was like a stick of dynamite with the fuse lit. He just exploded all over the place, and heaven help the guy who was in there with him. Terry McGovern was the same way," vociferated Dan as he paused for his second wind.

"Louis ain't so nervous, Dan," grunted the Gunner with a sly wink. Not the least bit disturbed by this apparent refutation of his theory, Dan answered this challenge as follows: "I call Louis a concentration hitter. There are two kinds, the nervous guys and the concentration guys. Louis pays no attention to anything or anybody when he's in that ring, all he has his mind on is hitting the other guy on the chin, and that's what makes him a great puncher. The crowd, his corner, the referee could all be in Ireland for all Louis cares. You could set the ring on fire and he wouldn't even know it. He's got a job to do, flatten the other guy and that's all he realizes.

"Jimmy McLarnin was a lot the same way, he concentrated on the other fellow's mistakes, and the first time he made one he was a goner. I never saw a fighter so quick to take advantage of a slip on the part of the other fellow as McLarnin, that's because he was all concentration.

"Now Billy Conn is just the other way around, he's a concentration fighter too is all defense, his mind is on boxing not belting, that's why he's no puncher. When he started out McLarnin concentrated on boxing and became a marvelous boxer, later on he concentrated on hitting and what a walloper he was!

"Benny Leonard and Tony Canzoneri did pretty much the same thing. When they started to concentrate on punching, they did a mighty good job of it," orated Daniel.

Gunboat Smith seized on this lull in Morgan's conversational torrent to inject a surprising observation. "The best one punch hitter of 'em all was Georges Carpentier," rumbled the Gunner. "The Gunner should know, he fought both Langford and Dempsey," put in Fleischer. "You bet I know, Carpentier hit me a punch in London and I thought Buckingham Palace fell on me. Why, he almost flattened Dempsey with a punch and he was four years past his prime then. Carpentier was the only fighter who ever lived who could lead with a right hand and get away with it. He nailed everybody with it. I sure know he clipped me," concluded Gunboat Smith. . . .

Carroll's writing would regularly turn to an analysis of boxing styles and techniques—in this example, discussing the secrets of hitting. *The Ring* (April 1941)

Knowing that Morgan was good for hours, I slipped out the doorway, and hot footed it over towards Broadway, where who should I run into but Benny Leonard, making his way over to his new eatery. "Hello, Ben," I opened, "I just left THE RING office where a bunch of the boys were talking over what makes a hitter." "Confidence," declared the peerless Benny. "I know that's what made me one. When I was a kid I could always hit because I was a weak kid without too much confidence. And let me tell you, I used to do plenty of running and hiding in there until I got strong and confident enough to let real punches go. Then I was all right, and I did pretty well. Did you know I knocked out seven in a row before I won the crown from Welsh? Most of them guys who had gone the distance with me before, too. But I had confidence and that made all the difference in the world," said Benny as he hurried along his way to his restaurant.

That same evening in Jack Dempsey's restaurant I spied Jack Kearns, the famous doctor himself, in a huddle with a party of friends. Joining the group, I brought up the subject that had been under discussion that same afternoon. "Don't let anybody tell you that Jack Johnson couldn't punch when he wanted to," [declared Kearns]. "He was such a marvelous defensive boxer. He was often satisfied to go along outboxing his man, but he could lay them in, when he cared to . . ."

The party was joined by the ageless dapper old professor of the fight business, popular Billy McCarney. . . . "What have you to say on the secrets of hitting, Bill," was my greeting to Mr. McCarney whose opinions are always interesting, seasoned as they are with the wisdom of his years in the boxing game. "Well, first, a man can't be too fast and be a hitter, too. You have to sacrifice some speed if you want to be a puncher," began dapper Will. "Leonard was the fastest kid you ever saw until George Engel had him grip the canvas with his toes and set himself for a punch. Then he lost some of his speed, but developed a punch. After that Benny, who used to outbox everybody, started knocking them all out.

"All the great hitters were body hitters. They threw the whole weight of their bodies behind a punch. That was the difference between McGovern and Armstrong, for instance, Armstrong was an arm hitter, Terry, a better puncher than Henry, fought like him but threw his whole body behind every wallop. So, Kearns says Johnson was a puncher, eh? Yes, he was with a right-hand uppercut, if he caught the other fellow coming in. Johnson was one of the few men who seemed able to anticipate a punch. He picked them off in the air and countered with a right-hand uppercut to the heart.

"The reason so many of those frail fellows can knock an elephant down with a punch, is the body drive they put in a blow. Abe Attell was a wonderful boxer, but he could hit like blazes when he had a mind to. But after all is said and done, the best hitters all came by their punching powers naturally," finished Mr. McCarney.

Thus we have a variety of opinions on what makes a boxer capable of knockout punching, . . . all of them logical.

AGES OF MATURITY

Why some athletes have seen their best days at 23 and others are better than ever at 33 has been a matter of puzzlement for years. In baseball, Bob Fellew had hit his peak at 21 while Satchell Paige was still on the rise in his thirties.

Fistic activity during 1954 provided a couple of interesting maturity variations, in the decline of Gil Turner and rise of Teddy "Red Top" Davis. The flailing Philadelphian, a battle worn and weary veteran at 25, and the ringwise and durable Davis, now No. 1 featherweight contender with some 31 summers behind him, afford intriguing contrasts.

Of course, the energy consuming style of Turner doomed him to a curtailed career. But who threw more punches than the late Harry Greb, and he was still an exceptional boxer 10 years after he had started out. Johnny Dundee never stopped moving from gong to gong every time he climbed through the ropes, and this old-time featherweight was still good enough to win the featherweight title 13 years after his first fight, in 1923. Mickey Walker, not exactly a lazybones in the ring, was a great fighter for nearly two decades. Louis "Kid" Kaplan, one-time featherweight king, was another bell-to-bell busy bee who hung around a long time.

Turner is alleged to fancy out of ring frivolity in such fashion as to guarantee him an early exit. But here again Greb and Walker, long-lasters both, took back seats to no man when it came to combining fun with fighting.

Teddy "Red Top," a gnome-like little man, just has come into his own. Like most ring relics the St. Louisan is hazy about how long he has been on this planet, but there are recollections of Davis, then called Murray Cain, boxing in boys clubs and settlement house tournaments, more than 20 years ago, around New York. "Red Top" does not deny this. He merely smiles off all queries about his age.

Davis is a Jersey Joe Walcott in miniature. He also has a large family, and like the antique Jerseyman, gave no evidence at the start of his recorded career that he would rise above mediocrity. He was always kept busy enough, being welcome fodder for his early foes. In 1948, he fought 25 bouts, averaging better than 2 a month, and lost 15 of them! Included among those who worked over "Red Top" that year was Willie Pep, a two-time foe. Strangely enough, despite Davis' ragged record, Willie—who is no fool in things boxing—must have seen something in Davis. Following a third meeting in 1949, the one-time wizard installed himself as "Red Top's" manager. He settled the wandering Davis, who had been gypsying about the country, in Hartford, and functioned as his pilot for some time thereafter.

Like most boxers who have fought under various names, "Red Top's" ring beginnings are obscure. As "Davis," he extends back to 1946, when he picked up his boxing career following his return from service in World War II. As Murray Cain, it is anybody's guess how far back his ring record reaches. As he has seen his opponent's hand raised 47 times, Davis will hold an unflattering record for defeats suffered by a ring champion if he can win the 126 lb. title.

But all this is beside the point. "Red Top" is a live contender, okayed by all boxing bodies and Ring Magazine as the world's foremost aspirant for Sandy Saddler's crown. Like most of the ring "mechanics," the most effective of boxers, he has mastered all the finer points of his trade, and is able to put them into execution. Percy Bassett is younger than "Red Top," and was a two-time conqueror of Davis, when the Philadelphia boy was checkmated at every turn by the late ripening Red Top in the Garden No. 26. Davis a fighter who couldn't win in 1948, was invincible in 1954.

As unusual as is Davis, he had a counterpoint last year in "Boardwalk Billy" Smith, an ancient warrior, who as "Oakland Billy" Smith did little better than "Red Top" when he was in those golden Twenties. Smith, who admits to 33 and may be older, up to 1954, had gained no more than a left-handed claim to fame as the fellow who "took a walk" out of the ring, when things got too tough for him while boxing Archie Moore in Portland, Ore., in 1951.

Smith, whose recorded career drifts back into 1941, appears to have been a victim of unusually severe competition, rather than any lack of ability, in his early years. Such formidables as Archie Moore, Charley Burley, Ezzard Charles, Bert Lytell, Jimmy Bivins, Bob Satterfield, and Jack Chase, accounted for most of his reverses. Since these are rugged customers, the fact that he was able to survive such a campaign to come on again at such an advanced fighting age is indeed remarkable. . . . Shakespeare once asked, "What's in a name?" and Smith, like Davis, is qualified from the West Coast to the East, as "Boardwalk Billy," of Atlantic City, discarding the "Oakland" appellation, he really has roared into high, with a string of four straight kayos at this writing. . . .

On the other extreme, no great fighter ever had an earlier ring maturity than the hero of grand-dad's day, Terrible Terry McGovern. By the time he had reached his twenty-first birthday, this ring immortal was over the hill. He already had won the bantam and featherweight titles, and was only 21 when Young Corbett knocked him out in Hartford in 1901. The way thereafter was downward. One-time heavyweight contender Tami Mauriello had seen his best days at 24, an age at which champion Rocky Marciano was still in the amateur ranks. Jimmy Slattery never regained the form he flashed at 19, his age when he defeated Jack Delaney in the old Garden back in 1924.

Filipino fighters usually reach their prime early. Pancho Villa, former fly-weight king, while still good, had passed his peak while still in his early twenties. The one startling exception, Dado Marino, won the world's flyweight title at 34!

Boxers of Irish descent seemingly take on a second wind late in their athletic lives. Tunney was just hitting his stride at 30, his age when he pulverized old Hard Rock Tom Heeney in 1928. Old Mike McTigue did his best fighting when past 35, and James J. Braddock came out of retirement to win the heavyweight title, a better fighter in his thirties than he had been a decade earlier.

Irishman Rinty Monaghan was 28 when he won the world's flyweight title in 1948. Little men supposedly master faster than big fellows, but this theory is also refuted by the present flyweight king, Pascual Perez, whose age had been estimated at 35. One-time bantam king Johnny Buff topped all the tiny ones in this respect. He came out of the Navy at the age of 30, started fighting professionally at this late stage, and became one of the best. Billy Petrolle, like Braddock, came out of retirement a better fighter at 30 than he had been at 25.

Recently retired Tony Janiro is a sharp contemporary case of a fighter whose career hits its crest when he was barely out of his teens. At 21, his future had passed. Tony, however, like Kid Chocolate, a generation ago, who also had seen his best days when still in his early twenties, packed so much outside meandering into his youthful years he hurried the aging process along.

Old Jersey Joe Walcott stands out as the pre-eminent prototype of late maturity, and will probably remain so till the end of time. The man from Camden, N.J., an indifferent unwilling performer in his youth, waited until middle age was closing in on him, before becoming good enough to win the heavyweight championship of the world. No fighter ever enjoyed a happier "old age," pugilistically speaking, than Gus Lesnevich. The former light heavyweight champion made more money, gained greater glory, and did better fighting when past 30 than he ever did in his twenties. Competent but unexciting for years, the old pride of Cliffside, N.J., became a public hero with a string of spectacular performances back in 1947 when he was 32 years old.

Just what the actual prime of life for an athlete is remains a matter of speculation. The 19-year-old sensation may simply have reached his peak at that immature notch, and may never improve. The plodder of 23 may blossom into a world-beater at 31. The time of athletic maturity remains a mystery.

The secret remains closed even to those who, like Jersey Joe, thumbed their noses at Time. One thing is certain. Fast living at 21 is not likely to produce fast movement at 31.

EVERY FISTIC GREAT HAS STYLE NEMESIS

Clay Proved That Again as He Ran and Jabbed Liston out of Title

The Clay-Liston fight again demonstrated that fighting styles make the surest of "sure-things" and the laying of "long odds" ridiculous. Everyone sees clearly now that Cassius Clay's prancing, elusive, brand of boxing was the antidote for the kind of fistic poison dispensed by the ponderous, flat-footed losing champion. Clay's agility, supplemented by nimbleness of foot, hand and head, made his ten to one pre-fight figure nonsensical.

Ring Magazine, while going along with the consensus favoring Liston over the apparently fragile and inexperienced challenger, nevertheless did not fail to warn against pre-judging the contest as too lopsided with such comments as " . . . no one can discount Clay's speed of hand and foot. . . . Liston, his feet flatter than postage stamps on an envelope moves as though mired on a mat of mucilage, slow even for a heavyweight." "In leg speed Liston is most vulnerable . . . as shown in his match with fast stepping Eddie Machen. This looks like the only chink in Sonny's formidable fistic armour . . . a weak link in a chain can always be exploited and it is there the chances of Clay lie. . . ."

Long odds find themselves at the mercy of fighting styles because no matter how great the fighter there always is a certain style that troubles him.

Although a result startingly similar to the Clay shocker had taken place before their eyes less than three months before, fight people and the general public had failed to "get the message." This was the middleweight title match between then champion Dick Tiger, who was being rated among the best 160 pound champions of all time and the battle-worn and weary relic of 15 years of ring warfare Joey Giardello at Atlantic City.

The odds on Tiger to beat Giardello changed from three to five to one. The tactics used by Clay and Joey were identical. Giardello, like Clay, had disclosed his plan of battle beforehand. "Tiger eats up those guys who stand there and fight him like Florentino Fernandez and Fullmer. He's going to have to chase me, and that's the way I'm going to win the title, by moving off." Giardello adherents were few but one of them, Rocky Graziano, former middleweight king, called the turn expertly. "I'm bettin' a few on Joey," he said. "He's in shape for this one and, he always made things tough for walk-in guys like Tiger." It turned out to be a matter of style. The supposedly over-the-hill Giardello moved and stuck his way to the biggest middleweight upset in years.

Ring historians were lax in their homework when they failed to take into account the most famous heavyweight title stunner of all, the Braddock-Baer title fight in 1935 in writing off Clay's chances. Not even James J. Braddock's repeated warnings in pre-fight interviews that Clay might duplicate his feat of twenty-five years ago swayed the judgement of the odds-makers. "It's all a matter of style," reiterated Jim. "Baer could punch. But I turned smart for that one, and that was the answer to his big right hand. I kept moving to my right with a long left sticking him."

"The old left hand" as Billy Conn used to call it, is the surest weapon with which big upsets are made. Billy himself came close but didn't quite make it against Louis the first time. Gene Tunney however, did in the most famous heavyweight title upset of the Twenties; his first meeting with champion Jack Dempsey at Philadelphia in 1926. Again fight veterans were guilty of oversight in reviewing the past. Tunney's key to success was the same that unlocked the door to the heavyweight throne room for Clay, fast footwork and a left hand.

Tunney simplified his job by getting the jump on Dempsey in the first round with a stiff right-hand punch which dulled the opening charge which had made Dempsey famous. From then on, leg speed proved the deciding factor against the aging Champion. There are many who claim that Tunney had the style to defeat the slugging "Manassa Mauler" at the peak of his career. The most outspoken of these, Jimmy Bronson, reminds us that Dempsey was never at his best against fast stepping boxers, and Tunney was among the best of these. Again it's a matter of style, repeats Bronson. "If his style is right the longshot becomes the favorite. People laid as high as ten to one on Dempsey, but it should have been the other way around," he insists.

Clay's 95-year-old grandmother was a young girl when the vulnerability of long odds to speed and cleverness first was demonstrated. Two legendary figures, James J. Corbett in the role of the despised underdog, and the mighty John L. Sullivan were the participants in the ring's first great upset. John L., bloated by excess, and drugged by over-confidence, was not unlike Liston in his frustration against the swift Corbett. Using a primitive form of Clay's style, Jim alienated thousands of Sullivan worshippers by defeating the fabulous Boston Strong Boy in 21 rounds at New Orleans on Sept. 7, 1892.

Styles embarrass the oddsmakers because even the greatest of fighters are not immune to the troublesome method. No fighter was ever more adept than Sugar Ray Robinson at adapting his own style to the problem of the moment. But even Ray, by his own admission, had trouble with "guys I have to look for."

By this he meant a bobbing and weaving target which refused to set itself up to be bullseyed and bombed.

Few expected Holly Mims to last the distance when he tangled with Robinson in Miami in 1951, but when everything was all over, Ray had to settle for a split decision! "I knew I had to stay close to the man and punch inside if I was going to stay alive," the genial Holly revealed, "but what made Robinson such a great fighter was that he could punch like the devil backing up. The trick was to keep your head low, bobbing and weaving all the time and not to get set up, whatever you did." Using a similar plan of battle Marty Servo forced Ray to go all out to beat him on two occasions in 1941 and 1942. Those who wagered on Robinson to stop Mims learned again that styles can beat the odds.

Louis opponents doing the unorthodox might befuddle both Joe and the bettors the first time around with the Brown Bomber but in the encore engagement Joe usually had everything nicely figured out. But even he could be baffled, as Arturo Godoy showed in Madison Sq. Garden in 1940 when crouching almost to the ground, he actually received the vote of one of the judges. Louis took good care of the rugged Chilean later on but he was always least impressive against a man who got down low against him, Tony Musto and Al McCoy being two more examples. "I would always figure on a guy who crouched going at least six rounds with Joe and that's the way I would lay it," a clever betting man once disclosed.

KOs THRILL BUT THE NAME OF THE GAME
IS BOXING AND BUCHANAN PROVES IT

The most frequently levelled criticism at boxing, and the most difficult to counter, is the charge that the ultimate purpose of the sport is the destruction of one's opponent. The knockout scorer is the automatic winner, no matter what has gone before. This is the gladiatorial concept, a holdover from the time of the Emperor Nero and the Roman arena.

Boxing, under the Marquis of Queensberry rules, is a sport of contradiction. The British nobleman intended the "Art of Self Defense" and not the coup de grace to be the prime factor in the sport. For many years, particularly on the Continent, and in England, purists insisted the ability to avoid punishment should carry weight, with the power to inflict it. This reasoning still prevails in Olympic boxing, to the dismay and amazement of statesiders who saw Britisher Chris Finnegan, battered and woozy, awarded the call over American Eddie Jones in the 1968 Games in Mexico City. The officials validated their verdict by crediting Finnegan with "superior defensive work."

The good Marquis and those of his leanings would have delighted in the recent lightweight championship contest between Scotland's Ken Buchanan and Panama's Ismael Laguna, two highly qualified experts of the boxing art.

This was to be expected, for there is plenty of ammunition for those who insist that boxing is a game of skill, to be found in the records of the lightweight division. In most cases the champion of this class is the cleverest boxer in it. Occasionally, as in the cases of Joe Gans and Benny Leonard, lightweight immortals, superb skill is coupled with power. But this is the exception rather than the rule.

Gans wasn't the first lightweight champion. Although he was a deadly puncher, his artistry was legendary and set the pattern for the better lightweight titlists who succeeded him. Gans' boxing was so consummate he was known as the "Old Master." Leonard, who vies with Gans as the greatest of the lightweight champions, was the Baltimorean's prototype in ring mastery but not in style. Leonard was a virtuoso who boxed on his toes. His movements were graceful. Gans was flatfooted, a shuffler who shed blows with slight moves of head and body. Both men were thinking fighters. A keen brain guided Gans' gliding movements as well as Benny's ballet-like brilliance.

The man Leonard defeated to win the championship, Freddy Welsh, was, according to the late Abe Attell, the superior of both Gans and Leonard for purely defensive skill. Abe should have known, since few could top him as a clever boxer. He received a lesson in the art when he met Welsh at the outset of his career. No one, insists confrere Jersey Jones, an authority on Welsh, could outbox the man from Wales when he was in top condition, which unfortunately was far too seldom.

Journeyman Jimmy Goodrich who won a tournament to decide Leonard's successor following Benny's retirement in 1925, and rough, tough Rocky Kansas interrupted the boxers' domination of the division until Kansas was dethroned by Sammy Mandell.

Mandell, a good-looking, black-haired movie type, was known as the Rockwood Sheik. Like Welsh he possessed uncanny skill but had no firepower to speak of. Sammy was a living rebuttal to the "opponent destruction" outcry of boxing's detractors. Mandell rarely hurt anybody in the ring but his defeats were even rarer. New York considered Sid Terris unbeatable at the time, but Mandell edged the Eastsider on his home grounds in a sparkling demonstration of boxing finesse by both men.

Though he appreciated a knockout finish, Carroll was unwavering in his preference for the more skillful aspects of the sweet science. *The Ring* (February 1971)

Tony Canzoneri, who called Mandell the "smartest boxer I ever met," could, when he felt like it, put all the nuances of the boxing art on display. Tony, who started as a bantamweight, as he grew heavier proved more and more inclined to punch it out with his foes. He decided one night to show the people just how accomplished a boxer he could be. On this occasion, his first meeting with Lou Ambers, with the lightweight title on the line, his performance would have convinced the most obstinate of boxing's critics that boxing is a game of skill and not a dogfight.

Canzoneri, one of the most versatile of the lightweight champions, often chose to slug it out, at which he was quite good. But in the really tough spots he would rely upon skill, as he did when he sidetracked the old Fargo Express, Billy Petrolle, in New York's Madison Square Garden. Tony had lost a slugfest to Jack Hurley's man in Chicago, so instead of trying to "destroy" Petrolle the next time around, he was content to stay away, move at long range and sharpshoot his punches.

Ambers finally caught up with Tony with an assist from Father Time, but his winning the lightweight title did not disrupt the boxers' continuity. Ambers was a speedster, a skilful one who knew what he was doing, and took relatively little punishment throughout his career.

Former 135-pound kingpins Ike Williams and Jimmy Carter were better than average boxers but primarily punchers, offensively oriented. Their hitting abilities did not keep them from being categorized as clever boxers.

Joe Brown had a radar guided right hand. This warrior had few superiors as a scientist. Brown, who came to ring glory so late he was known as "Old Bones," picked up many a pointer in generalship along the way. Whether it means slipping, ducking, blocking or moving, Brown knew his way around the ring.

Weary looking in action and frail appearing was Brown. Few men could pinpoint a kayo punch better than the Louisianan. Combining a canny defense with a striking rattler attack, Joe defended his lightweight championship successfully more times than any of his celebrated lightweight predecessors.

The debate over whether a boxing match is a "fight" or "game," which has gone on for decades, will never be settled to everyone's satisfaction. On whose side does the balance of proof lie? The skilled athlete who thwarts the offense with brains and skill or the aggressor who seeks to demolish his rival.

On the record in the lightweight class, the evidence is all in favour of boxing as a game of skill.

Nobody who saw the skilled Jem Driscoll, of England, the elusive Jimmy Wilde, Attell, or Welsh, could deny that the name of the game was boxing.

Driscoll was one of the greatest exponents of the boxing art in all the sport's history.

Although he turned tiger in the closing rounds to solidify his recent victory over capable former champion Laguna, Buchanan has already established himself as one of the cleverest boxers to hold the lightweight championship. He has disclosed that he has been greatly influenced by Sugar Ray Robinson, and availed himself of every opportunity to study the style of this boxing master. He must have paid very close attention for some of his moves—particularly along the ropes—are reminiscent of Sugar Ray.

It is always gratifying to see skill prevail in the ring, since it modifies a mistaken idea that force is the paramount factor in the sport, and the KO is boxing's dominant factor.

5

FIGHTERS AND FANS

Clean-living fighters live longest, Carroll claimed in *The Ring*'s July 1939 issue. They also looked years younger than their actual age. This applied as much to sluggers as to scientific boxers. By "clean-living," he meant "younger days free from dissipation," in particular no smoking and no drinking. By contrast to the "Boston Strong Boy," John L. Sullivan, dead from drink by the time he was fifty-nine, Jake Kilrain, who lasted seventy-five rounds against Sullivan in 1889 under London Prize Ring Rules, went on until he was seventy-nine. Heavyweights Harry Wills and Gene Tunney were addicted to clean living. The "Black Panther," Wills, throughout his long and fruitless pursuit of heavyweight champ Jack Dempsey, never touched alcohol and fasted for up to a month at a time. Tunney banned all hard drink from his training camps, and if no one else took it to such extremes, a long list of outstanding boxers, including Benny Leonard, Billy Petrolle, and Tommy Loughran, neither smoked nor drank, even after their fighting careers ended.

If clean living was vital for success in the ring and a long life thereafter, then a shrewd manager and an expert trainer were also essential, in Carroll's opinion. On at least four occasions, in August 1940, May 1941, August 1953, and September 1959, Carroll looked closely at what the best of them could do for their fighters. Managers had to be shrewd, persuasive, and aggressive, preferably at one and the same time. Jack Kearns helped Jack Dempsey, Mickey Walker, and himself, to make a fortune; Joe Jacobs "talked" Max Schmeling into the heavyweight title by shouting "foul" loud and long against Jack Sharkey in 1930 and ballyhooed Tony "I'll moider da bum" Galento into a title shot against Joe Louis in 1939; Jack Hurley turbocharged the stagnant careers of the "Fargo Express," Billy Petrolle, and Harry "Kid" Matthews; and Al Weill, a force to be reckoned with long before Rocky Marciano appeared on the scene, wheedled promoter Mike Jacobs out of a record $82,500 for lightweight king Lou Ambers back in 1937. Trainers who made all the difference included in their number

Jack "Chappie" Blackburn, on whose canny advice Joe Louis relied so heavily; Whitey Bimstein; Charlie Goldman; and Ray Arcel, expert conditioners and cornermen all of them. They generally laid down the law, right up to the point of banning women from training camps, in the belief that they sapped fighters' strength and edginess in the buildup to major bouts. It was a conviction that somehow survived the shock of Ingemar Johansson's stunning three-round KO of Floyd Patterson to win the heavyweight crown in 1959, all the more startling because the Swede, accompanied everywhere by his fiancée, had ignored every rule in the American trainers' handbook. With sex off the menu for most boxers in strict training, the only remaining pleasure was food, but that too was strictly controlled. Smaller fighters had to make stipulated weights, and all boxers had to watch what they ate—no fried food but as much steak as they could hold and plenty of green stuff.

The biggest challenge of all was knowing when to stop fighting. In January 1955, more than a year before Rocky Marciano announced his retirement from the ring as undefeated champion, Carroll reflected on the fact that great boxers seldom quit at the right time. Apart from Gene Tunney, everyone from Joe Louis onward got it wrong. Ezzard Charles's second fight with Marciano was a case in point. Widely praised after standing up to the "Brockton Blockbuster" for fifteen rounds the previous June, Charles's September 1954 rematch saw him panned for a hesitant if brave display. If only he had gone back to Cincinnati after the first match and retired, his sky-high reputation in the public mind would have been secure. Jersey Joe Walcott's last fight was particularly ignominious. His first-round surrender to Marciano, while kneeling on the canvas fully conscious as the referee counted ten, left him $245,000 richer but despised by fight fans across the country. Still fresh in many people's memory was the dismal close of Billy Conn's career. Having beaten the best in three divisions, middle, light heavy, and heavyweight, Conn gave Louis the fright of his boxing life in 1941, only to lose pathetically in the rematch four years later, a last performance which for many years overshadowed his otherwise stellar record. Although not all fighters ended up broke—the five-million-dollar estate left by Jack Dempsey's old opponent Luis Firpo evoked much discussion in the boxing world and was the subject of Carroll's December 1960 article in *The Ring*—"one more fight" was all too often because of financial need, keeping boxers in the ring beyond their sell-by date.

Less common but far from unknown was the problem of how to treat young and talented boxers as their careers took off. Should an under-age contender be allowed to take on the toughest competition over the full distance? Under New

York State Commission rules, fighters below the age of twenty were limited to six- or eight-round bouts, depending on their age. In March 1954, with Carroll asking "When is a Boy a Man?" undefeated Floyd Patterson, 1952 Olympic champion and 1953 "Rookie of the Year," was only eighteen. He was no less ready for the best in the light heavyweight division. Floyd was in good company. At the age of nineteen, Tommy Loughran was boxing the likes of Gene Tunney, Harry Greb, and Mike McTigue. Georges Carpentier, "The Orchid Man," whose right hand gave Jack Dempsey momentary pause for thought in their 1921 contest, was fifteen when he fought for the bantamweight championship of France, and by the time he was eighteen, he was European welterweight king. At twenty-one Carpentier was heavyweight champion of Europe. One way around the rules in laxer days included presenting an older brother's name and birth certificate. Other resourceful individuals added a few years to the fighter's original application. In this manner, Tony Canzoneri and Tami Mauriello were fighting professionally in New York's hardest arenas when they were both really only sixteen. As holding Patterson back until he was twenty might stifle his progress, the solution, Carroll concluded, was to regard him as a contender of such remarkable ability that an exception to the rules had to be made for him. In November 1956, Patterson would become the youngest man until then to win the heavyweight title, when he knocked out "Ancient" Archie Moore, nearly twenty years his senior, more if Archie's mother was to be believed.

Carroll never flinched from confronting the hardest question of all: did fans encourage brutality in the ring? Writing in June 1962, soon after welterweight champion Benny Paret was battered to death by Emile Griffith, described in *Ring* editor Nat Fleischer's ringside account of the fight as "a man gone berserk," Carroll's answer was as straight as an educated left to the jaw. YES, and no doubt about it: "The public wants blood and thunder and refutes exhibitions of skill as thoroughly boring." Using the ten-round bout in July 1961 between ranking heavyweight contender Eddie Machen and National Boxing Association light heavyweight champion Harold Johnson to make his point, Carroll emphasized what a superb display of the art of self-defense it had been. The match showcased two athletes in magnificent physical condition, both of whom were masters of slipping punches, feinting, and countering. The rules were observed at all times. There was no shoving, butting, elbowing, or kidney punches. And when the fight was over, won by Johnson on a razor-thin decision, what happened? Widespread unhappiness because of the lack of mayhem in the ring. Derided as "overcautious" and "in the wrong business," both Johnson and

Machen struggled to make a living from the sport. "Watching a smart fighter is like watching a guy read a book," sneered one reporter. With all but a minority of fans wanting gladiators not "glove-men," crowd-pleasing combat trumped exhibitions of scientific boxing. The style was set by the public.

———————

July 1939	Clean-Living Fighters Scorn Father Time
August 1940	The Manager's Role
May 1941	The Art of Training
August 1953	Food for Thought
March 1954	When Is a Boy a Man?
January 1955	One Fight Too Many . . .
September 1959	Training . . . Men vs. Women
December 1960	Not All Fighters End Up Broke
June 1962	Do Fans Make Brutality?

CLEAN-LIVING FIGHTERS SCORN FATHER TIME

Ring Career No Prelude to Slap-Happy Years, Johnson, Loughran, Leonard, McLarnin, Tunney Shout

Every now and then some writer, seized with a reforming spirit, emits a blast at the boxing business as a factory for mental and physical wrecks. Often the crusader is a former member of the writing fraternity who earned his livelihood reporting fights. No one can deny that many former fighters are unhappy relics. But whether the state of these unfortunates is due to the rigors of the business or careless living, is a moot question.

At the Louis-Farr fight a couple of years ago, no less than fifteen famous fighters and former fighters crowded into the ring before the opening gong for a mass introduction. Included were Gene Tunney, Jack Dempsey, Jack Johnson and Jack Sharkey. The most striking thing about these men was their physical appearance. Each looked years younger than his actual age. All had spent many arduous years in the ring, but it would have been difficult to find a like number of individuals picked from any other calling who would have presented as impressive an appearance.

At the age of sixty, Jack Johnson, former heavyweight champion of the world, is undoubtedly one of the best-preserved physical specimens in the world. As Lil' Artha steps jauntily down New York's Broadway, his famous golden smile still as scintillating as of yore, his spring step and graceful carriage is that of a man many years his junior. Invariably the passerby remarks, "Say, is that Jack Johnson? The old boy sure looks good!" With ten years to go of the allotted span of three score years and ten, Johnson is still a tremendously powerful man, surprisingly agile. Reflexes and eyesight are almost as keen as in his championship days, and his mind is eager and alert. Of course, Johnson's skill was so great he received a minimum of physical punishment in the ring. But he followed the wearing trade for more than twenty years and shows no ill-effects.

Harry Wills is another whose mental and physical well-being preach a sermon on the benefits of clean living. Unlike most of his boxing brethren of old, the Brown Panther doesn't have to worry about the landlord. He is one himself. As one of the largest property owners of his race in New York's Harlem, Harry enjoys these balmy spring evenings on the steps of one of his large apartment houses, his mind untroubled by economic worries. Wills' physical condition is on a par with his financial state. Clean of limb, trim of waist, and keen of eye, he looks about the same as he did when he was the Dark Menace of the Ring. The old Panther parlayed his long and unsuccessful pursuit of Dempsey into economic security. He should have no quarrel with anyone over his failure to ever get the Manassa Mauler into the ring.

During his fighting days, Wills became known as a physical culturist who made a fetish of occasional fasts of as long as thirty days. Harry still follows this formula. His long abstinences from solid food have become famous and people from all over the world write for advice on all manner of ailments. Besides his fasting, to which he attributes his marvelous physical condition, Wills, who is nearing fifty, always led a sober and proper life. The gin bottle was a stranger to him, and he never allowed himself to get out of fighting trim. The results of this mode of living are apparent in Wills, and his general appearance in 1939 is in sharp contrast to that of the careless livers of his fighting days.

No essay on the benefits of clean living and abstinence would be complete without mention of Gene Tunney, millionaire, country gentleman, business tycoon and former heavyweight champion of the world. Although gentleman Gene, as a distillers' executive, seems to have softened up in his uncompromising stand against Demon Rum, in his fighting days Tunney, patron saint of the early-to-bed boys, wouldn't allow any of the stuff in his training camps. Tunney's addiction to clean living has been so much harped upon that further comment is superfluous. That Gene had the right idea is strikingly evident. Handsome as of old, rich and respected, intelligent to the point where his opinions on all subjects are sought after, Tunney is perhaps the greatest living refutation of the "punch drunk, physical wreck" theory so often expounded by boxing's decriers.

Those who declare that boxing dulls the mental processes should have a hard time explaining away the case of Jack Dempsey. Back in his freight-hopping days, this famous ex-champion, according to old-timers and by his own admission, was a crude, unpolished, none-too-bright youngster. Today, Jack fits perfectly into any kind of discussion or gathering and the years seem to sharpen his mental faculties. Outside of a little added weight, Dempsey looks fit enough to step into the ring and he handles his multitudinous business interests with an ease and intelligence few could equal. It should also be noted that Dempsey was not clever and bore the brunt of bitter ring warfare. Today, his appearance and manner are typical of a master of ceremonies as he gladhands out-of-towners who flock into his New York establishment.

Getting a little closer to the present of fighters, Jimmy McLarnin has long confounded those who like to create the impression that all boxers are slap-happy, battered, stumbling wreckage. James' appearance is so directly opposite to this conception of a boxer that many to whom he is introduced refuse to believe he is the famous fighter. There is the tale of the Hollywood actress who, after seeing McLarnin's smooth, unmarked features and hearing his polished speech, figured she had heard wrong, and told everyone about Mr. McLarnin, the brilliant WRITER, she had met the previous evening. Independently wealthy, Jimmy fits in perfectly with the movie colony's country club set, although he is nothing like the broken-nosed cinema pugs that cavort on the screen. The viewers with alarm always steer clear of mention of McLarnin when they start shedding tears over the blight boxing casts over the mitt slingers.

Benny Leonard's case is almost a duplicate of McLarnin's, one of the greatest of all boxers. Benny's features, for all the 200 bouts he fought in the ring, are as unmarked as those of a newly arrived baby. Smart as they come in his ring career, Leonard still retains all his mental acuteness. Benny wasn't quite clever enough to beat Wall Street, but his intelligence is far above the average. Like all the others mentioned, Leonard took the best of care of himself, and this is paying him dividends today, even if some of his investments are not. Like McLarnin, Leonard never drank or smoked, and this is perhaps one of the main reasons why they look and act so much unlike the average idea of a retired pugilist. McLarnin in particular is a rare type of retired fighter. He golfs regularly and is a shrewd businessman in his ventures.

Because of his immunity to the temptations of the primrose path, someone once described Tommy Loughran as leading the life of a monk outside of a monastery. Tommy certainly knew what he was about, as anyone who speaks with him today soon realizes. The former light-heavyweight champion of the world, still a bachelor, fought for 18 years in the prize ring against the greatest men in three divisions, but for all the effects he shows of his long and arduous career, he might have been a clerk or a carpenter.

Most of the happy examples we have mentioned have been boxers of the scientific school. How have the men who waged war along more primitive lines been dealt with by the profession they followed? Not as well, in most cases, but this has mainly been due to the fact that the sluggers lacked the native intelligence of the clever men and were careless about their physical condition.

The rough and tough ones who knew enough to take care of themselves are nearly all in the best of physical and mental shape. Johnny Risko was anything but a smart performer inside the ropes, but outside of them it was a different story. It was more to John's advantage to use his head outside of the ring than in it, for today John is free from financial worries, thanks to a trust fund, and the careful life he led. Another member of the rough and ready school of scrappers who shows no ill-effects of the many gruelling struggles in which he engaged is Billy Petrolle, the old Fargo Express. Sight unimpaired, mind clear, and in the best of physical trim, Petrolle early learned the importance of proper conditioning and living a clean life, and he is reaping the rewards of this sane procedure. The case of Willie Ritchie, ex-lightweight champion of the world, is much the same as that of Petrolle. The rugged Californian participated in as many bruising encounters as any fighter of his day, but is in top-notch shape and fills his position as a California boxing commissioner very capably.

Like Jack Johnson, Frank Erne, at the age of 64, is a remarkably well-preserved physical specimen. The former lightweight champion still lives in Buffalo, comes down to New York occasionally for the big fights, and is a picture of health and contentment. James J. Jeffries, also at the age of 64, looks good for many years to come. Rugged and powerful in appearance, ol' Jeff looks as enduring as one of the redwood trees that surround his California home. The same thing goes for the ancient ex-star, Tom Sharkey, who is as robust as ever, although in his sixties.

As far as longevity is concerned, ex-boxers have little to fear from the rigors of the game if their younger days were free from dissipation. Jake Kilrain, who recently passed on, reached the age of 79, and this oldster belonged to the bare-knuckle era.

The list of old-time pugilists who have departed the fight game in about the same condition, physically and mentally, as they entered it, is an impressive one. Surely there seems to be nothing wrong, at least to the naked eye, with such well-known ex-pugs as big Jess Willard, Joe Jeanette, Tommy Burns, Tom Gibbons, Leo Houck and Tom Heeney. Jeanette, for example, survived a score of battles with men like Langford, McVey and Johnson to become one of the most respected citizens and ring officials of Hoboken, N.J. The Gibbons boys, Mike and Tom, look like a couple of average business men out of St. Paul, Minn.

Not all former fighters we have mentioned are free of financial cares, for, after all, how many of us are these days, but none of them show any physical disabilities for all their years in a business that many damn as demoralizing and detrimental in its after effects.

Those who followed the laws of correct living, as we have attempted to show by examples, are hale and hearty with prospects of living far beyond the span of the average man.

THE MANAGER'S ROLE

Plays an Important Part in Fighters' Careers—Kearns, Flynn, McCarney, Jacobs and Johnson Leading Figures in Last Twenty Years— Aggressiveness, Shrewdness and Persuasiveness Big Factors

"Why a fight manager?"

This innocent query, a laugh to the boxing conscious, is often heard from the lips of the uninitiated and uninformed. A goodly portion of the citizenry is prone to lump all the pugilistic masterminds into the "They can't hurt us" class of pilots who from a safe refuge outside the ropes exhort their struggling charges to greater efforts, then dash out for the payoff following the festivities and are not seen or heard of again until their battler's next appearance in the ring. Not many of the boys conform to this popular impression for the simple reason that in these days of tough competition, a mentor has to show plenty of ingenuity, manipulating prowess, non-stop hustling and what the fistic fraternity calls "cuteness" to keep a worthwhile bread winner out of the eager clutches of any one of a horde of rivals.

Most of the gags, schemes, and space grabbing tricks that make the boxing game pre-eminent on the sport pages the year round, are the products of the fast-working minds of the managers. For instance, wits have remarked that former champion Melio Bettina should fight his bouts on a vaudeville circuit, his magician manager, Jimmy Grippo, is so well publicized everywhere the Beacon boy goes. The old dodge of having a boxer in training rescue the fair heiress from drowning has come down through the years as an old standby in purloining training camp publicity. The name of the genius who first thought up this one has become lost in the mists of time, but it was no doubt born in the fertile imagination of some forgotten fight manager. Some of the publicity tricks employed by shrewd pilots have been so fruitful they have been appropriated by the members of various other professions, after free advertising.

Aside from their talents at grabbing free advertising, more important, many of the lads show genuine business ability in getting the greatest financial returns for their charges. Old Pop Foster had a stock answer to promoters who attempted to whittle down his demands for his Jimmy McLarnin's services. "James is the card," thrifty Pop would observe. "He's got to be paid." And James always was. Jack Kearns parlayed the talents of Dempsey and Mickey Walker into unheard of figures. Canny Al Weill is placed on a pedestal by even his se-verest critics for his trick of wheedling Uncle Mike Jacobs, no philanthropist, out of $82,500 for Lou Ambers in Jacobs' Carnival of Champions show in 1937. And there have been others.

What manner of men make up the ranks of the master minds who control the careers of the thousands of aspiring pugs all over the world? The movies to the contrary, there seems to be no standard type. Of course, you will find no dim wits or slow thinkers among the better-known ones, but this goes for almost any calling. Shrewdness is a necessary requirement in any kind of busi-ness nowadays. Some of the top ones are suave, smooth and dignified along the lines of James Bronson and Ancel Hoffman; others are garrulous, aggressive in the James J. Johnston manner. Like everyone else, the managers cover a wide range of characteristics and personalities.

Most ring students are agreed that the all-time money maker among the boxing managers was Jack Kearns. The dapper doctor, as he is known to the trade, must have cleared at least a million from his efforts on behalf of Dempsey, Mickey Walker, Jackie Fields, etc. A debonair fellow, well groomed, smooth spoken, Kearns reeked with the class that must be part of any one who makes big de-mands and gets what he asks for. But it must be remembered he had a fighter in Dempsey who really could sell himself. He was "color" personified. That made it easy for Dempsey. Kearns withheld Dempsey from the public view until the time was ripe for a peek at his super fighting machine, then he would talk box car figures—and get them. Kearns was paid high and he lived accordingly.

A good example of the Kearns style of doing things was the overseas junket the free spending Doc arranged and paid for when Mickey Walker went over to England to box Tommy Milligan back in 1927. Jack trundled some friends and several newspapermen aboard an ocean liner, entertained the party in the royal manner all during the trip for a couple of weeks in London, and footed the bill for everything right down to shaves and haircuts. In all things he attempted, Kearns spread it around with a lavish hand. A million-dollar manager, Jack lived the life of one and today has no regrets over the fortune that has fled.

Old Billy Gibson was another whose returns from the boxing game were among the largest. The great Benny Leonard and following him, Gene Tunney, were the instruments Billy's business acumen used in gaining wealth for him-self and them. With the possible exception of Roxborough and Black, Joe Louis' owners, the previously mentioned Al Weill is probably tops among the managers of today as a money maker. Weill's string of fighters from the most inconspicuous prelim boy up to Lou Ambers need never worry about getting the worse of any bargain. "The Vest" as he is more or less affectionately known by the fight crowd, hustles as frantically today as he did in the years when his waistcoat was a mess of vitamins, and he was from the Harlem dance halls, an ex-prize winning waltzer. No one would ever suspect, taking a quick gander at the thick set mentor today, that he was once a hoofer of gazelle-like grace. That was in the days when a "cut in" meant switching someone else's partner to Al, and had nothing to do with a fighter's purse.

Weill is miles removed from a free spending Kearns. In fact, harsh statements have been heard that he goes to the other extreme. But he is never deaf to a genuine call for help. Some years ago, the little ex-boxer, Andy Brown, a Weill roommate in Al's dancing days, departed this world, penniless and alone. Weill, who hadn't yet reached his present affluence, was right on the job taking care of all expenses for a decent funeral for his one-time benefactor.

No treatise on the fistic fraternity would be complete without mention of the Old Professor of Fistiana, Billy McCarney. Billy, who hasn't missed a hamlet in his treks up, down and around the country in the past forty years, is almost an institution in the boxing business. One of the last of the Old Guard, there is about the well-liked Will just a hint of W.C. Fields intermingled with a flair for showmanship of P.T. Barnum. Billy was one of the first of the old-time drum beating ballyhoo men of the profession. The ace story teller of the boxing world, there are as many stories of his own adventurous manipulations.

In the old days, Will often worked as a kind of uncoverer of heavyweight fodder for Jack Kearns, then engaged in maneuvering Dempsey to the top. Stymied in his search for a likely foe for a Tulsa, Okla., bout for the Manassa Mauler, Bill, detained in Kansas City at the time, dug up a German waiter with pugilistic ambitions.

German monikers were out of order back in 1918, so Will tagged the hopeful Kid McCarthy, assured him everything was all right and this guy Dempsey was just a beginner like he was. A minute after the opening gong, the waiter was in the lap of the mayor of the town, propelled there by Dempsey's first left hook. Some time later, the wandering Dempsey and Kearns wound up in Kansas City. Imagine Dempsey's surprise when he looked up and saw his erstwhile victim. "Hey," barked Jack, "haven't I seen you some place before." "Yah, Check," said the waiter, "in Tulsa, three weeks ago." A genius at odd nomenclature, Billy's forte in the old days was tagging his fighters with odd names. He called one of his charges, a colored battler with a pair of unusually long flat feet, the Virginia Creeper, because that worthy had a sliding sort of footwork in the ring.

Past the three-score mark, the Professor is still handsome, sartorially resplendent, and second to none as a ballyhoo merchant extraordinary. The late Joe Jacobs assimilated most of his knowledge of the ins and outs of the boxing business from his ten-year association with the astute McCarney. A native of Philadelphia, the amiable Will is known and welcomed everywhere. Long may he continue to trek the boxing byways.

The ways, means and methods many of the pilots use are as varied as the colors of the rainbow. Aggravation, or goat grabbing has been the means employed by the irrepressible James J. Johnston to gain his ends many times in the past. Derby aslant over one eye, his chest out like a belligerent bantam rooster, Jaunty James has goaded many an unsuspecting victim into acting as an unwitting tool to James' advantage. Johnston is never serious about his jibes and darts, as the learned judge informed the flustered Gen. John J. Phelan, in the New York Boxing Commissioner's recent court clash with James J. "Here is a man who must have his little joke. There is a mischievous gleam in his eye, only those with tender ears will be hurt by what he says or does," opined the jurist. Johnston's charges invariably wind up in lucrative spots. His cockiness has paid him and his battlers well for a long, long time.

Always-on-the-go, hustling is a highly successful formula for some of the boys. Always busier than a swarm of bees is the lively young looking Philadelphian, Chris Dundee. Like the fabulous Leo P. Flynn of yore, it's nothing unusual for the dark-haired, bespectacled, young Italian to have a fighter working every night in the week. One night in March Dundee had Eddie Dunne boxing Steve Belloise in a main event at the White Plains Community Center and George Abrams facing Ernie Vigh at the Bronx Coliseum the same evening. How he did it, nobody knows, but the ubiquitous Dundee showed up in both corners, although the arenas are ten miles apart. This is just a sample of the energy Chris expends in making boxing a good proposition for himself and his stable.

Of course, the patron saint of all the hustling pilots was silver-thatched Leo P. Flynn. Old Leo, whose middle name remains one of the ring's great mysteries, in later years turned over the job of handling his hinterland interests to others, and wound up as Dempsey's manager in both the Sharkey and second Tunney battles.

Managers and their varying roles in the fight game drew regular attention in Carroll's column for *The Ring*. *The Ring* (August 1940)

Tales about the great Leo are plentiful in ring lore. A golfer of some repute, he was one day accosted by a tall, good-looking stranger on the links, who forthwith invited Flynn to join him in a round. After a few holes, the stranger suggested that they add interest to the game by making small bets on each hole. The day following the stranger appeared again, this time suggesting that the ante be raised. "OK," said Leo, and that night Flynn went home $1,200 richer.

The next afternoon, the stranger propositioned Leo. "Mr. Flynn, you've been going quite well. What do you say, we play eighteen holes at $200 a hole?" Leo P.'s rejoinder floored the questioner. "Listen, Mr. Titanic Thompson," sneered Leo, "I KNOW you, and I'm $1,200 ahead of you, and that's the way we're gonna stay." Titanic Thompson, notorious gambler and golf expert, watched the flamboyant Flynn saunter away, beaten at his own game.

Some of the tricks imaginative mentors use in out-angling the opposition border on downright genius. For instance, Hymie Caplin, out on the Coast with Solly Krieger a couple of years ago, wanted a match with Champion Al

Hostak in the worst way. Wanting it and getting it were two entirely different things, until hand-talking Hymie thought this up. He approached the Hostak forces with overtures for a match with Krieger, after first allowing rumors to drift about that Sol could not make the 160-pound limit and be himself. He next made a match for Solly with a local rival at 165 pounds, putting up a $200 forfeit that Krieger would come in at this poundage. Solly entered the ring a pound over. Hymie blew his forfeit, and Hostak's board of strategy, figuring that the reports about Krieger's inability to make 160 pounds and be strong must be correct, fell into the trap and accepted Solly as a title foe. Krieger proved to be a bull at 159 pounds, pasted Hostak and Hymie had his fourth world's champion—in a lot of states, anyway.

Some of the boys rely upon the gift of gab in getting results. The voluble Dumb Dan Morgan, even though the years have given Daniel the general appearance of a small-town deacon, with his black fedora, square-toed shoes and dark ministerial garb. But be that as it may, Jack Britton and Bat Levinsky soared to fame on the power of Dan's vocal cords, and even today Dan commands plenty of space in the sports pages at every big fight.

Jack Hurley, who doubles in brass as a sports columnist and boxing manager, has a Jekyll and Hyde routine all his own. Outside the corner, the tall soft-spoken Hurley is the acme of gentleness, a Chesterfieldian fellow, from whom one would never expect a harsh word. Inside the ropes, though, the mild-mannered Hurley is transformed into a raging, acid-tongued Simon Legree, as he frantically goads his protégé on to greater efforts.

While on the subject of manners and particularly suaveness, one member of the fraternity stands out. James Bronson, a promoter at the moment, none the less for years stood as a symbol of the polished, smooth speaking, refined and dignified fight manager in the Adolphe Menjou manner. Mr. Bronson went from the boxing halls of Joplin, Missouri, to the post of boxing director of the A.E.F. in the first World War. Then followed a long and honorable stretch as a pilot for many top-notch ring-men. James is one of the few members of the trade to be taken up by society, having had Mr. Anthony J. Drexel Biddle of the Philadelphia Biddles, if you please, as a partner in the management of Abe Simon and Rene De Vos. Always impeccably clad, at home in any company, the bow-tied Mr. Bronson has added plenty of class to a business that can certainly use it, during all the years of his connection with pugilism.

Young Dewey Fragetta has gone his contemporaries one better by inaugurating a sort of chain-store system in boxing and managing the managers. From his central office in New York, Dewey contacts out of town entrepreneurs, then the local managers, and dispatches the desired talent to the port of call. In his early thirties, dark-haired Dewey, a former Utica boy who slid into the boxing business in the wake of Bushey Graham, is expanding his operations all the time. To give the impression of extreme activity, Dewey affects a tiny office in a Broadway building. This means that his office is always crowded, giving everyone the idea business is flourishing, as it usually is.

Probably no man ever performed his managerial duties better than frugal old Pop Foster. Not only did he adopt Jimmy McLarnin, but schooled him. He always got James the better of it, both on the scales and at the till, and retired his boy a rich man. If ever anyone made a case for a fight manager as an indispensable part of the business, it was old Pop.

Outstanding among the ex-pugs who have adopted managerial careers is dapper, unmarked Johnny Ray. Ray's eye for business is unusual for an ex-fighter, and he has imparted his own great defensive skill as a boxer to Billy Conn.

The Silver Fox of the business, Pete Reilly, has a flair for featherweights, owner of three recent title-holders in that division. White-haired Peter has an uncanny knack for coming up with the 126-pound incumbent. An incurable practical joker, Pete is generally credited with being the originator of the "hot foot." Laughing Lenny Sachs, the always smiling citizen who conducted Dempsey's farewell tour, which netted Jack and Lenny half a million, showed a keen sense of showmanship. He had a rare business acumen.

The stunning passing of colorful Joe Jacobs, one of the most picturesque managers of all time, has focused the spotlight on the pilots and the great part they play in the world of pugilism. If any one individual had to be picked to most typify a boxing manager as a great portion of the public imagines him, Yussel, as he was known, would undoubtedly have been the man. Quick-witted, inventive, aggressive when it was in line with his purpose, a natural showman, Jacobs' passing leaves a gap in the boxing world and the sports pages which will be hard to fill. His supreme achievement of yelling the reclining Max Schmeling into the heavyweight championship of the world alone justifies the existence of the managers in the pugilistic scheme of things, and answers the question asked in the opening line of this piece—"Why a Manager."

THE ART OF TRAINING

Boxing fans, critics and writers are agreed that the main reason for the scarcity of genuinely clever boxers and straight, hard, decisive punchers in the ring today can be found in the difference in methods of training and instructions between the fighters of today and years ago. Whereas trainers and teachers of the old school instilled the finer points of the art of boxing and keeping in proper condition into their charges by dint of long, rigorous hours of practice, this does not seem to be the case today. Young pugilists of the present era can't get through their conditioning chores quick enough before making a beeline to the nearest movie. In many cases those entrusted to the job of preparing them for the task at hand, are all too frequently lacking in the background necessary for readying a youngster for the arduous business of professional boxing.

The right education in the particular field is all important. This explains why Billy Conn and Joe Louis are so outstanding. It can hardly be called an accident that the handsome Pittsburgher is rated the cleverest boxer in the ring today. Billy was well schooled in the finer points of the art by Johnny Ray, who himself was one of the best defensive fighters in the lightweight class. Fortunately, unlike many other ex-boxers, Ray has been capable of imparting his knowledge to his protégé. The same thing goes for Louis. Jack Blackburn, one of the greatest boxers, turned in a masterful job in moulding the crude ex-Ford factory worker into the fistic marvel he is today.

The success of these two eminent men throws into bold relief the importance of proper training and instruction to a young boxer. Every now and then pugilistic sages voice loud laments at the disappearance of the art of scientific boxing. They point fingers of scorn at the back pedalling, hugging, floundering, slipshod antics of many of our present-day pugs, blaming the sad state of affairs on the lack of capable interpreters of the art of real boxing among the handlers of the lads. Of course, most of these critics concede that there are men around today as competent as any of the old boxing tutors of old, but sadly aver that they form a small minority.

"I go over to Paterson to look over a young kid a friend of mine tips me off to," groans one of the old line fight managers, "and what'd'ya think I find. The barber who cuts the kid's hair is his manager and trainer. He's a pal of the kid's old man, gives the family free haircuts, likes to go to fights, so that makes him an expert handler, and there he is showing the kid just how it should be done!

What can you do with that sort of thing going on! Today everybody who ever saw a fight, figures he can teach a kid boxing. Shoemakers, plumbers, waiters— they're all training fighters. Years ago that sort of thing never could happen."

"You're right!" sadly intoned Clarence Gillespie, "and what makes it worse, besides knowing so little about the business, those kind of guys give the kids too much leeway and baby them too much. How do you expect a fighter to develop his legs and wind when he's riding around in cars almost as soon as he can walk, like Pat Cominskey for instance! Where do you think the old-timers got the stamina to go those long distances? Not parked in a roadster, I can tell you."

So runs the course of conversation whenever boxing veterans discourse on the changes time has wrought in the game. In light of present-day conditions in the ring game, it must be admitted that their complaints are plenty sound, and bear examination. There is little doubt that on the average fighters of yore received the benefit of instruction and conditioning superior to that dealt out to present day boxers. This is proved by the obvious decline in the number of really clever boxers and straight hard hitters in the ring today. Today the youngsters who take up boxing as a profession do everything except learn the art of hitting from the shoulder and with force.

They learn how to clinch, hug, wrestle and shove, and they do all these things in the ring to the chagrin of the onlookers. The blows of a majority of the younger element are restricted to swings, slaps and pushes, and rarely is a punch delivered that has any force or weight behind it. These boxers have no future so far as winning a title is concerned, and they seldom get beyond the "preliminary" stage of the boxing business. The reason for the lack of accurate, forceful hitting on the part of a majority of the preliminary boxers is that the unfortunate youngsters are thrown into the ring and compelled to fight without instruction even in the rudiments of the art of boxing. If any of them manage to survive the preliminary stage of their career it is because they possess remarkable vitality and courage. Yet they seldom reach the top rung of the pugilistic ladder.

Years ago, boxers were handled by men whose lives had been spent mastering the rudiments of the trade. They knew little else and were real specialists in their field. Men like Prof. Mike Donovan, father of the famed referee, Arthur, for example, devoted a lifetime to the study of boxing and their complete command of the sport showed in the work of their pupils.

The noted Australian, Dan Hickey, is still recognized as one of the greatest of all, as a teacher and conditioner. His trick of transforming muscle-bound Paul Berlenbach from a left-handed wrestler into a world's champion boxer in the light-heavyweight division, has never been duplicated. For years it had been axiomatic that a wrestler could never be changed over to a fighter of ability. Hickey not only did this but he guided the plodding, stolid Berlenbach to a world's title. Hickey might have done the same with either or both of the Fullams, Dick and Frank, now a referee, as both had more potential ability than Paul, but the ambitions of both brothers lay in other directions and neither took the ring game seriously enough.

Hardest boiled and strictest of all the old-time trainers and conditioners was the late William Muldoon, for many years head of the New York Boxing Commission. Modern boxers would have been amazed at the iron tactics of the Iron Duke, as this one-time Greco-Roman wrestling king was nicknamed. Muldoon wasn't averse to enforcing his dictates with a baseball bat, old-timers tell us, and he was the only man alive who could make roistering old John L. Sullivan behave himself and get down to business.

More than a half century ago, Spider Kelly out in San Francisco built up a world-wide reputation for his ability at turning out well conditioned, well-schooled boxers.

Although in recent years George Blake of California has concentrated his efforts on refereeing, Blake was for many years recognized as one of the greatest teachers and trainers of boxers in the country. Quiet, reserved and gentlemanly, Blake served in army camps during the last war with distinction and gained high praise for his work as a physical director and boxing instructor for the lads in khaki. Following the war, he took Fidel La Barba off a California high school campus, through a career that saw the curly-haired coast boy crowned first Olympic flyweight champion and then world's champion in the same division.

Frank "Doc" Bagley combined the jobs of managing, teaching and conditioning to a rare degree. This west side New Yorker became famous for his dexterous work in the corners. As a patcher up of battered gladiators, the Doc has had no superiors, and of modern-day handlers only that deft corner-surgeon, Ray Arcel, compares with him. George Engel was another of the old line conditioners who had mastered his trade, and Doc Robb, who is still active today, was one of the best, still is, in fact. Over in Stillman's and the Pioneer Clubs, where all the star boxers train when in New York City, you'll find some of America's best trainers handling the boys.

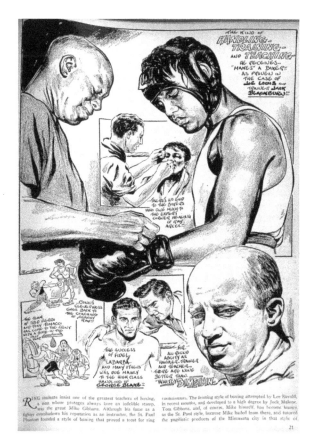

Ted Carroll would also highlight the crucial role played by trainers and corner men. *The Ring* (May 1941)

Ring students insist one of the greatest teachers of boxing, a man whose proteges always bore an indelible stamp, was the great Mike Gibbons. Although his fame as a fighter overshadows his reputation as an instructor, the St. Paul Phantom founded a style of boxing that proved a treat for ring connoisseurs. The feinting style of boxing attempted by Lee Savold, in recent months, and developed to a high degree by Jock Malone, Tom Gibbons, and, of course, Mike himself, has become known as the St. Paul style, because Mike hailed from there, and tutored the pugilistic products of the Minnesota city in that style of milling. Joe Welling was another ex-fighter who possessed the ability to pass on his ring ability to others.

These are but a few of the many outstanding exponents of the art of teaching and conditioning pugilists of the past. They are typical of the type of men who coached and handled most of the great fighters of the past. Let it not be misunderstood that the ranks of trainers and teachers of today are totally lacking in men of high ability and knowledge in their field.

Blackburn, of course, who is very much a part of the modern scene, is one of the greatest of them all as a teacher or body conditioner. No pugilistic trainer past or present has anything on Whitey Bimstein. This likable New Yorker is one of the few today who is readily recognized by the fight public when he climbs into a corner. The customers know that with Whitey in there, they can't miss seeing a well-trained, competent boxer, and throughout the fight world it's taken for granted that if "Whitey has him," everything will be all right.

No one, not even previously mentioned Doc Bagley, ever doctored a wounded eye as expertly as does widely publicized Ray Arcel. Arcel is the closest thing to a surgeon working over a battered charge in the business. He is a picture of smooth efficiency and expertness under pressure as he goes about the task of repairing damaged features. As time goes by Ray seems to get better and better, but then again this may be because he is frequently in the other corner when Joe Louis goes to work. Ray has done his healing routine over no less than 10 of Bomber's victims which may account for his highly developed skill. Be that as it may, Arcel has built up a reputation that is country wide as a conditioner and corner man, and is in greater demand than anybody in the business.

Veterans of the boxing game concede to a man that Hymie Caplin . . . rates as one of the greatest as a tutor of boxing and training. That always obliging, much quoted saga of fistiana, our unfailing friend, Dan Morgan, is even more vocal than usual on the subject of Hymie as a boxing Svengali. "I call Hymie Caplin the best of the modern boxing teachers," stoutly declares Mr. Morgan. "Look what the guy has done. He took Ben Jeby, who never figured to get out of the preliminaries, and brought him along to the title. Jenkins was nothing but a guy fighting for eating money who had been licked by everybody in Texas, and look what Hymie did with him. Solly Krieger was a grandfather, as fighters go, when Hymie took him over, and the first thing you know the guy was champion of the world. He did the same thing with Lou Salica, who looked all washed up two years ago. Hymie always used to say, 'I know what to show my fighters.' I don't know what it is but it must be all right." Dan's audience nodded ready assent to the words of the authority, indeed there was nothing else for them to do, for the records prove convincingly that Caplin is one modern who belongs in any company when it comes to teaching the fine art of fisticuffs.

Contemporary trainers and handlers who always send their proteges into action as well prepared for the task at hand as any of the old-time standouts are the competent Florio brothers, Nick and Dan. This pair of west side New Yorkers do not work as a team, preferring to go their separate ways, but each performs the varied and important duties of a boxing handler in first rate fashion. Izzy Klein, who has the not too easy task of keeping the irrepressible Maxie Baer in line, has a national reputation for his work. Freddy Brown goes about his job of readying Bob Pastor for his ring endeavours with great efficiency. His namesake, Charles Brown, applies the knowledge gained through years of keen study of the game to the training of fighters with fine results.

One of the outstanding teachers of defensive boxing in the country is ex-New York City fireman, Jess Harrington, who doubles in brass between his professional duties and coaching the eastern Golden Gloves team. Young Otto is another highly regarded tutor of boxing, whose services are always called upon by the *Daily News* in preparing the amateur warriors for the big inter-city Golden Gloves matches. Al Ramo, one-time Y.M.C.A. instructor, brings a high order of intelligence to the performance of his duties as a trainer of boxers. Larry Amadee is one of the most capable of the modern handlers. Still another ex-fighter who has shown much aptitude at the job of training and teaching young boxers for many years is former featherweight Artie Rose. Harry Gordon one time star bantamweight has proven equally successful in his new field of pugilistic handler.

The past year saw the highly regarded team of Freddy Fierro and Tony Tomacci forge to the front ranks in their calling. This pair number a pair of champions among their successful charges, in Fritzie Zivic and Billy Conn, since both Pittsburgh boys turn over complete charge of their training chores to Fierro and Tomacci for all their big bouts. Tomacci, gassed and wounded war veteran, has been around for some time, but it is only in recent years that he has received the recognition he has deserved for a long time.

Frankie Doyle, to whom is entrusted the unending task of keeping Chris Dundee's string of always busy fighters in fighting trim, takes care of this formidable job in fine style. Rotund Eddie Ross gives Red Burman A-No. 1 care and attention. Willie Ketchum does the same for Lew Jenkins, Fat Benny Greenfield, Red Kelly, Al Silvani and Johnny Russell, a trio (*sic*) of capables who know what it's all about. Al Weill, an astute gent where anything at all is concerned, has had little Charley Goldman take care of his large stable of hired hands for years, and that alone is high recommendation for this diminutive former Brooklyn bantamweight ace. Jack Moore is a highly regarded student of boxing.

One of the big reasons for the high quality of the fight cards at Madison Square Garden since Nat Rogers' elevation to the post of matchmaker is the importance attached by Nat to the fighters' trainer. "If I know the trainer is a good one," says Rogers, "I know the fighter will come into the ring in the best possible shape and a good fight is bound to be the result." . . .

The importance of proper handling, training and instruction to a boxer cannot be overestimated, and the ring game is fortunate in that there are still those around who perform these duties as well as even the best of the old-timers did them.

Gene Tunney set an example of training sensibly and seriously. Contrary to the old training theories, he drank quantities of milk after exercising. Vegetables replaced meats. Tunney's theory was to conserve as much strength as possible. The most beneficial part of his training was the rest it afforded him. He knew how to relax when training, and his schedule of exercises was a means of attaining the proper rest and relaxation.

Schmeling took a leaf out of Tunney's book. He was a sensible eater, and vegetables and milk constituted a large part of his menu while training. Like Tunney, he relaxed at golf, and he took plenty of rest and got plenty of sleep to conserve his energy.

Dempsey always took his training seriously and worked hard, sometimes too hard. He did most of his hard work when the crowd wasn't around. Carpentier surrounded his training with mystery. He talked about how much training he did, but no one saw it at Manhasset. Harry Greb did no training at all to speak of at their camps. Trainer Muldoon had to work harder to make John L. train than John L. worked in the ring against his opponents.

FOOD FOR THOUGHT

A long time ago somebody said "Tell me what you eat and I'll tell you what you are." The insurance companies have come up with their own paraphrase of this, "Tell us how much you eat and we'll tell you how long you'll live." Over-weight, direct result of over-eating is, according to the newest revelations, the greatest danger to a lengthy stay on this planet, and that explains the interest of the underwriters—and the medical profession—in the diet of all of us.

The big brains of big business are just getting around to finding out what fight people have realized ever since the first punch was thrown in a boxing ring, that the kind and the amount of food we take in is all-important to our physical welfare.

Typifying the amount of thought given the subject by boxing people, able trainer Jimmy August, one of the keenest students of the proper care and feeding of fighters, has in the course of a long career learned many things about diet of benefit not only to his charges but to the average person. August, an alert and articulate chap, doesn't go in for three substantial meals a day for his battlers. "Along about 9 or 10 in the morning, the kid should get a good solid breakfast, he's gone for a long time without a real meal, and has already done his roadwork so his appetite is sharp and he can take in plenty. Like all people using a lot of energy, boxers need plenty of proteins, and that means plenty of eggs in the morning along with the other usual breakfast foods, like cereals, milk, fruits and such. He lies down to help along the digestion of the meal and by 1 or 2 o'clock he is ready for his workout. A fighter uses up a tremendous amount of energy in training, so by 6:30 or so he is as hungry as a tiger and ready for a very big meal. If the fighter is a heavyweight you can turn him loose at the table and let him go to town. Give him as much steak as he can hold, but be sure and surround it with plenty of green stuff. Salads, vegetables, they give the roughage which helps him digest the proteins easier, and at the same time they have minerals in them which are good for him—or anybody—for that matter. Most fighters like sweets, and ice cream is the best bet there. If your fighter is a little fellow you may have to watch more closely. A fighter is a lot like an automobile. The food he eats is his fuel. A big fellow like a big car will get less mileage out of what he eats than a lightweight so he can stand a lot more food."

I wondered about the value of starches in a fighter's diet. "Well, that depends a lot on the individual fighter. Steaks and green stuff are good for anybody but starches affect different people different ways. You have to watch them. If your guy is a fellow built like Sugar Ray Robinson, you can let him get away with potatoes and macaroni now and then, but if he's built like Tami Mauriello or Jake LaMotta, watch out!"

"What happens to a fighter's diet when he's 'drying out'?" I wanted to know. "No starches at all then," explained Jimmy, "how you feed a boxer when he has to make weight depends a lot on how much weight he loses working out. I worked with Melio Bettina, a fellow who'd lose as much as six pounds after a single workout, you could keep feeding him like always right up to the day of the fight."

"I've been told that drying out can be harmful if done too frequently," I persisted. "Yes, it's true that drying out and fasting to make an unnatural weight can hurt a fighter if done too often, but the problem here is to bring your kid in at the weight at which he fights best. A weak fighter at 129, who should be 133, is just as bad off coming in at 138, 'cause he'll be sluggish at that weight. If your fighter is big for his class limit like, say, LaMotta was for a middleweight, you have to skip that one big meal the day before the fight and feed him concentrated proteins like beef tea."

"Is there any difference to an athlete between boiled and fried foods?" I asked. "Not as far as the food itself goes," answered August, "but boiled foods are so much easier to digest, trainers like to give them to their kids. Fried stuff is much more likely to cause an upset stomach." Jimmy continued, "Proper food is one of the greatest problems in out of town fights. I've always said one of the real reasons a fighter will drop a fight he figures to win in a strange city is the trouble in finding the proper restaurant. In a strange place you still have your fighter to feed, and it's up to you to get him the same kind of food and cooking he's been getting all along. If you don't, you may be heading for trouble. I have less trouble finding good places for my fighters to eat in Chicago than any place else."

Is alcohol very damaging to a fighter's chances of reaching a ripe old age? "Alcohol is an artificial stimulant which is very bad for anyone using up as much energy as a fighter does. They tell me some of the old-time trainers used to believe in letting the boys have a few shots between fights, but I can't see it and neither can any of the other trainers around today that I know of," said Jimmy.

I recalled that many years ago, well preserved Harry Wills had deplored the use of coffee by boxers because it also stimulates. I asked Jimmy about this. "Give me a milk drinker every time, I feel the same way Wills does about coffee. A lot of kids already have the coffee habit when you get them and since it might hurt them mentally to take it away from them, you let them go ahead and try to cut down on it as much as possible," he answered.

"Down in the business districts like Wall St.," he continued, "I see great big healthy-looking guys eating like little birds. They're smart. Some of them are old football players and as big as heavyweights, but they shouldn't eat like heavyweights because they all have sit-down jobs and are not burning up much energy."

Inquiring *about* among other conditioners I found them all in pretty much agreement. The between-meals eater is a bit of a problem, because depriving him of various tidbits may not work out well psychologically. Most of them agreed it was necessary to cater to such taste but only to a limited degree. Especially since such things as ice cream and candy usually are the boxers' cravings.

All of them sounded solemn warnings against eating too much by the average unathletic person. Most of them took issue with the general practice of three meals a day. "You have to be doing heavy work to take in three meals a day. Most people do light work and all that food is not good for them," advises well-preserved Jack Moore, a 70-year-old conditioner who looks years younger.

Most people who have seen him at the table call Rocky Marciano the biggest eater of all the heavyweight champions. Besides the king-sized meals he puts away the Brockton Blockbuster is always hungry and is a champion between-meals nibbler. "The only arguments me and Rocky ever have is over that eatin' between meals. I'll go up to his room and under his pillow I'll find a bunch of bananas he's hidin' from me. I've found a lot of fighters have to be made to eat certain things and to work hard, with Rocky it's just the opposite, you have to keep after him all the time to keep him from eatin' too much and workin' too hard," discloses trainer Charley Goldman.

Marciano is able to assimilate large quantities of food because he is an unusually vigorous gym worker and burns it up as rapidly as he puts it in. The Massachusetts Italian who is a typical New England Puritan in a lot of ways, not only doesn't smoke or drink, he doesn't even cuss! The heavyweight champion is also fond of swimming, and it comes as a surprise to most folks when Goldman says he approves of his going in for this. It has been a long-time belief with many people that swimming is not good for a boxer since it tends to soften the muscles. Goldman doesn't go along with this theory. "To me it's good exercise, Rocky really believes that swimming helped his punchin' and who am I to stop something which he thinks is doin' him a lot of good. The only stuff I don't like for fighters is weight lifting and things like that that put too much strain on a fighter's muscles," declared little Charley.

In their off moments many fighters are movie fans, although Marciano is not. He likes to read and is a detective story devotee. Condition is so important to a boxer that his day-to-day doings seldom deviate from a rather dreary routine. That is the price that must be paid for success in the ring. Early to bed, early to rise isn't just a motto for a pugilist, it's a must. Lee Oma, Tony Janiro, Charley Weinert, Kid Chocolate, Lew Jenkins, Jimmy Slattery, all did well in the ring but nowhere near as well as they would have done had they been willing to adhere to the Spartan life the ring demands.

Outside of meal time there are few pleasures suitable for the ambitious boxer. Dancing is frowned upon by most trainers, "keeps 'em out too late!" they tell you. For a time, it looked like Kid Gavilan was going to rhumba himself right out of the picture, but the kid got married and caught hold of himself.

Too much car riding, disturbs the conditioners also. "It makes 'em lazy and a lot of them like to drive too fast, look at ol' Jack Johnson. He'd 'a lived to a hundred but he had to go 90 miles an hour whenever he got behind a wheel." In spite of the trainer's uneasiness about cars, they haven't been able to do much about it. Since their fun is so limited, and this is the age of the automobile, the first thing a boxer usually gets when he can afford it is a car. Roland LaStarza has gone them one better, he is now flying his own plane, as Manager Jimmy De Angelo, a man who will invent worries if none exist, gets greyer every day.

Trainers and managers are thankful for the movies which take care of much of the fighter's spare time harmlessly, and for television which keeps him contented at home and out of the way of temptation. There probably never was a greater movie fan among the boxers than Joe Louis. Joe never got tired of seeing them, particularly westerns.

Frustrated ball players are frequent among fighters, going as far back as John L. Sullivan and James J. Corbett, a couple of ring immortals who had professional ambitions. It is well known that Marciano was a ball player long before he took up boxing, and Joe Louis had baseball leanings too. Joe once toured the country with a soft ball unit, and he was the No. 1 rooter for the Detroit Tigers for years. Boxers are regular attendees at baseball games, this, of course, meets with the complete approval of trainers and managers.

Not all of the hobbies of famous fighters add to the trainers' peace of mind. There was nothing anybody could do about Lew Jenkins dashing madly about town on his motorcycle, and the task of getting Maxie Rosenbloom to bed before midnight was finally given up as a hopeless job. These were exceptions though.

Most boxer's pastimes must be geared to his daily routine of physical hard-ness and health and for this reason it is to the advantage of the average person to study them and take heed. Meals are regular and adjusted to the amount of energy burned up by the individual, with proteins and minerals in abundance. Plenty of rest never hurt anyone, fighters have to go to bed early since day-break finds them on the road running. While no such demand is made of the ordinary citizen, extra hours of sleep will do him good too. Frequent physical check-ups are mandatory for fighters. They are vital to pugilists, but at the same time mighty important for all of us, particularly those of middle age. . . .

WHEN IS A BOY A MAN?

Patterson Case Poses Problem

In most parts of the civilized world, 21 is the magic age which transforms an adolescent into an adult, although many a teenager makes the sudden transition from childhood to maturity by way of a military uniform. The argument that if an 18-year-old is ripe enough to be shot at, he should be old enough for anything else is always cropping up here and there. A similar situation has plagued the boxing overseers for many years. Namely, should an underage contender be allowed to meet the sternest competition in long contests?

The New York Commission and other official boxing bodies have in the case of Floyd Patterson, teenage pugilistic prodigy from Brooklyn, a puzzler which figures to keep them awake at night. The undefeated 1953 Rookie of the Year is obviously ready for the best of the light heavyweights, but he is only 18, which means that if the New York rules are adhered to, he won't be allowed to fight a ten rounder for two more years.

Under the Empire State boxing bylaws, 6 rounds is the longest any 18-year-old can box professionally, 8 rounds is the limit for a boy of 19, and he must have passed his 20th birthday before he can box a ten round bout. Technically 6 of Patterson's bouts have been 'illegal' as they were of 8 rounds duration, and it now turns out that instead of being legally old enough to go that distance, he was 18 instead. Jacking up a fighter's age is a time-honored trick in the boxing business, and there have even been cases where birth records of older persons were used by under-age applicants for licenses.

While the intent of the 20 year rule in New York is very good, being clearly designed to protect the physical development of the youngster, and also to prevent his being subjected to pressure too great for such tender years, its idea runs contrary to the careers of most of the great boxers of the past. Patterson is far from being the first teenager to show the kind of promise he is showing. That all-time great of the featherweights, Terry McGovern, would have been in a tight spot had such an edict been operative when he was fighting. The old Brooklyn Terror, was World Bantamweight Champion at 19, World Featherweight Champion at 20 and was past his prime at 21! The natural conclusion here would be that such an early finish makes the modern ruling look very good, but in contradiction to that opinion, consider the case of the old Phantom of Philadelphia Tommy Loughran.

In 1922, at 19, Loughran was tangling with such titans as Harry Greb and Gene Tunney. Every bout he had that year was against a champion or near-champion. Besides Greb and Tunney, such names as Mike McTigue, Lou Bogash and Bryan Downey were included in his list of foes of 32 years ago. A year later, Loughran made his first appearance in New York. His opponent, none other than Harry Greb! When Loughran climbed through the ropes, the old Madison Sq. Garden crowd gasped in amazement. "What—there must be some mistake! This choir boy can't be the fellow who's been fighting guys like Greb!" said a startled old-timer. Before he had reached his 21st milestone, Loughran had been through five scuffles with Greb, three with McTigue, two with Jeff Smith, and has also boxed Young Stribling, Ted Moore, and the great Jack Delaney.

How did such rugged early years affect Loughran's career? In strong contrast to McGovern, Tommy thrived on it, remained in the ring for 18 years and in 1942, at the age of 40, was in such remarkable physical condition he was accepted for service in the U.S. Marines. Loughran's career would seem to be a boost for the "tougher-the-better" school of thought, which argues that a kid either has it or hasn't, so toss him in there with the tough ones as soon as possible and get it over with.

Loughran himself is inclined to believe this, using his own history as Exhibit A. Unlike McGovern, who was all offense, Loughran took the Art of Self Defense literally, and he was geared to withstand his rugged youthful campaigning. By concentrating on superb boxing Tommy was able to remain undamaged in his tough early bouts. Tommy mastered the fine points of defensive boxing so well, he added years to his career. His early battles against the big timers helped rather than hurt him.

Those old time California aces, Eddie Hanlon and Abe Attell, had experiences paralleling those of McGovern and Loughran. Hanlon, like Terrible Terry was the dynamic type battler, while still in his teens he was engaging top-notchers in gruelling twenty round contests and he was through at 21. Attell also got a very early start, but soon realized that to last in the business, you had to learn something about avoiding punishment. In 1900 at the age of 18 he was meeting the great but fading George Dixon for the vacated featherweight title. Attell credits Dixon for making him see the light, and he began to really work on his cleverness. Abe got so good at it, he went on to become one of the greatest boxers of them all, and lasted 13 years as a top-notcher.

Georges Carpentier was one of the boy wonders of the ring. At 15 he was meeting Charles Ledoux for the bantamweight champion, at 19 he was meeting men like Willie Lewis and former middleweight champions Billy Papke, and Frank Klaus. He was only 21 at the outbreak of World War I and was already heavyweight champion of Europe, with remarkable showings against U.S. heavies Joe Jeanette and Gunboat Smith behind him, although he was still only a middleweight. In 1927, 19 years after his first bout, the Orchid Man campaigned in the States, performing credibility for a man of his years. In his last visit to this country in 1948 Georges looked surprisingly well preserved, youthful, and handsome at 54.

A quarter century ago the New York Boxing Commission was putting restrictions on the fighting routes of the teeners. The two bouts with Jack Delaney which made Jimmy Slattery a reigning fistic sensation for a time were both limited to 6 rounds because the Buffalo boy was underage. The deliberate Delaney couldn't catch up with the flashy 19-year-older the first time they met in 1925, and 5 months later, Slattery's speed carried him to another victory over the hard hitting Bridgeporter. Being exposed to tough competition at an early age didn't particularly harm Slattery. Young Stribling and Harry Greb were among his rivals when he was only 18. Slattery won a claim to the light heavy title later on and boxed for 12 years. A performer of fantastic grace and skill, Jimmy had the potential to have scaled even greater heights had he taken things more seriously, and conditioned himself more thoroughly.

The famous New York neighborhood classic between Sid Terris and Ruby Goldstein at the Polo Grounds in 1927 had to be cut to 6 heats because Ruby was only 19, and there were numerous other such cases back in those days.

Some far-seeing souls got around this age restriction by adding a few years on the boxer's original application. Tony Canzoneri is said to have been only 16, instead of the required 18, when he made his professional bow. If this is so, and the record book confirms it, by the time he was 19 Tony was boxing Bud Taylor for the world's bantam title and was already recognized as one of the outstanding boxers of the period. Canzoneri fought for 15 years. Tami Mauriello, who was only 16, got around the ruling, by simply presenting an older brother's name and birth certificate. Tami's teens were taken up fighting people like Billy Soose, Gus Lesnevich, Steve Belloise, and other high-ranking battlers of the time. He was over the hill at 24.

Tony Janiro, who still looks cherubic after all these years, was another who got around the underage rulings in one way or another. A sparkling performer in his kid days too, Janiro like Slattery, loved fun more than fighting and this rather than being rushed along, crimped his career.

Jimmy McLarnin looked so young boxing the likes of Bud Taylor and Pancho Villa on the coast, he was tagged "Babyface."

There is a unanimity of opinion among the various boxing bodies relative to restricting the operations of "under-21" boxers. Down in New Orleans, 18 year old Ralph Dupas is only permitted to go 8 rounds, in New York 6 rounds would be his limit. This flashy youngster, like Patterson, is going to give the bigwigs something to think about very soon, as he is closing in on the topnotchers, and since he won't be eligible to fight ten rounds for a couple of years, some exception will probably have to be made in his case as well as Patterson's.

A quick riffle though the *Ring Record Book* reveals that many famous fighters ranging all the way back to the last century were knocking on the champions' door long before their 21st birthday. Decades ago, the great George Dixon had established himself as the best little man in the U.S. while still in his teens. Dixon was a world's champion, before he reached the age of 20. Despite his early maturity in the ring, Dixon fought for 20 years. Lasting this long even though he could have taken far better care of himself. There were no restrictions on age or the distances of bouts in that long-gone era and Dixon engaged in a bout lasting 26 rounds while still 18 years of age! Such a contest today, involving a boy of this age, would bring the cops on the run, with life suspensions or even jail sentences handed out to all implicated.

Billy Conn, according to the records had whipped three former world middleweight kings before reaching his 20th birthday, Babe Risko, Teddy Yarosz and Vince Dundee. Back in the Twenties, one time lightweight king, Sammy Mandell had gained national prominence, and top ranking as a contender, at just 19 years of age.

Pugilistic prodigies are much more frequent among the littler fellows as bigger men mature much more slowly as a rule. Heavyweight champion Rocky Marciano, who started out at 24, wasn't even thinking about being a fighter, at an age when many small men had already seen their best days.

Patterson's manager Cus D'Amato is naturally wary of hurrying things along too fast, thereby risking the ruination of a rare prospect. The commission is in a real dilemma, since the only opponents capable of meeting him are the topliners, with those of lesser merit being unacceptable. To curtail his activities for the next two years, or until he reaches 20, would probably hamper his progress. It seems that the only solution here is to forget in his case and taking him at face value, regard him as any other contender, a contender of such unusual qualifications, that exceptions must be made in this case.

The precedent here is the success gained by such prodigies as Loughran, Canzoneri, Dixon, Attell, Carpentier, Conn and others in the past. None of them suffered through being given premature tests of fire.

ONE FIGHT TOO MANY . . .

Great Fighters Seldom Quit at the Right Time

Just as a losing last round in a boxing bout often unduly influences the decision by offsetting several earlier winning ones, so does a disastrous finale to a fighter's career often obscure many brilliant former efforts.

As a rule, a whole new generation of fans is on hand to witness the downfall of a once great veteran and that is the picture they retain of the ex-star. This is most unfair to the former champion, but that's the way it is much of the time. Gene Tunney's prestige grows with the years because there is no recollection of him as a battered past-his-prime victim of Father Time and young, on-the-way-up opponent. Gene, smartest of all boxers, didn't give anything like that a chance to happen. He called it quits while still on top, and made his decision stick. Not so, poor old Joe Louis, who, balding and blubbery, bumbled into blasting defeat at the hands of Rocky Marciano. Joe, turning a deaf ear to the advice of Tunney himself, refused to stay retired, and his final fight is a mournful memory to many who exulted in his long tour of triumph.

The old chestnut about the pitcher going to the well once too often, must have been thought up, with most of our great fighters in mind. Just about all of them have worn out their welcomes in the ring, by not getting out when the getting was good. Of course, practical people point out that some of them were well paid for hanging around past the point of no return, but only in the boxer's mind can be found the answer as to whether the resultant damage to his professional standing was worth the price he received.

The case of Ezzard Charles is a prime example here. A few months ago, Charles, after years of getting the unwanted stepchild treatment from the public found himself hip-hoorayed as a hero everywhere, following his blistering battle against champion Rocky Marciano last June. Had he then taken himself back to Cincinnati, and called it a career, the final picture of Charles which would have persisted in the public mind would have been a most flattering one of gallantry and fortitude under fire. But it was not to be! Ez, taking as his theme song, the once popular ditty "Just one more chance," tried it again with Marciano. His September performance against the champion was as timorous as his June joust had been tremendous. So far as Ez was concerned, the aftermath of the second go was just like old times, with press and public writing off his earlier effort as a temporary transformation of a tabby-cat into a tiger, and accepting the more recent affair as typical of the real Charles.

This shouldn't be so, as Ez Charles, in a long career during which he faced the toughest men available, carved out a record which in the words of Marciano's trainer Charley Goldman—"makes the guy a great fighter no matter what anybody says. They tell you what a great fighter Archie Moore is. Well, Charles licked him every time they fought. Then there were guys like Charley Burley, who nobody wanted to fight. Charles licked all of them kind of guys. He was only a light heavyweight, but he beat all the heavyweights. The guy was really good," pointed out Mr. Goldman. For all of that, the last fight is the one that carries a lot of weight, as Ez will no doubt realize as the years march on. Charles got some $85,000 for his September set-back—no mean purse—but he is well fixed anyway, and with income tax brackets being what they are today, only he can decide, whether what he had left from the second Marciano fight purse made up for his loss of the public esteem it took him so many years to gain.

No fighter was ever more victimised by a sorry finale than Billy Conn. The career of the good-looking Pittsburgher, one of the best boxers of all time, is all too often confined to the pathetic second Louis-Conn fight in 1946, to Conn's detriment. This is ridiculous, since Conn was beating first-rate middleweights like Vince Dundee, Young Corbett, and Solly Krieger while still in his teens. As a light-heavyweight he was invincible, and the opponents he turned back—Apostoli, Bettina, and Lesnevich—weren't soft touches by any means. He outclassed most of the heavyweights he faced, and proved a formidable foe for Louis the first time they met.

Despite all this, that last punt performance against the Brown Bomber, fought after 4 years of inactivity and easy living, is held against him. It is allowed to overshadow one of the most impressive records of any modern fighter.

That is the way those last ones usually pan out, and although Conn got more than $100,000 for the 1946 fiasco, he is a proud fellow and possibly wishes that something could have prevented that Louis return.

Over in Camden, N.J. old Jersey Joe Walcott, as he pumps gas in his deluxe filling station and motel, probably ponders over the way his last fling at the ring knocked the props out from under his popularity. For a time, the antique Jerseyman was one of the most idolized fighters ever. He appealed to many varying groups. As a father of six children, he aroused the sympathy and well wishes of women everywhere. Those of middle age or verging upon it, threw out their chests a little further while reminding doubters they still had plenty left. "Just look at the way this old guy Walcott is beating up these young fellows." Down-and-outers took a new toehold on life as Jersey Joe climbed off a dump truck, to gain fame and wealth.

His stunning title-winning kayo of Charles captivated the country, and on top of everything, he was actually an amazing fighter for one of his years, both as a puncher and boxer. He maintained his high position in public favor even following the loss of his title to Marciano. The thrilling nature of the bout added to, rather than subtracted from, his popularity. Well-spoken and well groomed, at ease in any company and of pleasant personality, Jersey Joe Walcott rode high as a popular favorite.

But Jersey Joe's last appearance against Marciano in Chicago in the spring of 1953 took care of all of this. When he sagged to the floor and remained there though perfectly conscious, while the referee tolled off the ten seconds, he was $245,000 richer—minus all deductions when he arose, but he had also picked up a one-way ticket to oblivion. His public appeal was squashed as completely as though it had been a balloon he had sat upon as he squatted upon the canvas. Today, Walcott, once Camden's most celebrated citizen, seldom wanders far from his home town. His public appearances since the second Marciano fight have been most rare. At last reports he was said to be preparing to enter the ministry. At any rate he has kept under cover since his last "fight."

Financial pressure often forces our ring greats into the danger zone of "one more fight." Tony Canzoneri was a sad case here. In the last bout he had, the former champion was knocked out by wild swinging Al Davis, in 3 rounds in Madison Square Garden back in 1939. Canzoneri was fighting on borrowed time. He was just a caricature of the brilliant ringman he had been, the purpose of the match was a payday, pure and simple.

Mickey Walker's predicament was just about the same. Mickey had been around for 16 years, but had little or nothing to show for his years of big-time battling and living. German Eric Seelig halted Mickey in 7 rounds in the old St. Nicholas Arena in 1935, and Walker never tried it again.

Benny Leonard once disclosed that he had made a half-million dollars in the ring, but 4 years after he retired, following the great crash of 1929, he was starting from scratch all over again. This forced the great undefeated lightweight champion back into action. Like Walker and Canzoneri, he was also a kayo victim in his last bout. Jimmy McLarnin packed far too much power for the worn and weary one-time wonder of the Roaring Twenties, when they met in the Garden back in 1932. Leonard's comeback while a fistic fizzle, was no financial failure. He picked up a sizable purse for his swan song. The Garden was jammed to the rafters with his old-time rooters the night he called it a career.

Luckily their unfortunate finishes had no adverse effects on the high rankings of Leonard, Walker or Canzoneri in the eyes of the public, which took cognizance of the fact that urgency had forced them back into action.

Willie Pep's last try at big time boxing was a sorry one for a boxer of his superlative skill. Although he has been attempting a comeback, he has been almost a recluse from the fans and friends who once hailed him as a ring marvel, since the fromagenous affair with Lulu Perez in the Garden.

In announcing a return to the ring, Sugar Ray Robinson is defying that "one bout too many" hoodoo which has claimed most of the great fighters of the past. Before embarking upon his none-too-successful stage career, Ray's last bout had not been a winning one. This was the "kayoed by the heat" hassle with light-heavyweight champion Joey Maxim in June 1952, when the thermometer flattened both Referee Ruby Goldstein and Sugar Ray. The ending was unorthodox and is in the record as a K.O. for Maxim, but Sugar Ray had outboxed the bigger man so completely his reputation as one of the greatest of them all was not lessened by the sour ending. In daring the comeback nightmare which has shattered so many dreams in times past, Ray runs the risk of similar loss of prestige which befell such as Joe Louis, Ezzard Charles, Walcott and Conn in their final bouts.

TRAINING . . . MEN VS. WOMEN

Is that last stronghold of male seclusion, the fighter's training camp, along with its die-hard defenders, the managers and trainers, yielding at long last to the unrelenting pressure of the Twentieth Century female?

Shaken, but still unconvinced, fight people find themselves less amazed by the outcome of the Patterson-Johansson bout, now that the first shock has worn off, than by the training routine—if it can be called that—of the surprising Swede. But the boys are making it clear, that Johansson's methods, however successful in his case, aren't going to revolutionize the training regimen on this side of the water. . . .

Fighters in this country, at least, are going to continue in a straightjacket of strict denial of most of life's pleasure if the managers and trainers have anything to say about it. As is usually the case, the fighters haven't been heard from, although it might be imagined Ingo is viewed with envy by many of them.

The Spartan system of fight conditioning over here, goes back a long way, one of its earliest and most vigorous proponents being the old "Iron Duke." William P. Muldoon, one time head of the New York Boxing commission, and years before that, the trainer of John L. Sullivan, [who] was such an unwilling subject, that old time wrestler Muldoon was not above enforcing his routine on the bulky Bostonian with threats of rough and tumble action backed up by a baseball bat.

The conditioning creed of self-denial has been generally followed rigidly with a few exceptions. What good-timing there may have been, was reserved for intervals between fights, when nothing was pending.

There have been some exceptions to the ban on women in the training camp, however, one of the most notable being a man whose attraction for, and admiration of the fair sex is legendary, Jack Johnson. Johnson's uncanny mastery of defensive boxing made him a superb gym performer, and it was his practice to install the current Mrs. Johnson in a first-row seat, while with one eye on her and the other on his sparmate, he exhibited his superlative skill. One of the victims of this old champion's showboating was the late Harry Wills, who as a gangling youngster served as a Johnson sparring partner, for Jack's fight with Fireman Jim Flynn way back in 1912.

This experience provided one of Wills' favorite tales. "When I was young," Harry would say, "I had the best right hand to the body you ever saw. I figured I could nail anybody with it. I was working with Johnson one day out in New

Mexico, and sure enough I caught him perfect with a right under the heart. His eyes got big as pie plates. I thought they were going to come out of his head. Well, I was a cocky kid, and I tried it again, but this time old Jack just reached down, caught my hand like you catch a baseball, and threw it back at me, and at the very same time, he turned, grinned, and said something to his wife." Such displays were dear to the heart of Johnson, especially with ladies present. In conversation years after his fighting days, Johnson would boast: "My sparring partners always knew they were in for a hard time, if women were in my company in camp. It made me think fast, and I'd be at my sharpest."

There may be a connection here with the after-fight observations and comments of many—including Patterson himself—that Johansson is a "thinking fighter." This would certainly be in line with old Jack's statements of long ago. What applied to Johnson apparently didn't work out so well for Louis, who for the first and only time in his long and lustrous career, had his wife, the attractive Marva Louis, in camp for the first Schmeling fight. Not only that, but Joe's preparation for this one, ran neck and neck with Johansson's for jaunts to the city, golfing, dilatory sparring sessions, and feminine distractions.

The Schmeling disaster etched an imprint on Louis which he never forgot, and while he may have let down a bit between fights, his training periods from then on, were most severe. Not too long ago, the old Bomber complained: "The trouble with being a fighter is that you're an old man from the time you start, 'cause you can never have much of a young fellow's fun."

Not so Maxie Baer, who always diluted his training with dalliance, and as if to ridicule it, came off an Asbury Park, N.J., frivolity-filled "training period" to knock out the dedicated Max Schmeling, who, with the exception of Tunney, was just about the most conscientious of all fighters when preparing for a bout.

For the Carnera fight in which he won the title, Baer's preparation was in the same playboy pattern, but for Louis, the "Livermore Larruper" was bundled off to an isolated spot in upstate New York and old Papa Baer was hustled fast from the coast to act as a kind of warden over the meandering Maxie. For the only time in his career Baer then really trained, as a fighter should. He whipped his magnificent physique into its finest condition, discarding the caperings of the clown for the rugged routine of the trained athlete. And what happened?— Louis stopped him in four rounds!

In a well-received series of articles on the recent title fight, Rocky Marciano, famous for the sternness of his training approach, commented both wittily and plaintively, after everything was over, and Johansson had been crowned champion, " . . . all I could think of was me waking up in Grossingers when I trained.

I'd see Charley Goldman—before he shaved—and then go the road. When I'd get back from running, Al Weill—also without a shave—would be up and ready to give orders. Ingo—he saw his mother. And Birgit. Now, tell me, who had the best training methods? Ingemar with his Birgit or me with my Charley Goldman and Al Weill?"

Among the last firm believers that woman's place is in the home, fight managers have had a long-time phobia about the fair sex being included in a training retinue. The appearance of Mama Jackson laden down with home cookery headed for son Hurricane's setup in Greenwood Lake, always brought a hurried call for the aspirins from harassed manager Lippy Breitbart. For many years one of the main training camp functions of suave but caustic Louis co-manager Julian Black, was the discouragement of designing damsels who, long after the bulk of the week end visitors had departed, would be flitting about Joe's training quarters, eyes shining in anticipation.

The late Hymie Caplin, a man who usually had an answer for everything, found the presence of Katie Jenkins in hubby Lew's training camp, a problem he couldn't solve, combined as it was with the problem of Jenkins himself who like Johansson, had some highly unorthodox ideas about how to get ready for a fight.

Outstanding boxers who were not averse to feminine companionship during the training period are in a minority, but show some great names. Besides Johansson and Johnson, whose similarity in nomenclature also carries over into a similarity in other ways—Harry Greb was notorious for such desires and it is marvelled that he remained a good fighter as long as he did, considering the conditions under which he trained. Georges Carpentier, in a Paris autobiography some years ago, confessed some three thousand romantic affairs, in his dazzling career as the "Idol of France." Then there was Baer, and Louis was not completely unaware of feminine charms despite the bird-dogging on his heels of Black and Blackburn. But Joe learned his lesson in the first Schmeling fight, and used considerable restraint from then on.

Much was made of Johansson's cha-cha dancing up at Grossinger's. Just how much of this the new champion did is obscure, reports ranging from just a couple of turns around the floor, to regular exhibitions in the resort ballroom. But here he probably runs a poor second to Cuba's Kid Gavilan, whose flashy footwork was directly borrowed from the fancy twist and turns of the dances of his native Cuba. Not a few of the Kid's unexpected setbacks were charged to his addiction to the delights of the dance at an hour well past a boxer's bedtime.

Johansson's habit of nightly excursions into the nearby village of Liberty, N.Y., where, in company with his beauteous Birgit, he indulged in herring and ice cream at a local delicatessen was likewise quite an innovation, nor did Ingemar seem much concerned with curfew time. Otherwise, the new champion's approach to the business of getting ready for the greatest opportunity of his lifetime contrasted as sharply with American customs, as his luxurious training quarters did with the cell-like atmosphere of Patterson's cubbyhole in Summit, N.J.

Ingy's explanation for these unconventionalities was always the same— he liked people wearing skirts. Nor was the feminine scenery any ordeal for visitors. When one tired of looking at bounteously bestowed Birgit, there was brother Rolf's fiancée, a Hollywood-Propositioned blonde, Mama Johansson, aglow with handsome maturity and curvaceous and comely Sister Johansson, already famous as Ingy's pick to beat Britisher Brian London.

With such eyefuls in evidence, thoughts arose of other days in other camps, peopled by such figures, as Weill and Goldman, Jake Mintz, Jack Blackburn and Mushky Jackson, Joe Jacobs and Felix Boccichio. As these apparitions flashed across the mirror of memory, one could resist the thought that this extreme contrast in environment could have contributed a great deal to the carefree manner and casual confidence which played such a large part in Johansson's victory.

Ingemar really made the old adage about "All work and no play . . . " stand up.

NOT ALL FIGHTERS END UP BROKE

The recent passing of Luis Angel Firpo provided a revelation which brought an amazed reaction throughout the world. The one time "Wild Bull of the Pampas" left an estate estimated at five million dollars.

The public, more familiar with such unfortunate circumstances surrounding a fighter's passing as those attending the untimely demise of Tony Canzoneri who had nothing left of the fortune he earned in the ring, found Firpo's huge wealth a real shocker.

Firpo's affluence had its roots in the canny conclusion that the money he made while fighting was meant for saving and not for spending, unlike too many of his less farsighted fellow fighters. Firpo's philosophy made his frugality legendary among boxing people. But the same ones who waxed sarcastic about his death grip on a dime back in his fighting days, later on were among the first to single him out as a "smart fella" who saved his dough.

Although he did not give that impression in general appearance, he had a business acumen second to none. This showed up early in his career when he tied up the pictures of one of his early fights and peddled them in the Argentine at an enormous profit. This same sagacity marked his commercial manipulations following his ring career. Although the perfect picture of the shaggy-haired lumbering yokel, completely out of place in the cutthroat competition of modern business, Firpo possessed a guile in his dealings which was in strong contrast to his primitive methods of waging ring warfare. Like Sugar Ray Robinson, Gene Tunney, Jake LaMotta, Ingemar Johansson and other strong-willed money-conscious personalities, the manager's conventional one-third cut of his purses caused Firpo considerable pain, and he took early steps to eliminate this—to him—exorbitant stipend. Consequently, he escaped to South America with the major part of his large U.S. earnings, outmaneuvering any stateside sharpies who had designs on his hard-earned dollars.

Firpo's case reinforces the fact that public opinion notwithstanding, not all fighters are pigeons asking to be plucked when they venture into the high flying—and finagling—world of business. The classic case here of course, is Gene Tunney, who not only made his boxing career pay off in a manner unheard of before or since, but added to his fortune as the years went by to earn a current rating of millionaire. Tunney's importance in the world of finance has reached a point where his support was recently sought in a proxy fight for control of the Alleghany Corporation, a holding company which controls

N.Y. Central Railroad and Investors Diversified Services. Since the opposition to Tunney's group is spearheaded by the multi-millioned Murchison Texas oil interest, it is apparent Gene has reached main bout status in the Wall St. arena by facing such contention. . . .

The current condition of most of our former heavyweight champions happily isn't that of the stereotyped tough-time-making-ends-meet ex-fighter. Besides Tunney, Jack Sharkey is well off. He lives a pleasant existence as a country squire in a New England suburb. Between refereeing stints and Outdoor Show fishing and casting exhibitions throughout the country, he keeps active and adds to his fortune. Dempsey is considered wealthy. Carnera, on the strength of his boxing reputation, cleaned up as a wrestler, and is well paid for supporting roles as the "Giant" in various movie spectacles. Marciano, according to ex-manager Al Weill—who should know—is well fixed despite a few business reverses since quitting the ring. Poor Max Baer, cut down untimely, left his family well provided for with lush annuities. Old Jim Jeffries was well-to-do at the time of his death due to real estate holdings in Burbank, Cal., where he had lived for many years. Another famed heavyweight of bygone years, Harry Wills, went to glory, leaving behind property probated at more than $100,000. Harry was one of the few Negro fighters to live his retired years in affluence.

Jimmy McLarnin, probably the best managed fighter in ring history, has no worries. To his own assets, which are considerable, were added a $200,000 inheritance from Pop Foster, his old manager. Pop did not allow a feud which had alienated the two for some years, to corrupt his concern for the future of McLarnin's family whom he made the recipients of his bequest. Billy Petrolle is reputedly one of the wealthiest of the ex-mittmen due to the success of various enterprises in Duluth, Minn., notably an iron foundry. Manager Jack Hurley did an excellent job of shepherding the earnings of the old Fargo Express.

For years the New York Yankees Baseball Club has been pressuring Jake LaMotta to sell them property belonging to him adjacent to Yankee Stadium. From last reports Jake still has the land, which speaks well for his financial position, since he could hardly sustain so independent an attitude without being substantially solvent.

LaMotta's old pen pal and playmate, Rocky Graziano, is another of the rough and ready school who apparently is doing quite well, thank you. Rocky made a great deal of money in his explosive career and despite a naïve free-handedness to pals and admirers, retained enough of it to live very well. He still drives a Cadillac and does enough state and TV stints to keep his nest egg intact. He has a beautiful home in the canal section of Long Beach, Long Island.

One of boxing's all-time greats, dazzling Packey McFarland, was just as clever a businessman as he was a boxer. Packey was only 26 when he quit the rugged profession to invest his earnings in a varied assortment of profitable business ventures in Illinois, among them a bank, a brewery and real estate. . . .

Few men are in better position to discourse on monied fighters and those who should have money—but don't—than trainer Whitey Bimstein, himself well-off, after a lifetime of working with most of the noted boxers of the past four decades.

"The fellows you mention as doing well," begins Whitey, "aren't always the ones who made the most money. They're simply the ones who realized that it wasn't going to last forever and made provisions. I say now like I've always said. Any first-rate fighter can make and save enough to take care of himself later on, if he is lucky enough to handle it right or have somebody handle it for him. As for the old timers around the Twenties and Thirties, none of the good ones should have ever been broke. Even during the depression, they made big money with milk ten cents a quart and no taxes to pay.

"Take Al Singer for instance, he's a good example, he made a fortune in hard times, so did Tony Canzoneri. In those days if there had only been some kind of trust fund for them, there would no such thing as a broke ex-fighter. Believe me, they made it! I know, I worked with all of them. I can also tell you that they spent it in a way they shouldn't have," concluded Mr. Bimstein.

DO FANS MAKE BRUTALITY?

**The writer says, "YES." The public wants blood and thunder
and refutes exhibitions of skill as thoroughly boring**

The television broadcasting networks castigated by high placed criticism of the violence which dominates their most popular programs, can find ready sympathizers in the ranks of fight people everywhere. Under continual constraint to concentrate more on programs of intellectual and educational merit, the tormented telecasters strike back at the critic with the foolproof rejoinder that no power in existence can keep the great mass audience from switching the dial from the high-minded cultural offerings, to the action-crammed, "rock-and-sock," westerns and murder mysteries.

This—experience has shown—is invariably what happens, as proven by the "ratings" the industry swears by. These electronic age moguls are finding out what boxing managers and promoters discovered decades ago, that the public appetite for entertainment despite the refinements of Twentieth Century civilization remains as primitive in its preference for "blood-and-thunder" divertissement as it did ages ago.

It was the doubtless intent of the Marquis of Queensberry, father of the modern gloved version of fisticuffing, that the "scientific" or skilful phase of the sport be developed after the archaic "London Prize Ring" rules had been discarded. Indeed, England, the birthplace of pugilism, clung tenaciously to this concept of it for many years, and even in this country such pioneers as Corbett, Peter Jackson, Gans, and Jack Johnson attempted to make skill the prevailing technique in the sport. But it was not to be. Like a young fellow college-bound, who, forced by economic necessity winds up working in a slaughterhouse, "boxing" under public pressure became "fighting." The people demanded a "gladiator," not a "glove-man."

Televised boxing has also afforded another interesting revelation. It has long been the custom of scornful observers to saddle boxing fans with the charge of "sadism"; singling them out as a segment of the populace no different in its tastes from the tiny minority which in "pre-TV" times attended fights in the flesh. Never was this fact so convincingly brought home as in the after-fight reaction of the living room audience to the Harold Johnson-Eddie Machen match on July 1, 1961.

One would have thought the armchair millions were under compulsion to see it or had paid their way into their own living rooms, judging from the complaints cascading coast-to-coast over the lack of mayhem in the match. "My boyfriend and me put up better fights than those two fellows on TV last night," giggled an office-bound secretary sardined amidst New York's stifling "subway rush." "OOY, that Machen, with him who needs a sleeping pill?" grumbled a retired oldster as he settled down to sunning himself in a neighborhood park the morning after the bout.

The press can also always be counted upon to come up with clamorous echoes of public disappointment when a boxing bout features finesse rather than ferocity. In no other sport do we find a more frequent target of ridicule and wisecracks in sports columns than the defensive-minded boxer. He is always available as the butt of jokes when ideas run short; he is decried as timid, frightened, over-cautious, and being in the wrong business. Such jibes as, " . . . watching a smart fighter is like watching a guy read a book . . . " result from the display of his talents. Nor are fight people themselves free from blame in their harsh appraisals of clever men who are actually the sport's most solid asset. In the unpolite parlance of pugilism these are often referred to as "stinkos" who instead of bringing customers in, chase them away.

The Johnson-Machen bout suffered the censure of all these varied factions. Actually—when analyzed—this match really represented what its founder, The Marquis, and truly discerning critics—of which there are a limited few—intended boxing to be.

To begin with, it brought together two magnificent physical specimens, either of whom could have modelled a statue by Praxiteles, finely conditioned and in top shape. During the match in which the accent was on defense, all the moves and stratagems of the accomplished boxer were exhibited. The sidestep, hand, elbow, and arm blocking, the left jab, shifty movements of the head designed to break the force of a blow, punch slipping and ducking, feinting, countering, economy of effort with all waste movement eliminated, the sharpshooting straight right, not a single nuance necessary to boxing mastery was omitted.

On top of that the rules were observed with an impeccability rarely seen in a ring. Completely lacking were the shoving, mauling, butting, wrestling, elbowing, heeling, kidney blows, sneak hitting, and wild swinging, which have become so common, and with which the public seldom finds fault, as long as it is animated by fury. The men fought like automatons completely devoid of any emotion or ill feeling which is, as it was meant to be, in a boxing match.

And when the Johnson-Machen display of the "Art of Self Defense" was over, what happened? Dissatisfaction was general, no one had been hurt, so the public was outraged!

Few boxers in ring history have suffered more from the public predilection for bloodshed in the ring than Harold Johnson. Admittedly an outstanding ringman, press, public and promoters are as one in their objections to him; because his defensive skill does not churn up the eddies of excitement which channel the customers through the turnstiles. In 1959 and '60 Johnson had a total of three fights although ranked as the No. 1 contender in the lightheavy division during this time. For years he was forced to concede great gobs of weight to giant heavies whenever he was able to get any fights at all. If anyone wants a living proof that the public and not the sport is responsible for the so-called "brutality" of boxing they need look no further than Harold Johnson, long unable to make a living in his own profession because he attempted to make a science and not a brawl of boxing.

Almost coincident with the unfortunate Griffith-Paret tragedy and the resultant furor over the punishment absorbed by the luckless Cuban, was the passing of one of the all-time masters of defensive boxing, former welterweight champion Jack Britton at the considerable age of 74. Britton perfected the art of self-protection in the ring to such a degree that in more than twenty-five years of boxing, taking in more than 300 bouts, he probably received less physical punishment than the average professional football player does in a season: enjoying good health and no ill effects from his long career, for almost three-quarters of a century.

It is also ironic that Griffith, taken to task by some for the fierce fusillade he directed at Paret while the champion was in a helpless position, has been chastised by both press and fans in the past for failing to force his advantage against a stricken foe. In the first Paret match long-time and respected N.Y. Journal-American columnist, Frank Graham, was one of the few who saw the decision which originally cost Griffith his crown as correct; claiming that Griffith had not extended himself sufficiently in much of the fight to warrant retaining his title. In his last bout previous to regaining his title, Emile was brought to book over a lacklustre performance against war worn Isaac Logart, a bout in which he barely gained the decision. Not enough drive and determination was the complaint.

For many years British boxers have run into the problem of changing their styles from the so-called "classic" manner stressing skill and defense, acceptable in England and on the continent, to the power-driven, head-on, tactics so dear to stateside audiences.

One-time welterweight champion, many time foe of Britton, and probably best of the British boxers to campaign in this country Ted 'Kid' Lewis once confided to eminent authority-confrere Mr. Jersey Jones, "When I set foot in your country, I make a complete change from a boxer to a fighting man. There's a difference you know." Like Jack "Kid" Berg, the old "Whitechapel Whirlwind," another Britisher who enjoyed great success in the States speedily adjusted from the clever methods he used in his homeland to the busy, "club fighting" style which caused American newsmen to give him his colorful nickname.

One of the reasons why ageless Archie Moore had to travel such a long road before finally attaining a pugilistic pinnacle was his unwillingness to treat boxing as anything but a game of skill. Archie showed he still retained the knack by outsmarting Italian Guilio Rinaldi while coasting to an easy win in the Garden last June; but not even Archie for all his likeability and popularity could draw forth any hurrahs from public and press for such polished technique. They were hungering for something more violent, and dissatisfied crowd mumbles marred an amazing exhibition by a middle-aged man against an opponent half his years.

Pugilists from whom no violence could be expected whatever their skills have found themselves performing in the privacy of half empty arenas, with the fans finding other things to do on that particular evening. Tommy Loughran, the boxing master, comes to mind in this connection.

Furthermore, an outstanding boxer, suspected of refraining from knocking out a rival by the customers, will speedily find himself the object of hooted disapproval performance. Both Benny Leonard and Ray Robinson often found themselves in this position.

Way back in 1926 Sailor Jack Sharkey, one-time heavyweight kingpin, in a Garden bout with Sailor Eddie Huffman had his opponent so far outclassed that, following the bout, he was hit with a barrage of criticism by press and public for not stopping Huffman, although his exhibition of boxing had been sparkling enough to satisfy anyone. Called on the carpet by the New York Commission, Sharkey, to avert a suspension and get himself out of hot water, gave unprecedented testimony against his own punching power; using his record up to then as proof that he was not a hard "enough" hitter to have knocked out Huffman in any case!

Many have claimed that Jack Dempsey's savage style, reaching a roaring climax in the "Massacre of Maumee Bay" against big Jess Willard in 1919 converted the people for all time into worshippers of ferocity in the ring. While this may have been a factor, the same change has also taken place in other sports, as in baseball for instance, where the crashing homerun has long since supplanted the pitchers' duel as the sine qua non for the onlookers.

Public preferences being what they are, the old-time clever boxing teacher, such as Jack Blackburn, Bill Miller, Jess Harrington, Bobby Dobbs, et al., has all but vanished from the scene; since his instructions if thoroughly mastered are more likely to result in a boycott for his pupil as a "sleep inducer" than in any demand for his services. Billy Bello, young New York middleweight is a case in point, possessing natural boxing skill, he must in these times cater to the crowd by concentrating on punching and offense.

The modern mania for violent action in a civilization reckoned effete by the standards of the rugged pioneering past, is worthy of study by the most noted psychologists. Boxing if allowed to progress on its original course would have wound up as a pure game of skill, instead of crowd-pleasing combat. The sport has had to go along; the public sets the style.

APPENDIX

Complete Listing of Ted Carroll's Published Articles
for *The Ring* (1936–1972)

PUBLICATION DATE	TITLE OF ARTICLE IN *THE RING* (*appears in this book)
June 1936	Fighters Who Fight
July 1936	Thumb-Nail Sketches
September 1936	Has Unique Record
October 1936	Fighters Who Fight
November 1936	Another Lewis in Spotlight
December 1936	Playboy of the Ring
January 1937	Pedro Montanez, the Tropical Terror
February 1937	Negroes Who Starred in 1936
March 1937	Colored Boxers Make Progress
April 1937	New York's Budding Tale
May 1937	New York's Lightweight Classics
June 1937	New Jersey's New Title Contenders
July 1937	Farr's Rise Stirs Empire
August 1937	Bob Pastor's Rise
September 1937	"The Fighting Champion"
October 1937	New Terror of the Ring
November 1937	New Knockout Artists
December 1937	They Figure in the News
January 1938	Heavyweight Comebacks
February 1938	Old Timers Compare 'Em
March 1938	California Boxing Aces
April 1938	The Road Back
May 1938	Feared Fighters
June 1938	Lightning Changes in Heavyweight Set-Up
July 1938	Schmeling vs. Louis, Right vs. Left
August 1938	"Hurricane Henry" Came Up the Hard Way
September 1938	A Great Champion Arrives

PUBLICATION DATE	**TITLE OF ARTICLE IN *THE RING*** (*appears in this book)
October 1938	Joe Louis Compares to Titans of the Past
November 1938	The Indoor Season Is Open
December 1938	Garcia's Rise Recalls Other Famous Filipinos
January 1939	The Crowd-Pleasing Good Club Fighters
March 1939	Sepian Sockers Supreme*
April 1939	"Sucker" Often Socker
May 1939	Neighbourhood Feuds
June 1939	Puncher Always Has a Chance*
July 1939	Clean-Living Fighters Scorn Father Time*
August 1939	Nova and Tunney
September 1939	Lustrous, Even in Defeat
October 1939	South America in Pugilism*
November 1939	The "Foul" Problem
December 1939	In the Spotlight
January 1940	Feathers Fly Again
February 1940	Thrills of 1939
March 1940	New York Stars*
April 1940	Stamina Is a Great Ring Asset*
May 1940	From All Walks of Life
June 1940	They Work Both Ways
July 1940	Fine Summer Talent
August 1940	The Manager's Role*
September 1940	Louis Proves Greatness
October 1940	Troupers of the Ring
November 1940	From Obscurity to Fame
January 1941	Hidden Talent
February 1941	Dramatic Kayoes
March 1941	Ring Ratings Arouse Interest in Boxing
April 1941	Secrets of Hitting*
May 1941	The Art of Training*
June 1941	Soose Heads List
July 1941	Canada Lee Scores Stage Triumph
August 1941	The War Babies
September 1941	Bantams in Favor
October 1941	Nova's Yogi Cult
November 1941	Cochrane Came Out of Grab Bag

PUBLICATION DATE	TITLE OF ARTICLE IN *THE RING* (*appears in this book)
December 1941	Outdoor Fights Made Three New Champions
January 1942	Golden Glovers Hit the Spotlight
February 1942	Fortune's Favorites of '41
March 1942	Watch Those Comers
April 1942	Winning Streaks
May 1942	Disparity Matches
June 1942	Boxing Styles
July 1942	Gestures of Mercy
August 1942	Army Gets East Side Jewel
September 1942	Service Stars Shine
October 1942	Jersey Fighters
November 1942	Turning the Tide
December 1942	Scrappy Skeeters
March 1943	Man of the Year in Boxing
November 1943	On World Boxing Tour
May 1944	Apostoli Award Pride
June 1944	One Round Kayoes
February 1947	Golden Boys of Boxing
March 1947	Sable Sockers to the Fore*
April 1947	Cerdan's Visit Recalls Other Foreign Stars
May 1947	The Merry Madcaps
June 1947	Stories of the Roped Square
July 1947	A Champion to Remember
August 1947	Golden Age for Lesnevich
September 1947	Defensive Tactics
October 1947	Happy Going for a Dead End Kid
November 1947	Fighting Filipinos
December 1947	Joe, a Real Champ, Has Met 'Em All*
January 1948	An Irish King At Last
February 1948	"Ring and Glove"
March 1948	Battle of Question Marks
April 1948	"Bowtie" Jimmy Bronson
May 1948	Jackson Johnson Best
	Gus Is New Ring Idol
June 1948	Cerdan, the Rage of Paris
July 1948	Laughs, Drama, Color in Heavyweight Title Bout

PUBLICATION DATE	TITLE OF ARTICLE IN *THE RING* (*appears in this book)
August 1948	Ring Skyscrapers
September 1948	Times Have Changed
October 1948	The Modern Miracle Man
	Things They'll Remember
November 1948	Which Would You Prefer—Nice Guys or Tough Guys?
December 1948	Modern Champs Rate High
January 1949	Promotional Rivalry Peps Up Boxing
March 1949	Featherweight Class Tops
April 1949	Down Memory Lane with Hurley
May 1949	Some Get By; Many Fail in Acid Tests
June 1949	It's Up to the Small Fry
July 1949	Sugar Ray Has His Say
August 1949	Maxim Cashing In on Decade's Effort
September 1949	Where Strategy Failed
October 1949	Belloise Still Hopes
November 1949	South America's Bid
December 1949	Old Versus New
January 1950	They Seldom Make It Stick
February 1950	Middleweight Prospects High for 1950
March 1950	It's Golden Gloves Time
April 1950	St. Paddy's Day Parade
May 1950	From Boxer to Ace Business Executive
June 1950	Oldest Living Champion
July 1950	Marvel of the Roped Square
August 1950	The Yanks Liked 'Em
September 1950	Boxing Playboys
October 1950	Louis' Spectacular Success on His Rich Exhibition Trail
November 1950	Heavyweight Highlights
December 1950	Forgotten Men
January 1951	Perennial Challenger
February 1951	Memorable Fights of 1950
March 1951	Robinson's European Tour Heightened His Ring Presence
	They Ripen with Age

PUBLICATION DATE	TITLE OF ARTICLE IN *THE RING* (*appears in this book)
April 1951	Welters in Title Scramble
May 1951	Olympic Trio's Success Story
June 1951	History Repeats with Light Heavyweights
July 1951	British Prestige Booms*
August 1951	The Ring Wins with Carter
September 1951	Avast, Belay, Now Comes Murphy to Blow 'Em Down
October 1951	Beg for Elusive Chances
November 1951	The Man at the Helm in Europe
December 1951	Luckless Challengers
January 1952	Unhappy Champions
February 1952	Standout Bouts of '51
March 1952	Pilots Who Kept the Pot Boiling
April 1952	Home Town Prides
May 1952	They Barred Nobody
June 1952	The Way to Success
July 1952	Louis Picks 'Em
August 1952	Welters Busiest Class
September 1952	Middleweights Rule the Roost
October 1952	Money Fighters
November 1952	Cuban Bout Recalls Foreign Ring Oddities
December 1952	Southpaw Favorites
January 1953	Desert Dramas
February 1953	Standout Fights
March 1953	Tom Collins—KO Punch
April 1953	Might Have Been Champ
June 1953	Gone Are the Boxing Teachers
July 1953	U.S. Title Revival
August 1953	Food for Thought*
September 1953	Turpin Tries Again
October 1953	Marciano Popularity Puzzle
November 1953	Leonard Remembered
December 1953	The Golden Bantams
January 1954	Unsung Champions
February 1954	Standout Fights of '53
March 1954	When Is a Boy a Man?*
April 1954	Showboats . . .

PUBLICATION DATE	TITLE OF ARTICLE IN *THE RING* (*appears in this book)
May 1954	Paging . . . Ponce De Leon!
June 1954	Middleweights Keep Boxing on Top
July 1954	Managers Vital in Heavyweight Success
August 1954	Quick Kayoes
September 1954	Brave Men
October 1954	Hurricane Jackson May Blow Back
November 1954	Ring Mechanics Rule TV Era
December 1954	Marciano, the Human Blockbuster, Has Experts Wondering, What Style Would Stop Rocky?*
January 1955	One Fight Too Many . . .*
February 1955	Standout Fights of 1954
March 1955	Age vs. Experience*
April 1955	Moore Campaign Clicks
May 1955	Fatherly Fight Managers
June 1955	It Appears That the Path to the Heavyweight Title Is Open to Any Heavyweight Who Can Do Any One of Several Things Well Enough
July 1955	Boxing Not Lost Art
August 1955	160's Rarely Covet Lt. Heavy Title
September 1955	Those Handsome Light Heavyweights
October 1955	When Lightning Strikes
November 1955	Self Managing Fighters
December 1955	Friendly Feuds
January 1956	Patterson Has Big Potential
February 1956	Fistic Follies of 1955
March 1956	Fans Sure Have Changed
April 1956	The Fighting Irish*
May 1956	Meet the Ladies
June 1956	What Price Records?
July 1956	Italians Make Ring History
August 1956	Ring Stars' Dads Usually Unobtrusive
September 1956	U.S.—Happy Hunting Grounds
October 1956	Those Philosophic Fight Managers
November 1956	Big Outdoor Fights Had Stirring Sidelights
December 1956	Ray Robinson Is Superstitious!
January 1957	Bob Baker Lazy? Well, He's No Dynamo

PUBLICATION DATE	TITLE OF ARTICLE IN *THE RING* (*appears in this book)
February 1957	1956—A Real Gone Year
March, 1957	Louis and Patterson Compared
April 1957	The Cauliflower Set
May 1957	When "King Kap" Reigned
June, 1957	Knack for Nicknaming
July 1957	It Might Have Been . . .
August 1957	Heavy Calibre Same
September 1957	No Longer "Unknown Champ"
October 1957	TV Amplifies Decision "Beefs"
December 1957	Kanthal Modern Mendoza?
January 1958	Welter Crown Grab-Bag
February 1958	Fistic Follies of 1957
March 1958	A Perennial Rose
April 1958	Unhappy Hero
May 1958	McLarnin, Depression Time Hero
June 1958	Marco Polo With Gloves
July 1958	Paolino July 4th Hero
August 1958	Olympian Hidge to the Fore
September 1958	Ruby Goldstein
October 1958	Loughran, Boxing Master of Yore
November 1958	Krieger, "Fighter's Fighter"
December 1958	Cowboy Hero Who Might Have Been— George Courtney
January 1959	Norway's Golden Bantam
February 1959	It Happened in 1958
March 1959	Everybody Likes a Fight
April 1959	Rosensohn—New Promotional Power
May 1959	Triple Champ Armstrong Has "No Regrets"
June 1959	The Versatile Powell
July 1959	International Fights Drip with Intrigue
August 1959	Last Laugh for Maxie Baer
September 1959	Training . . . Men vs. Women*
October 1959	Delaney—Ring Wizard
November 1959	The Moore The Merrier
December 1959	The Yankee Dollar What a Character!

PUBLICATION DATE	TITLE OF ARTICLE IN *THE RING* (*appears in this book)
January 1960	Liston Poses Problems
February 1960	It Was Really Odd . . .
March 1960	Out of the Past . . . Jack Fugazy
April 1960	Harold Johnson—That Old Run Around
May 1960	Irish Echoes
June 1960	Philippines Are Back
July 1960	Rough and Ready
August 1960	Joe Louis . . . Mr. Dignity
September 1960	Heavyweight Situation Recalls Ancient Trio
	Quotable Quotes
October 1960	Boxing Sets Pace in Fair Play*
November 1960	A Matter of Personality
December 1960	Not All Fighters End Up Broke*
January 1961	Is Fighting Fun?
February 1961	Oddities of "60"
March 1961	Tony Canzoneri
April 1961	Mickey Walker: D'Artagnan of the Ring*
June 1961	Joe Gans . . . The Mystic Hero
July 1961	The Strange Career of Al Singer
August 1961	Billy Conn: The Collar Ad Hero*
September 1961	Rocky Graziano, the Dead End Kid
October 1961	Fun and Frolic
November 1961	Ugly Duckling Lays Golden Eggs
December 1961	The Strange World of . . . Charley Rose
January 1962	The Strange World of . . . Charley Rose (Part II)
February 1962	Silly Symphony of Sixty-One
March 1962	Ray Robinson: The Greatest Champion Since 1922?*
May 1962	Outstanding Merit from 1922, the Birth of the Ring, to 1962 Not Confined to the Celebrities Singled Out for Super-Star Status
June 1962	Do Fans Make Brutality?*
August 1962	They Don't Hardly Come Like That No More
September 1962	Joe Louis 1937 to 1962
October 1962	The "I" in Boxing
	The Ring's Survey Favors Patterson
November 1962	Underrated Champions

PUBLICATION DATE	TITLE OF ARTICLE IN *THE RING* (*appears in this book)
December 1962	Patterson-Personality Puzzle
January 1963	Men of Africa!
February 1963	Big Men
March 1963	Greatest of the Irish: Mickey Walker
April 1963	Fate. Fate. Fate . . .
May 1963	Ring Triumph's Spawn . . . Heroes World Over
June 1963	Revive Towel Tossing?
July 1963	Are Fighter's Suckers?
August 1963	Artie O'Leary's Still Going Strong
October 1963	How Good Is Liston?
November 1963	Thanksgiving
December 1963	Big Guns of World War II
January 1964	Boxer vs. Puncher (Archer vs. Carter)
February 1964	Another Early Night Got Liston? Maybe Not
March 1964	Is Liston Too Slow?
April 1964	Erin Go Bragh!
June 1964	Every Fistic Great Has Style Nemesis*
July 1964	How Vulnerable Is Clay?
September 1964	U.S. Fans Soon Forget Olympic Boxing Feats
October 1964	Groans Now, Cheers Later
November 1964	To Fight, Or Sit Tight?
January 1965	Many Football Heroes Have Eyed Ring Titles
February 1965	Slugging Irish? Clever Jewish Fighters? Who Said So?
March 1965	Big Laughs of 1964
June 1965	Science Lacking? Baloney!
August 1965	"Toughest? Gavilan"—Ray
September 1965	The Italians, Past and Present, Hold Special Niche in Boxing History*
October 1965	Jim Norris in New Light
December 1965	Floyd's Position Unmatched
January 1966	Greb, Griffith—A Parallel
March 1966	Carroll's "Follies of 1965"
April 1966	Tiger Living Proof That Nice Guys Do Finish First
May 1966	Army Call Clouds Clay's Career
July 1966	How Would Clay Have Done Against Stars of Past?*
October 1966	"Dark Hopes" Showed Great Boxers with Pittance Pay*

PUBLICATION DATE	TITLE OF ARTICLE IN *THE RING* (*appears in this book)
November 1966	Controversial, Colorful Mike McTigue Left Behind Many Lurid Experiences
December 1966	Fistic Analysis Conceded Chance to "Big Cat" in Title Encounter
January 1967	Rip Van Winkle Awakes to Astonishing Boxing Picture
February 1967	Victory over Lincoln Revealed New Persol as Ring Ballet Dancer
March 1967	Sportsmanship Backs Up Skill to Make Tiger U.S. Favorite
May 1967	How Stillman Saved Money
June 1967	Spendthrift Fighters Gone
August 1967	Carroll Analyzes Merits and Failings of Heavies
September 1967	Benvenuti May Be Tops among Italian-Born Boxers
October 1967	Fighters Who Scorn Clock Invariably Pay High Toll
November 1967	Dame Fortune's Smile Has Eluded Ring Heroes Galore
December 1967	Expo 67 Not Canada's Only Claim to Fame
January 1968	Ancient Ballyhoo Gimmicks Pulled Out of Moth Balls
February 1968	All-Time Championship
March 1968	Silly Symphonies of Sixty-Seven
April 1968	"Luck Of Irish" Not Always Outstanding in Ring History
May 1968	The Good Losers
	Leonard Underrated
June 1968	Promotional Skills Set Off Heavyweight Class Explosion
July 1968	Negro Ring Achievements Unequalled
August 1968	Garden State Proud of Its Heavyweight Heroes
September 1968	The Man in the Broadway Window: Matchless Dempsey*
November 1968	"California, Here I Come," Still Popular
December 1968	Texas, Big State, Big Men!
January 1969	Philly's Fight History Features Greats Galore*
February 1969	Old New Orleans, Rich in Ring Tradition, Carries On
March 1969	Oddities of '68
April 1969	Erin Go Bragh!

PUBLICATION DATE	TITLE OF ARTICLE IN *THE RING* (*appears in this book)
May 1969	Names Make News All the Time, Here's a Batch Done in Rhyme
June 1969	The Record Book and the Knockdown Rule
July 1969	The Fantastic World of Floyd Patterson
August 1969	Japanese Boxing, Born in 1905, Has Enjoyed Spectacular Success*
September 1969	Violence Victims
October 1969	The American Black Man and Boxing (I of VII)*
November 1969	Johnson, Gans, Walcott and Langford Salient as Negro Stars Embellished Ring Annals (II of VII)*
December 1969	Rocky Marciano 1923–1969
	The Joe Louis Era (III of VII)*
January 1970	Television Helped Vastly in Destroying Color Line; Robinson Reign Spectacular (IV of VII)*
February 1970	Charles, Patterson Too Quiet; Liston Too Involved; Then Came Brash Mr. Clay (V of VII)*
March 1970	Fistic Follies of '69
	Clay's Rise to Championship Climax of Negro Takeover in Heavyweight Excitement (VI of VII)*
April 1970	Negro Achievements Galore in Boxing Have Battered Down Old Racial Barriers (VII of VII)*
May 1970	Is Incredible Olivares Best Bantam of All?
June 1970	Laguna, Paduano Throwback to Ring's Beautiful People
July 1970	Argentina's Hall of Fame Made Illustrious by Firpo, Who Belted Jack Out of Ring
August 1970	Carpentier's Skill, Debonair Quality, Dominant in France
September 1970	Der Mox, Once Champion, Still Germany's No. 1 Idol*
October 1970	Darcy Standout Down Under Where Tragedy Stalks Stars
November 1970	Turpin, Farr, Mills Help Britain to Stand Up to Failures with Heavyweights
December 1970	Wilde, Driscoll Gave British Boxing Rare Classic Stamp
January 1971	Carroll Lists America's 50 Leading Ring Heroes
February 1971	Upsets Galore Spiced Title Combat During Hectic 1970

PUBLICATION DATE	TITLE OF ARTICLE IN *THE RING* (*appears in this book)
March 1971	Silly Symphonies of 1970
	Frazier's Body Attack, Clay's Left, Dominate Analyses of Their Styles
April 1971	Want to Live Long and Be Fame's Close Pal? Win Heavyweight Title
	Robinson Blasts Turpin
May 1971	The Ring Begins Its Golden Year
June 1971	"Take Charge," Sadler Tells Foreman, But How To Do It Fighting Frazier or Clay?
July 1971	Frazier Might Do Worse Than Quit Ring Unbeaten
August 1971	Clay Fight Wilt the Stilt? D'Amato Defends Notion but Realism Rules It Out
October 1971	Jewish Fighters Have Achieved Fame beyond Their Limited Numbers*
November 1971	At Long Last, Underrated Charles Gets His Just Dues as Heavyweight Champion
December 1971	KOs Thrill but the Name of Game Is Boxing and Buchanan Proves It*
January 1972	Was Greb Really Best Fighter For His Pounds?*
February 1972	Boxers of Central Europe Descent Merit Richer Glory
March 1972	Incredible Inklings of '71
April 1972	How Griffith Rates Monzon
May 1972	Fickle Fate Has Given Many Greats "Bum Raps"
June 1972	"Greatest Of Gaels" Still Going Strong
August 1972	De Jesus Puerto Rico's Latest On Glory Path
September 1972	Pioneer Stock Vital in Development of American Supremacy in Heavier Ranks
November 1972	Marciano, Pep Brilliant Stars of Italian Descent in Our American Galaxy

---

| April 1973 | Obituary for Ted Carroll, by Dan Daniel |

NOTES

INTRODUCTION

1. Nat Fleischer, *Fifty Years at Ringside* (New York: Fleet, 1958).

2. Tim Jackson, *Pioneering Cartoonists of Color* (Jackson: University Press of Mississippi, 2016).

3. John Hansan, "Greenwich House, New York City," Virginia Commonwealth Libraries, Social Welfare History Project, 2017, https://socialwelfare.library.vcu.edu /settlement-houses/greenwich-house-new-york-city/ (accessed June 2020).

4. Gerald McFarland, *Inside Greenwich Village: A New York City Neighborhood 1898–1918* (Amherst: University of Massachusetts Press, 2005).

5. Tamiment Library and Robert F. Wagner Labor Archives, Greenwich House Records, TAM. 139; "History of Greenwich House," http://www.greenwichhouse.org (accessed May 2021).

6. *Ebony*, December 1959.

7. Jackson, *Pioneering Cartoonists*.

8. *Ebony*, December 1959; *The Ring*, April 1973.

9. *The Ring*, October 1969.

10. *The Ring*, April 1973.

11. Ted Carroll, *Ring Career: Jack Dempsey, Joe Louis* (New York: publisher unknown, 1947).

12. *Ebony*, December 1959.

13. Foreword, *Ring Career*.

14. *The Ring*, April 1973.

15. *The Ring*, April 1973.

16. *Ebony*, March 1960.

17. *The Ring*, April 1973.

18. *The Ring*, April 1973.

19. *The Ring*, December 1962.

20. *The Ring*, December 1962.

21. *The Ring*, April 1973.

22. *The Ring*, April 1973.

23. *Ebony*, December 1959.

24. *The Ring*, December 1949; *The Ring*, April 1952.

25. *The Ring*, October 1963.

26. *The Ring*, October 1969.

27. *Ebony*, December 1959.

28. *Ebony*, December 1959.

29. *The Ring*, October 1969.

30. Springs Toledo, *Murderers' Row: In Search of Boxing's Biggest Outcasts* (Boston: Tora, 2017).

31. *The Ring*, November 1974.

32. *Ebony*, December 1959.

INDEX

ABOUT THE EDITORS

Ian Phimister and **David Patrick** are both members of the International Studies Group at the University of the Free State. Ian has written widely on African and world history, while David's research interests focus on media representations of historical phenomena, including mass violence and contemporary politics. He is the author of two books. They share an obsessive interest in professional boxing. David's library contains hundreds of books on the Noble Art, and Ian was in the crowd that watched Muhammad Ali beat Brian London in 1966.

9 781538 164792